INFALLIBLE?

INFALLIBLE?

An Unresolved Enquiry

New expanded edition,
with a preface by Herbert Haag

Hans Küng

CONTINUUM • NEW YORK

1994
The Continuum Publishing Company
370 Lexington Avenue, New York, NY 10017

Originally translated by Eric Mosbacher from the German *Unfehlbar?*, © 1970 by
Benziger Verlag, and by Edward Quinn from the German *Kirche–gehalten in der
Wahrheit?*, © 1979 by Benziger Verlag. Other material translated by John Bowden from
Unfehlbar. Erweiterte Neuausgabe, © R. Piper GmbH & Co. KG 1979, 1989.

Translations © William Collins Sons & Co. Ltd 1971, © The Seabury Press, Inc. 1980,
© John Bowden 1994.

Printed in the United States of America.

Library of Congress Cataloging-in-Publication Data

Küng, Hans, 1928–
[Unfehlbar.   English]
     Infallible? : an unresolved enquiry / Hans Küng. — New expanded
ed. with a preface by Herbert Haag.
          p.   cm.
     Includes bibliographical references and index.
     ISBN 0-8264-0669-6
     1. Popes—Infallibility—Controversial literature.   2. Catholic
Church—Infallibility.   3. Church—Infallibility   4. Catholic
Church—Doctrines.   I. Title.
BX1806.K8613   1994
262'. 131—dc20   94-8577
                                                                        CIP

CONTENTS

Further let me ask of my reader, wherever, alike with myself, he is certain, there to go on with me; wherever, alike with myself, he hesitates, there to join with me in enquiring; wherever he recognizes himself to be in error, there to return to me; wherever he recognizes me to be so, there to call me back.

ST AUGUSTINE, *De Trinitate*, I, 5

PREFACE: AN UNRESOLVED ENQUIRY

Herbert Haag

This book is a singular document in the history of theology. Since it was first published in 1970, it has sparked off an international and interconfessional debate without precedent in more recent theology. Hence its republication here.

There are three good reasons for this new edition:

First, the author of *Infallible?* was constantly being asked about the substance of his criticism of the doctrine of papal infallibility. Since earlier editions of the book are out of print, it is very difficult for readers now to make up their own minds on the basis of the evidence. This new edition should solve that problem. The original text has therefore been reprinted unchanged (with the omission of the 'Portrait of a Possible Pope').

Secondly, in 1989, as I write, ten years after Hans Küng had his *missio canonica* withdrawn (in December 1979), it is quite clear that none of the problems tackled at that time with disciplinary sanctions have been solved (all the documents of 1979/80 were published in *Der Fall Küng. Eine Dokumentation*, ed. N. Greinacher and H. Haag, Munich 1980). On the contrary, it is now becoming increasingly clear how the measures taken then were canonically illegitimate, theologically unfounded and counter-productive as church policy. To put the reader in the picture about the formal basis for the Roman proceedings, the two texts which the Curia used as a pretext for its intervention at the time are printed here as documentation.

Thirdly, attentive observers of the Church scene all over the world are disturbed that ten years of the pontificate of John Paul II have not removed the crisis in our Church which was already beginning to break under Paul VI, but rather have intensified it. It is no exaggeration to speak of the indignation with which both scholars and the faithful generally are reacting

to the present course adopted by Rome. Letters published in
German newspapers are full of the disappointment or res-
ignation of Catholics who lament the change in climate in the
Church since the Second Vatican Council and John XXIII,
such a different Pope. Conferences on the crisis have been held
in Catholic academies (Rottenburg-Stuttgart and Munich)
and Catholic Associations (the Austrian Academic As-
sociation). Articles have appeared in Catholic journals like
Christ in der Gegenwart and *Publik-Forum*. New critical journals
are springing up: *Kirche intern* in Austria and *Aufbruch* in
Switzerland. Indeed even Catholic theologians and journalists
who in other respects are restrained and tend to be more
conservative are making critical comments – not only on the
controversial nomination of bishops and the disciplining of
professors but also on the style in which the Roman teaching
authority is exercising its office.

In January 1989 the chief editor of the Catholic *Herder-
Korrespondenz*, David Seber, complained about the rise of a
'fundamentalism' in the Catholic Church: 'In the absolutizing
of certain traditions or papal doctrinal statements with no
consideration of the historical context in which they appeared
and no sense of the hierarchy of individual truths within the
structure of Catholic faith or even Christian faith generally, we
have Catholic variants of a religious fundamentalism with no
proper biblical basis which is spreading all over the place and
becoming an increasingly significant factor.' Indeed Seber did
not hesitate to criticize certain forms of contemporary 'papal
piety': 'Distorted forms of veneration . . . (e.g. the many *totus
tuus* banners on papal trips), from which it can be seen that it is
not so much the trinitarian God as the Pope, thought of in
monocratic terms, who is the real point of reference for religious
feelings and Catholic devotion with all the consequences that
has for the Church. A prior decision which in principle is
irrational goes with fundamentalism. It leads to the arbitrary
replacement of reality as a whole with a particular reality, and
anything which does not fit in with this one absolutized reality
as a sole norm is excluded.'

Even clearer statements are to be found in *Academia*, the
journal of the German Catholic student associations, which in
June 1989 devoted a whole issue to the question of where the

Church is going: '*Quo vadis ecclesia?*' The leading article lamented 'a frosty climate' in our Church. A statement by the Central Committee of German Catholics was quoted with approval: 'Is not a false opposition being built up between binding church instructions and the claim of the individual conscience? Is there not a one-sided emphasis in the Church on the virtue of obedience at the cost of the virtue of Christian freedom of spirit?'

A stir was also caused by a well-argued article by the Regensburg dogmatic theologian Wolfgang Beinert, which appeared in the Jesuit journal *Stimmen der Zeit* in April 1989, under the title 'Church and Anxiety'. Terrifying results from demographic surveys were making it clear to the author that solidarity with the Church was rapidly disappearing. He speaks of many complaints among church people and the 'markedly aggressive attitude of the church government'. A divergent, inconvenient and nonconformist view immediately incurs the suspicion of disloyalty to the Church, disobedience and deviation. The number of processes against theologians, bishops and priests is on the increase. They are largely, or completely, anonymous. There is also a tendency towards ideology. It emerges in the efforts to restrict free discussion as far as possible by central measures. Anxiety seeks to beget anxiety so that 'the sought-after state of consolidation is achieved'. That can even extend to the *damnatio memoriae* which was already practised in antiquity: 'Certain authors may not in fact be quoted any longer, even if in specific instances they testify to orthodoxy.' No wonder, then, that many effects of the real church system 'cause anxiety even today': 'so the institutional Church is frightening – in particular to sensitive Christians.'

The critical remarks by the distinguished Catholic ecumenist Professor Heinrich Fries of Munich, published under the title 'Suffering over the Church', are no less fundamental: 'The present state of the Church is essentially also brought about from within, caused by the Church itself, through the measures and decisions of the hierarchy in the Church, through the way in which the Petrine office is perceived and presented, through a defective realization of what *communio* and people of God means as the basic structure of the Church – through continuing to fall short of the intention and the aim of the Second Vatican Council, to offer a spirit of hope, encouragement and confidence. It is the continual falling short of what was once a concrete reality in the Catholic Church and led to a high degree of assent, identification and credibility for the Church – which today have almost turned into the opposite' (*Christ in der Gegenwart*, 12 December 1989). This reads like an echo of the volume of essays *Katholische Kirche – wohin? Wider den Verrat am Konzil* (1986), edited by Norbert Greinacher and Hans Küng with the collaboration of many well-known theologians.

All these are disturbing alarm signals. So disturbing that the Bonn moral theologian Franz Böckle feels led to ask, 'Is the Pope provoking a split in faith among Catholics? Unfortunately this question must be taken with deadly seriousness' (*Die Zeit*, 3 March 1989). How seriously is shown by a comment from the doyen of Catholic moral theology, Professor Bernhard Häring, under the headline 'I am Deeply Disturbed'. Häring complains about the present conservative, even reactionary, course of the church government and concludes: 'We need patient mourning for our past sins, but also mourning by the Church, by head and members, for the many serious false doctrines which are constantly reasserted. The most serious was perhaps the doctrine constantly inculcated anew by dozens of papal bulls, that witches had to be tracked down and compelled by torture to speak the truth. Granted, recently Popes have spoken humbly about the case of Galileo, but they have never spoken specifically about very much more regrettable wrong decisions. And these in particular are a heavy burden on the papacy in an ecumenical perspective – indeed on the understanding of the Petrine office within the Church' (*Kirche intern*, March 1989).

Now others are experiencing what certain theologians already experienced years ago. The Pope did not think it worth answering the letter of Bernard Häring, who at one time was even invited to lead spiritual exercises for the Pope and his curial staff in the Vatican, any more than he thought the protest letter from thirty-four Christian Socialist deputies from the Bavarian Landtag worthy of a reply. Their spokesman, Peter Widmann, commented: 'If a letter from thirty-four Landtag deputies of the Christian Social Union who publicly represent

Christian positions no longer receives a reply from the Pope, then we may as well shut down the Church. In that case it is no longer a Church in the spirit of Jesus Christ' (*Kirche intern*, ibid.).

But what was the occasion for all these alarming statements? Along with scandalous nominations of bishops and measures taken against professors, the provocation for them has been two addresses which the present Pope gave on Pope Paul's 1968 encyclical *Humanae vitae* on birth control. A worse time for these addresses could hardly have been chosen. Whereas according to the most recent reports 100 million children worldwide are living a wretched life on the streets (the topic of a UNICEF and Childhope conference in Catholic Manila, cf. *Die Zeit*, 19 May 1989), the Vatican has no greater concerns than to urge the banning of methods of birth control which are indispensable today. A congress of moral theologians met in Rome from 8 to 12 November, which had been called by the Study Institute for Marriage and Family at the Papal Lateran University and by the Roman academic centre of the secret organization *Opus dei*. Only carefully chosen supporters of the papal doctrine were invited. The whole undertaking was financed by the reactionary American 'Knights of Columbus'.

One of the two addresses was the foundation address which the Pope delivered personally to the participants in this congress on 12 November. In it he not only praised Paul VI's encyclical for its 'clarification and somehow prophetic value'. He went far beyond Paul VI in respect of the foundation of *Humanae vitae*: 'It (*Humanae vitae*) is not about a doctrine devised by human hand; rather, it has been written by the creative hand of God in human nature and endorsed by him in revelation. To subject it to discussion is therefore tantamount to refusing God himself the obedience of our understanding. It means that we prefer the light of our reason to the light of the divine wisdom, and thus fall into the darkness of error, finally to attack even more fundamental cornerstones of Christian doctrine.' In other words: a rejection of *Humanae vitae* amounts to a rejection of Christianity generally. Catholics who use 'artificial' means of birth control thus to some degree depart from God's order of creation and redemption!

Alarmed by this address, the moral theologian Franz Böckle immediately went on to draw the consequences which follow from it: 'A moral doctrine hitherto proclaimed as an authentic interpretation of natural law or the law of reason is elevated to the status of an indubitable doctrine of faith revealed by God. The decision for the choice of a method of birth control thus becomes a challenge of faith for the believing Catholic. This is an unheard-of event compared with the doctrinal proclamation of the late Pope Pius VI, and one which is nowhere attested in the sources of revelation. The consequence is clear to anyone: the majority of believing Catholics would in that case – in the Pope's view – no longer be orthodox in a not insignificant part of the Christian faith' (*Die Zeit*, 3 March 1989).

No wonder that Catholic theologians were deeply disturbed by the papal statements. In addition, they were disturbed by reactionary nominations of bishops in the Netherlands, in Austria, Switzerland, and finally Cologne. Once again it is Professor Franz Böckle who draws attention to the ominous connections between personal papal policy and theological policy: 'One must bear in mind that the controversial appointments to sees in Austria, Switzerland and Germany, and the Vatican objections to appointments to professorial positions in the theological faculties, are the expression of a deliberate personal papal policy. In the end, the pure "doctrine of marriage and family, especially the prohibition of any active contraception", is to be imposed. Anyone who attracts even the slightest suspicion that he is not in full accord with the Pope on this point is no longer considered to be a candidate for a see or a chair of moral theology. A letter has been published from the nuncio, Archbishop Dr Uhač, in which he invites certain professors, apparently loyal to him, to "name colleagues who are no longer faithful to the teaching of the Church". One such replied that he could not in conscience denounce a fellow citizen since this went against the whole teaching of the gospel' (*Die Zeit*, 3 March 1989).

This is the background to the Cologne Declaration of 27 January 1989, 'Against Disenfranchism in the Church' (published in Hans Küng, *Reforming the Church Today*, Edinburgh and New York 1990, 187–91). The first part is about the nomination of bishops, the second part about the granting of the Church's licence to professors of theology, and the third part about the competence of the magisterium in matters of birth control. This Cologne Declaration, which was signed by 165 theologians from German-speaking countries and the Netherlands and had the support of numerous often highly prominent French, Italian, Spanish, American and recently also Brazilian theologians, with its widespread press coverage, was a bombshell for the Vatican. It accused the Pope of having made illegitimate use of his magisterial competence in connection with *Humanae vitae*. For, it stated, according to the Second Vatican Council there was a 'hierarchy of truths'; theological statements had varying degrees of certainty; the limitations of theological knowledge in medical and anthropological questions had to be noted; the papal magisterium had given theology the role of examining the arguments for theological statements and norms; the conscience was not an executive assistant to the papal magisterium. The criticism culminates in the statement: 'The Pope claims to exercise the office of unity. In cases of conflict, therefore, it is part of his office to bring people together. In this, he went to excessive lengths with regard to Marcel Lefebvre and his followers, in spite of Lefebvre's fundamental challenge to the teaching magisterium. It is not part of the papal office to sharpen conflicts of a secondary nature without any attempt at a dialogue, to resolve such conflicts unilaterally and by official decree, and to turn them into grounds for exclusion. If the Pope does what does not belong to his office, he cannot demand obedience in the name of Catholicism. Then he must expect contradiction' (191).

This declaration was desperately necessary. I subscribed to it, and I stand by it with utter conviction. And yet one must be allowed to ask a question which relates to this present book by Hans Küng. In connection with *Humanae vitae*, did the Pope really make 'illegitimate' use of his magisterial competence? In this instance did he do something 'that does not belong to his office'? From the Roman perspective, certainly not. Experts on Roman theology already knew that the substance of the more recent statements of the Pope on *Humanae vitae* were nothing 'new', but reflected the teaching which had long been put forward in Rome. For it was still the case for Roman theology that while the encyclical *Humanae vitae* on birth control is not infallible, the doctrine which stands behind *Humanae vitae* is. It is to be regarded as *de facto* infallible, even if it has not hitherto (or not yet) been defined *ex cathedra*. And it was this, precisely this, that Hans Küng had made the focal point of his argument in his 1970 book *Infallible? An Enquiry*: Paul VI had issued the encyclical *Humanae vitae* as he did because he was fully convinced of the *continuity, authority and infallibility* of this doctrine (i.e. of its inerrancy guaranteed by the Holy Spirit) – and was so convinced *because it had constantly been put forward as binding teaching by his predecessors and all the episcopate*. For Paul VI it was clear that to revoke the teaching of the Church on matters of birth control would be to concede that on this important point of moral doctrine the magisterium had erred, and therefore had not been guided by the Holy Spirit. But that could not be. So in his address to the moral theologians, John Paul II was only repeating in substance what had always been Roman doctrine.

Rudolf Schermann, the pastor and editor of the Austrian journal *Kirche intern* (which within a few months reached a circulation of more than 20,000), grasped the central point better than some professors of theology, who in questioning not only the encyclical *Humanae vitae* but also papal infallibility were similarly threatened with the withdrawal of the Church's licence to teach: 'So why did Paul VI decide against the use of artificial means of contraception? Out of anxiety for women's health? Certainly not. He was not just concerned about the pill, the medical risks of which both women and doctors soon recognized, with the result that the pill boom waned of its own accord, but with all artificial means. The Pope was not making a medical statement but a moral statement. Why did Paul VI go against the advice of the experts whom he himself had invited? The answer is as banal as it is significant: he decided as he did in order to be able to maintain the prestige of the papacy, in order to be able to say: "As our predecessors of blessed memory have repeatedly confirmed . . ." For what would people all over the world have thought – at least that was the notion haunting the curial minds which, it is said, put the Pope under pressure – if Paul VI had suddenly given the green light for artificial contraception against the clear statements by his predecessors? It was indeed well known that Pius XII (who was Pope from 1939 to 1958) regarded artificial birth control as fundamentally evil' (*Publik-forum*, 22 July 1988).

Indeed, at the time Paul VI had already based his decision on matters of birth control on the infallibility of the everyday, '*ordinary*' teaching office (the *magisterium ordinarium*) of the Pope and the bishops, a highly problematic neo-scholastic doctrine, which – unfortunately – also found acceptance in the Second Vatican Council's Constitution on the Church (*Lumen gentium*, no. 25). This states unambiguously: 'Although the bishops, taken individually, do not enjoy the privilege of infallibility, they do, however, proclaim infallibly the doctrine of Christ on the following conditions: namely, when, even though dispersed throughout the world but preserving for all that among themselves and with Peter's successor the bond of communion, in their authoritative teaching concerning matters of faith and morals, they are in agreement that a particular teaching is to be held definitively and absolutely.' And as the present book shows, precisely this happened in the case of what Schermann has called 'this baneful encyclical'. In the debate on infallibility which centred on Hans Küng's book, people would not perceive that on this point Hans Küng has reproduced the Roman teaching precisely. He was accused of a 'distorted' understanding of the Roman magisterium. It was believed that one could get round the fundamental problem of the question of infallibility by excluding *this* doctrine from the claim to infallibility.

And what about the present Pope? One has to concede that John Paul II has simply hammered home once again the Roman doctrine of infallibility endorsed by the Second Vatican Council. He did this in an address which he gave to the American bishops on 16 October 1988 and which with good reason preceded that to the moral theologians. Here the Pope spoke unmistakably, with reference to the moral teachings of the Church which were being scorned in America, of the 'charism of infallibility' that is not only present in the 'solemn definitions of the Roman Pontiff and of ecumenical councils, but similarly in the 'universal ordinary magisterium, which can be regarded as the *usual* expression of the Church's infallibility' (cf. *Osservatore Romano*, 16 October 1988).

Nevertheless it must be asked: has not a new situation arisen over the question of infallibility as a result of the most recent statements by the Pope? Yes and no. No, because – as I have indicated – Pope Wojtyla in his statements has only endorsed the *de facto* infallibility of the doctrine of *Humanae vitae*, which had always been presupposed in Rome. Yes, because the Pope from Poland has put two new emphases in his most recent programmatic statements.

1. He is now declaring specifically that the ordinary magisterium of the Church must be understood and accepted as 'the usual expression of the Church's infallibility'.

2. In his address to the moral theologians on the basis for *Humanae vitae* he shifts the emphasis from natural law to revelation itself and makes the prohibition of birth control a 'basic cornerstone of Christian doctrine'.

That, on sober consideration, is the 'new' situation with which one has to grapple in the sphere of Catholic theology. And only someone who has avoided a fundamental debate on the problem of infallibility all these years can be surprised at this development. In a brave Open Letter to the then President of the German Conference of Bishops (Bishop Karl Lehmann), the Catholic dogmatic theologian Peter Hünermann from Tübingen complained about the most recent development, and indeed with good reason expressed fears about the outbreak of a 'third Modernist crisis' in our Church. But instead of looking behind the Roman doctrine of infallibility, he stated in consternation: 'If one reads the Pope's address to the moral theologians as quoted, it is almost uncanny how far Rome has followed the understanding presupposed by Hans Küng.' Hünermann evidently cannot understand that it is not Rome that has adopted the understanding attributed to it by Hans Küng, but that in his book *Infallible?* Hans Küng was merely reporting the understanding of infallibility which has always prevailed in Rome and which moreover Rome has never contradicted. No, Küng's book does not contain any 'distortion' of the Roman doctrine of infallibility, but reproduces it exactly – as is now also expressly confirmed by this Pope. Also in his address to the moral theologians the Pope refers almost

solemnly for the teaching against birth control given by himself
and his predecessors to the 'constant teaching of tradition and
the magisterium of the Church . . . which may not be doubted
by a Catholic theologian'. Indeed he does not hesitate to add:
'Here we are touching upon a central point of the Christian
doctrine of God and man.'

It should thus have become clear that if Catholic theology is to
remain credible, it can no longer avoid the basic problem: what
is the foundation of infallibility, particularly the infallibility of
the ordinary, usual, everyday magisterium? How is it
guaranteed by scripture and tradition? The question raised by
Hans Küng twenty years ago in this book has still not been
answered. It remains an unresolved enquiry.

I hope that I may be allowed to recall here a proposal which
Hans Küng already made at the end of his 1979 work *The Church
– Maintained in Truth?* In connection with this issue – as formerly
in the question of birth control – he wanted to see the
appointment of an *ecumenical commission* which would consist of
internationally recognized experts from the various disciplines
(exegesis, history of dogma, systematic and practical theology
and relevant non-theological disciplines). This would do both
the Catholic Church and the worldwide ecumene a service. I
might also recall what I and my colleague Norbert Greinacher
wrote in the conclusion to our documentation *Der Fall Küng*
(1980): 'In view of this, as teachers of theology and priests of the
Church we make ourselves the spokesmen of the protest
articulated in this book and throughout the world, and address
the Pope directly: Holy Father! Take up the case again without
delay! Appoint an unprejudiced commission of bishops and
theologians to examine properly and not under the pressure of
time the theological questions which have been raised! We
appeal to your responsibility and your conscience: make good a
wrong that has been done! Do not leave the rehabilitation of
Küng to history! Make your personal action a blessing for the
Church' (p. 546). The state secretariat acknowledged receipt of
the letter, but no answer ever came.

In conclusion, I would like to quote a leading article dated 10
June 1989 from the distinguished old London journal *The
Tablet*, which is distributed all over the British Commonwealth:

'Theologians dedicate their lives and laborious hours to bringing out the truths to which the Church is committed. They ask questions because that is the way to advance. They ask questions because they have been asked questions. They ask questions because the questions are there, hanging in the air, and will not go away because authority discourages and dismisses them. Repressed questions poison the inner life of the Church.' As Professor Ulrich Horst recently said at a conference of the Catholic Academy in Bavaria (in the context of the present crisis): 'Questions do not disappear; the past never ceases, and it stands there unnoticed in our midst with its unresolved claim. All the crucial points in the history of theology bear witness that it is only rarely the lack of courage or the arrogance of theologians that brings back conflicts which had once been pushed aside. The subject matter finds its own hearing' (*Zur Debatte*, March/ April 1989). Can the Pope understand this language?

A CANDID FOREWORD

The renewal of the Catholic Church willed by the Second Vatican Council has come to a standstill, and with it ecumenical understanding with other Christian Churches and a new opening out towards the contemporary world. Five years after the Council ended this is a situation that can no longer be ignored, and for churchmen and theologians to remain silent would be unwise and harmful. After long years of waiting, patiently, but in vain, the time has come to speak out more plainly and more openly, so that the gravity of the situation may be made clear and those responsible may perhaps take heed. The reasons for the present stagnation must be exposed, for the sake of the Church and the people for whom the theologian does his work, so that hope and action may again break through in force in the post-conciliar period, as they did before the Council and during it. To anticipate ever-recurrent criticisms and reproaches, let no one assume lack of faith or charity on our part in a situation in which awareness of and concern for so much human suffering in the Church call, not for soothing words and glossing things over, but for courageous and hopeful outspokenness (*parrhesia*). Is it necessary to insist that what follows is an attempt, not to foster unrest and uncertainty in the Church, but merely to give expression to the unrest and uncertainty that already exist on all sides; that the author is not motivated by presumption, but wishes merely to help gain a hearing for grievances of the faithful to which it is impossible to be deaf; and that if sometimes, perhaps, the tone is sharp and the manner harsh, that is a reflection, not of the author's aggressiveness, but of his deep concern?

No progress is being made at present in a number of questions the solution of which seems overdue to most people inside and outside the Catholic Church, and there seem to be two main reasons for this.

1. In spite of the impulse given by the Council, no significant change, in the spirit of the Christian message, has yet

been brought about in the institutional and personal power-structure of the government of the Church. Notwithstanding the inevitability of change, the Pope, the Curia and many bishops continue to behave in a largely pre-conciliar fashion; little seems to have been learnt from the Council. Both in Rome and elsewhere in the Church the levers of spiritual power are now, as before, in the hands of personalities more interested in the maintenance of a comfortable *status quo* than in a serious renewal. Now, as before, obstacles are put in the way of significant institutional reforms that would enable less conservative, conformist, Roman-minded men to rise to key positions. Now, as before, the canon law that prevails (its place should be taken by a new 'basic law') is of such a nature that it prevents the renewal of the Church that is aspired to by wide and active circles among laity and clergy from making a breakthrough in relation to the most urgent problems.

The author has stated elsewhere what needs to be done in this field. In his book *The Church* (1967) he developed an interpretation of the Church for modern times based on the biblical message and said what had to be said about the service of the Church and a renewal of the Petrine ministry. In his *Truthfulness: The Future of the Church* (1968) he tried to apply these principles and to work out the practical requirements that logically follow in the light of the gospel from the Second Vatican Council. (One of the most urgent needs that we may mention here is a reform of the system by which popes are elected. Under the present system they are elected by a totally antiquated body, consisting largely of pensioners and still dominated by a single nationality and a single mentality.) What was said in those two books will not be repeated here, but the general principles will be reaffirmed.

The bishops, all of whom have borne joint responsibility for the Church as a whole since the Second Vatican Council, should be concerned to see that justified demands are put through in Rome, and at the same time should courageously and resolutely press ahead with renewal in their own countries and dioceses. Nothing will be achieved without tireless struggle and patient effort and constant legitimate pressure on ecclesiastical authorities by individuals, clergy and laity, men and women, and by the various newly created bodies in parishes and dioceses and in the Church as a whole; or if counter-organizations are not set up – groups of priests and laymen with specific aims in relation to such matters as mixed marriages, co-responsibility, and the celibacy of the clergy; or without prudently considered, massive self-help, if necessary against specific regulations in cases in which further delay is unacceptable because of the human plight involved.

2. So far, in spite of the impulse given by the Council, there has been no critical consideration or redefinition of the nature and function of the Church's teaching authority in the spirit of the Christian message. In the field of doctrine also surprisingly little seems to have been learnt from the Council; to a far-reaching extent the *magisterium*, the Church's 'teaching office', is still interpreted by the Pope and also by many bishops in a pre-conciliar, authoritarian fashion, without the co-operation with theology that was attested at the Council and became much more necessary after it. Now, as before, a pre-conciliar theology, slightly polished up in individual instances, prevails in Rome, the Church is still presented with encyclicals, decrees and pastoral letters which in vital matters are not supported by the gospel, are not really understood by most people today, and cannot be substantiated by theology. Now, as before, the Holy Spirit and delegated apostolic plenary powers are quoted as authority on all sorts of issues great and small, and such a display of infallibility is made in practice that five years after the Council the authority and credibility of the Catholic Church have rarely been exposed to such a test.

The whole question of the teaching authority of the Church will therefore be submitted to constructively critical theological examination in this book. The author did not seek out this dangerously hot potato; the subject simply imposed itself on him, as on other theologians, as a result of the needs of the Church and the requirements of the time. In 1970 the centenary of the First Vatican Council might perhaps have been passed over as unceremoniously as the fourth centenary of the Council of Trent was at the time of Vatican II. But in the post-conciliar period no one has done more to stimulate critical thought about Vatican I and its decisions than the Vatican itself. In recent years no one has done more to provoke the demythologization of the ecclesiastical teaching office than the teaching office itself;

and no one has done more to raise the question of the infallibility of the Church than those who give themselves out to be
infallible in all sorts of questions of Church doctrine, morality
and discipline.

Many will perhaps regard this book as provocative, though it
is intended to be constructive, but if we look back – not 'in
anger', but certainly with deep concern – the context in which
it was written becomes clear. Our purpose is certainly not to
romanticize the conciliar period and the pontificate of John
XXIII, and consequently to create animosity against the
present occupant of St Peter's chair. But it is essential to paint
the true picture, warts and all. By his whole attitude, by his
words and actions, John exercised the Church's teaching office
in a new, Christian fashion – or perhaps basically in a more
primal fashion, one therefore so potent for the future. Countless
numbers of people, both inside and outside the Catholic
Church, listened to him. Together with the Council, he brought
about an astonishing increase in the internal and external
credibility of the Catholic Church; and many who actively
co-operated in this renewal had cause to grieve at seeing the
store of confidence accumulated in those few short years
squandered in a yet shorter period and noting how much hope
and joy were and are still being shattered thereby.

Paul VI is a man of integrity, who suffers under his load of
responsibility and perhaps feels overburdened by it. Personally
he is motivated by a selfless desire to do only the best for the
Church and for humanity, and he sincerely believes he must act
accordingly. Where he does not feel bound by dogma or
Church policy he has shown this plainly, as in his initiatives for
world peace and disarmament, social justice, the Third World
and development aid, the continuation of liturgical reform and
a limited reform in the personnel and structure of the Roman
Curia, and so on. In comparison with some high Curial
advisers, he must be described as a moderate. Though to many
in the Church and in the world he seems to be of the extreme
right, to many inside the Vatican ghetto he is a man of the left.
Just as John XXIII was not without his faults, so Paul VI is not
without his strong sides. No one should dispute or belittle all
this. And yet – would it help the Church to pass it over in
silence? – it is impossible to go on shutting one's eyes to the fact

that, in spite of his and his advisers' best intentions, the longer
the teaching office is exercised by this pope and his curia, the
more damage is done to the unity and credibility of the
Catholic Church; and, yet again in history, this damage is done
from within Rome itself.

The most important facts are familiar, and no one can be
criticized for enumerating them, for they show the trend of the
official Church in the post-conciliar period better than any
theoretical discussion. A negative development was plainly
signalled at an early stage when the newly-elected Pope Paul,
after his great and hopeful address at the opening of the second
session of the Council in 1963, began roughly half-way through
that session – whether because of increasing anxiety, theological uncertainty, Curial tradition, regard for his environment or
the fluid political situation in his native Italy, or whatever the
reason may have been – to speak in a very different tone. As
opposed to the Council, which had set its heart on renewal, he
more and more often supported the Curia, to which he had
himself belonged for about thirty years – the backward-looking,
unecumenical, traditionalist Curia, that thinks in terms of
nationalism and power politics. He rejected the proposal
backed by many that the Council should freely elect the
presidents of its commissions, which would have resulted in a
renewal of those commissions dominated by the Curial machine.
In a personal address to the Council he committed himself to the
schema on missions, which was conceived purely from the
standpoint of the Roman Congregation on Missions and was
subsequently rejected by a large majority in the assembly as
being totally inadequate. There were acts of real Curial
sabotage against the Declaration on the Jews and the Declaration on Religious Liberty, and only massive protest by bishops
and theologians prevented the resolutions on these important
matters from being torpedoed. At the last moment the Pope
introduced changes into the schema on ecumenism, which the
Council had approved many times, that were scarcely friendly
towards other Christians and had only ostensibly been approved
by the Secretariat for Unity.

On certain questions (not least those discussed in this book)
the commissions of the Council, and in particular the theological commissions, were plagued by demands from higher

authority which were inspired by Curial theologians, and on sundry occasions these led to changes for the worse in the text. Discussion of the birth-control issue was forbidden by the Pope and referred to a papal commission, just as the question of mixed marriages was by the Council itself; the post-conciliar Church was to pay dearly for these two steps. Names of bishops who wanted to raise the question of the celibacy of the clergy were deleted from the list of speakers, and at the papal behest no discussion of the celibacy question as such took place in the Council, so that the burden of grappling with it was again passed to the post-conciliar Church. On the question, vital for the future constitution of the Church, of the relationship between pope and bishops, the Pope sent the Council a *nota explicativa* watering down the principle of episcopal collegiality. This was never submitted to a vote, but provided an ideological defence of all single-handed, uncollegial papal actions in the period to follow. Against the express will of the majority of the Council, he announced the misleading description of Mary as *Mater Ecclesiae*, which roused great resentment and misgivings about the genuineness of his desire for ecumenical understanding, and this not only outside the Catholic Church. At the end of the third session of the Council in 1964 the author published these notorious facts[1] and drew attention to the dangerous consequences for the credibility of the Church and the Pope himself that would flow from them, with the result that he was called to account in Rome and had an interview, first with Cardinal Ottaviani and then with two commissioners of the Inquisition, which however took place in an atmosphere of mutual respect.

With the fourth session the Vatican Council came to an end. In spite of all difficulties, setbacks and failings, as a whole it was a magnificent success. This cannot be sufficiently emphasized, especially at the present time. No doors were shut and innumerable doors were opened – in regard to the other Christian Churches, the Jews, the great world religions, and the problems of the secular world in general, and finally the internal structure of the Catholic Church itself. A new spirit, a new freedom of thought, discussion and action, and also a new relationship with truth had come about. For all their negative features, the Council's declarations contained so much that was positive that in summing up its work[2] at the time it could be claimed with good reason that 'in spite of all, what is now important is not to complain of the indisputable obscurities, compromises, omissions, imbalance, retrograde steps and mistakes as defects of the past, in a critical manoeuvre directed backwards, but to see them in forward-looking hope as *tasks of the future*, in the spirit of the Council which did not want to close any doors. For in a sense the Council, the true realization of the Council event, *began* on 8 December 1965. And precisely in order to prepare the better future, we must at the present time not make the better the enemy of the good, but the good the herald of the better.'

The Council put forward a magnificent programme for a renewed Church of the future,[3] and in innumerable parishes and dioceses throughout the world people set to work energetically to implement it. The Pope himself exhorted his reluctant Curial officials to take the Council's conclusions seriously, and in due course he appointed new, more moderate men, including foreigners, especially Frenchmen, to some important posts. The Roman central administration was reformed in various respects, but it was also strongly centralized. In a short time a new view of the Church established itself, at any rate theoretically, in the Catholic world; the Church was regarded as consisting of the people of God and ecclesiastical office as consisting of service to them. The reform of the Mass liturgy and the replacement of Latin by the vernacular, with a new arrangement of Scripture readings, represented an advance the importance of which could hardly be exaggerated. Ecumenical co-operation, both at parish level (joint activities and services) and at Church level (reciprocal visits and mixed study commissions) was encouraged. The reform of priests' seminaries and religious orders was energetically pursued. Diocesan and parish councils with strong lay participation were founded and began to be active. A new vitality made its appearance in theology, and a new opening out of the Church became plainly evident in relation to the problems of contemporary humanity and contemporary society. Nothing of all this was perfect, but it was all basically good and hopeful.

Meanwhile important problems were left unsettled as a result of the attitude of the Pope and the bishops, who at the time did not protest. These came to occupy a bigger place in the

public mind than any others. They were the questions of birth
control, mixed marriages, celibacy of the clergy in the Latin
Church, the structural and personal reform of the Roman Curia,
the effective involvement of the localities concerned in the
appointment of new and suitable bishops. These were certainly
not the central theological questions of the Christian message.
Nevertheless they were of the utmost urgency for the credible
proclamation of that message in the contemporary world and of
deep concern to the countless numbers of people affected by
them. But it was precisely in these sensitive areas, in every one of
which solutions are basically possible, that the leadership
failed. The firm, strong, hopeful spiritual leadership provided
by John XXIII was lacking. Instead, a growing stream of
sometimes very sombre warnings, jeremiads and imputations
was addressed to bishops and episcopal conferences, to theologians, priests, and to the young people of the Church and of the
world. The personal and structural reasons for this reaction are
manifold. As usual, instead of piloting by the pole-star of the
bold message of Jesus and the new challenges of a new age, there
was an ever-increasing anxious and nervous concentration on
the maintenance of the *status quo* and the maintenance of
spiritual power, no part of which would be willingly surrendered.
The traditional Curial policy and theology again prevailed,
and to a large extent a relapse took place in Rome into pre-
conciliar absolutism, juridicism and centralism, all in accordance with the saying that was quoted at the time of the Council
itself: 'Councils come to an end, popes pass away, but the
Roman Curia goes on.' The Curia was expanded instead of
being cut back and its centralization in the Secretariat of State
meant a setback for all other Curial authorities, with the result
that, as in the time of Pius XII, the most important decisions
are once more made in practice, not so much by the appropriate congregations as by a number of secret but well-known
'super-experts'.

Faced with this rigidity in Rome, many bishops and bishops'
conferences behaved irresolutely, hesitantly, and passively.
Instead of boldly and immediately setting about putting the
Council's decisions into practice in the various countries, a
policy of wait-and-see was adopted. Exceptionally and admirably, the Dutch bishops seized the opportunity to identify

themselves with the cares and needs of their clergy and people; elsewhere the opportunity was missed. Some bishops attempted a new style, while others reverted to an undisguised pre-conciliar authoritarianism. Rome remained the model. The co-operation between bishops and theologians that had worked so well at the Council and had so largely contributed to its success withered away. What was wanted was a return to the familiar, and the results were what might have been expected. Theological aid was welcome only in emergencies or, as happened at the Council, when Latin documents were needed; otherwise theologians were regarded by many bishops as an awkward species of humanity whom it was as well to avoid. It was easy to charge them with lack of humility, faith, and love of the Church; it was less easy to admit that they had not caused the crisis but merely given warning of it. Seven post-conciliar years were to pass in Germany before the holding of a synod was finally announced for 1972, though this could have been planned as early as 1965. In many other countries nothing at all has yet been done in this respect. But the hope that everything would remain as it had been turned out to be illusory.

Meanwhile, the Roman Curia tried to retain pre-conciliar-minded bishops in office beyond the age-limit envisaged by the Council (in principle, seventy-five); the old Roman system of royal dispensations and privileges got to work again. In so far as Rome had a free hand, new bishops were selected preferably according to the two tried and tested principles of sound moral standards and the uncritical loyalty to Rome which is called 'obedience'. Fortunately, mistakes were made in some instances, and some men were appointed who subsequently distinguished themselves by their independence of mind, courage and unexpected initiative. Rome did not appreciate this at all – the unobjective reactions to the moves made by the Dutch episcopate and Cardinal Suenens's celebrated, so moderate and objective interview (to which we shall return later) will be recalled. It preferred compliant bishops, even though – as is strikingly obvious in many cases – this results in the real diocesan leadership slipping from their hands.

In these circumstances, the growing trend to solidarity, particularly among the younger clergy, and the formation of organizations of priests and also of laymen, were a necessity, and

to many were a hopeful sign in a Church system that was
relapsing into rigidity. Even the Church authorities must
surely admit that most of these priests' organizations have
behaved with an exceedingly reasonable and constructive
moderation.

All the blame for the present critical situation should not of
course be attributed to Rome. The many theologians who kept
silent when they should have spoken out bear their full share of
responsibility. But it cannot be denied that the chief responsibility for the present intensity of the crisis devolves upon the
reactionary attitude of Rome. The Pope obviously believes he
has done much, very much, for the renewal of the Church. Let
us repeat that his integrity and his good intentions are not for
one moment in question. But what appears to be revolutionary
from the narrow viewpoint of Rome – the long overdue shaking
of a number of Vatican court traditions, the simplification of
clothing and titles that still seem strange, the appointment to
the Curia of foreign, but obviously very Roman-minded,
prelates – counts for hardly anything in the eyes of the world
and the greater part of the Church. To these there are more
important things that matter.

True, the Index has been abolished, and the Inquisition is
now called by another name. But inquisitional proceedings are
still taken against troublesome theologians, and the regulations
governing the Congregation for the Doctrine of the Faith have
not yet been published, though the Pope approved them in
1965. True, an international commission of theologians has at
last been appointed, but conciliar and post-conciliar theology
has made practically no headway in the Curia, as is shown,
among other things, by the painful incidents connected with
the Dutch catechism. Theologians such as Daniélou, who used
to be persecuted by the Inquisition but now bring an aura of
pseudo-learning to the role of Grand Inquisitor, are appointed
cardinals of the Holy Roman Church and fulfil its expectations.

True, a synod of bishops has twice been held, and in general
the importance of the episcopal office is spoken of with great
deference. But even the modest recommendations made by this
high representative body of the Church make little visible
impact, and vanish into the files of the Vatican, where for
intelligible reasons the intimation of a personal wish is if

possible preferred to the statement of a position publicly
arrived at. True, some rights, generally insignificant, have been
restored to the bishops, for example in the matter of dispensations, but, at the same time, contrary to the wishes of the
Council, the position of nuncios was strengthened by a *motu
proprio* (1969); and a papal commission for the reform of
canon law – from which all representatives of public opinion
in the Church, including progressive specialists such as those of
the Canon Law Society of America, were excluded – was
appointed to draft a basic law of the Catholic Church that
would make use of the words of Vatican II to reconsolidate
Roman absolutism. True, the Church calendar has been
reformed – in the most inept fashion – at the expense of some
unhistorical saints, but at the same time relics found under the
main altar of St Peter's are officially identified as the bones of
the apostle, though this is rejected by the best qualified historians. The reform of women's orders has been encouraged, but in
America, where it was most seriously attempted, a stop was put
to it by the Congregation for Religious and Secular Institutes.
Cardinals' trains have been shortened, but not done away with;
indulgences have been 'reformed', but not discontinued; the
expenses of canonization have been reduced, but not abolished.

True, during the Council the excommunication of the
Patriarch of Constantinople and his Churches was rescinded
after more than nine hundred years, and mutual visits arranged.
But after the lifting of the excommunication intercommunion
was not restored, and maintenance of all the Roman privileges
and prerogatives which have been customary since the Middle
Ages were rigidly insisted on. True, relations were established
with the World Council of Churches, and a call was paid on the
General Secretariat of the World Council on the occasion of
a visit to the International Labour Office at Geneva. But all the
ecumenical words have hardly been followed by ecumenical
deeds. A recent *motu proprio* (1970) attempts by a discriminating
use of dispensations to continue to avoid and prevent general
recognition of the validity of mixed marriages, ecumenical
marriage services based on equality of rights between the
Churches, and responsible parental decisions made in the light of
their conscience in regard to the baptism and education of
children.

True, a papal visit was paid to Jerusalem and the Israeli government was greeted. But, as before, recognition of the State of Israel was withheld for political reasons, and the response to the threat to annihilate the people of Israel was, following in the footsteps of Pius XII, prudently to send both sides the same exhortation to adopt peaceful ways. Visits to the United Nations and addresses on human rights contrast with diplomatic silence on the persecution and torture of Catholic priests and laymen under South American military dictatorships; and on a trip to Portugal, where freedom in Church and State was being suppressed at the time by the crudest totalitarian methods, this was likewise passed over in silence, tribute being paid instead to a Marian shrine that historically and theologically is dubious in every respect. The introduction into Italy of a reasonable civil divorce law, of a kind that has long existed in wide areas of the world, was the subject of the most vigorous protest and opposition, while non-recognition of the validity of so many mixed marriages serves as a positive encouragement to frivolous divorce. Visits to Africa, Asia and South America achieve great publicity success as efforts on behalf of the Third World, while the solution put forward for the central problem of these continents, the population explosion, is continence and prohibition of the use of contraceptives.

It is extremely depressing to have to look on at all this, but it brings us back to our chief point, which is that the greater the Pope's efforts to take his teaching office seriously, the more they seem to take place at the expense of the credibility of that office and the inner cohesion of the Church. Papal doctrinal statements seem to many to be inspired by a narrow Roman theology and ideology which then fail to make the intended impact on the Church. Only in the dogmatically innocuous field of the encyclical *Populorum Progressio* (1967), and of development aid, did the Pope venture to make any advance, without, however, drawing any very clear conclusions on the role of the Church and the Vatican in regard to immediate aid. The other important doctrinal documents, however, basically display a reactionary trend. The very first encyclical, *Ecclesiam Suam* (1963), was disappointing because of its unecumenical Romanism and its insnffiicent documentation from Scripture. The encyclical *Mysterivm Fidei*, on the Eucharist (1965), which, to the indignation of many bishops who had their eyes on Holland, Paul VI published just before the Council assembled for its fourth session, also showed him to be tied to a textbook theology on which neither the exegesis nor the historical studies of recent decades had made any sort of impression; John XXIII's statement that the clothing of the formulation of faith might change while its substance remained the same was denied. The encyclical *Sacerdotalis Coelibatus* (1967) made desperate efforts to use the supreme truths of the gospel to demonstrate the undemonstrable, namely that the meaningful free choice of celibacy of which the gospel speaks justifies the imposition by ecclesiastical authority of a law that eliminates freedom of choice in the matter. The encyclical *Humanae Vitae* (1968) exposed to an astonished world the weaknesses and backwardness of Roman theology and roused unprecedented opposition among ordinary Church members, theologians and bishops, and at bishops' conferences. In the papal *Credo* (1968) the Pope in typical Roman fashion identified himself with the Church without consulting it, for he declared it to be the 'credo of the people of God'; and he completely ignored the hierarchy of truths established by Vatican II and put questionable theologumena of the Roman tradition on a par with the central statements of the Christian faith. Finally, the latest decree on mixed marriages (1970) again shows the profoundly unecumenical attitude of the Roman central administration that underlies all its ecumenical protestations.[4]

It is consistent with all this that Paul VI responded to the just and reasonable plea of the Dutch bishops and their Church for a re-examination of the law of celibacy with an abrupt 'no' from the window of his palace, as if doubt had been cast on a dogma of the Church or this were an issue to be decided by himself alone; and that instead of seeking a dialogue with his Dutch episcopal brethren he sought one with the Cardinal Secretary of State on the floor below, to whom he wrote a letter; and that finally as a repressive measure betraying a profound mistrust of the whole clergy, he tried to impose an annual renewal of their priestly vows in connection with the Maundy Thursday service, as if to make up by vows and oaths for lack of reason and documentation from the gospel.

'*Quousque tandem . . .*' We might well be tempted to quote the

words of the Roman Cicero did we not know that we are not
confronted here merely with the failure of an individual acting in
good faith, but that the whole thing is connected with the
Roman system, which is still characterized by a spiritual
absolutism, a formal and often inhuman juridicism, a terrifying
spiritual absolutism and a traditionalism fatal to genuine
renewal that are truly shocking to modern man. To eliminate
any misunderstanding and dispel doubts expressed in letters
from pious souls, let it be said that, for all his criticisms, the
author of this book is and remains a convinced Catholic theologian. It is precisely because he is a Catholic theologian with a
profound obligation to his Church that he believes it to be his
right, and also unfortunately his duty, in all modesty and in full
awareness of his own human inadequacy *and* fallibility to raise
his voice in unequivocal and unignorable protest against the
fashion in which – blindly, though with the best intentions – the
people of God are being deprived of the fruits of the Council. A
Petrine ministry in the Church makes sense, and every Catholic
accepts it. But the Pope exists for the Church, and not the
Church for the Pope. His primacy is not the primacy of
sovereignty, but the primacy of service. The holder of the
Petrine office must not set himself up as overlord either of the
Church or of the gospel, which is what he does today when, after
all the negative experiences of the past and the positive experience
of the Council, he interprets theology and Church policy in the
light of an uncritically adopted tradition. It was primarily this
Roman theology and Church policy that bequeathed us the
separation from the Eastern Churches, and later the break-
away of the Reformed Churches, and finally isolated our
Church in the ghetto of the Counter-Reformation. In this fresh
crisis provoked by Roman intransigence, is it not better to speak
out plainly and openly and in good time, before more priests
give up the ministry, more candidates for orders go away, and
more people noisily or quietly turn their backs on the Church,
while the latter continues its decline to the level of a sub-
culture? The extent to which disappointment, a sense of
paralysis, and actual defeatism and hopelessness, have spread
recently, particularly among the best of our clergy and people,
is indescribable.

The crisis must be endured and will be overcome. Without

bitterness or animosity, and also without being impressed by
sanctimonious exhortations to keep silent and practise obedient
'humility' and 'love' of the Church, we shall continue to stand
up in word and deed for the reform and renewal of our Church
on the lines of the Second Vatican Council, by the power of the
message of Jesus and his Spirit. Reform and renewal is our
watchword. But let this also be said. Just as we have no time for
reaction in the Church, so do we have none for revolution, that
is, the violent overthrow of the Church's government and
values. Certainly the question may legitimately be asked
whether an absolutist system – for the Roman system is the
only absolutism that survived the French Revolution intact –
can be overthrown without violence. But the Christian message,
which aims at radical but not violent change, suggests an
opposite question. Should not the supersession of an absolutist
system without violent revolution, but by changes of personnel
and structures (which seems to be such a rare phenomenon in
the world and in world politics), be possible in the Church by
virtue of the Christian message? We must not give up the
struggle for renewal and reform, but neither must we give up
dialogue and hope of mutual understanding.

In this book the whole question of the Church's teaching
authority, and in particular the question of infallibility, will be
discussed. In our previous book on the Church we dealt only
marginally with infallibility, for good reasons. But, for equally
good reasons, a number of reviewers encouraged a specific
treatment of the subject, and present developments in the
Church call for such treatment. Roman absolutism and
traditionalism in theory and practice will be subjected to
theological examination at the point where they stand out
most sharply and also make maximum impact. Even when the
Church's claim to infallibility is not explicit, it is always
subliminally present. It is this claim to infallibility that we shall
examine here, taking as our starting-point the encyclical of
Paul VI that by its dogmatic rejection of all 'artificial' methods
of birth control so greatly shook the credibility of the Catholic
Church and its teaching office. It became clear at this point that
an insufficiently considered view of its continuity, authority and
infallibility had led the Catholic Church into a dangerous
impasse. If we have the strength (and the humility) to escape

from it by our own efforts, in the long run more good will be done than harm. For it will open up to us a wide expanse of territory on which we shall be able to walk freely, without being compelled perpetually to keep to the side-lines, perpetually looking over our shoulder for reassurance that we are covered by authority; and there we shall again meet our Christian brethren, who for a long time have not understood us on this matter.

No imprimatur will be sought for this book; not because it is not intended to be Catholic, but because – as we hope – it is Catholic without it. In recent years the imprimatur has become increasingly meaningless. It did not prevent my book *The Church* from becoming involved in Roman inquisitionary proceedings which have not yet closed. On the other hand, more than one bishop has asked authors to refrain from seeking an imprimatur, which might be interpreted in Rome and elsewhere as implying episcopal recommendation of the book. We know from experience that in many cases the imprimatur in practice means precensorship of one theological school by another, and its abolition has long been a matter of urgency. But the Roman tendency to think in terms of centuries often means that there is no time to tackle the problems of the hour. In the age of absolutism it was usual to seek permission to print publications of all kinds, and in this matter the Church was no exception. But in the contemporary world the free expression of opinion is a basic human right that cannot be denied even to a Catholic theologian in the ecclesial community when he is striving after the truth of the Church's proclamation.[5]

At the end of this candid foreword it is perhaps permissible to quote some words used in another context by Cardinal Bernhard Alfrink in his important closing address to the Dutch Pastoral Council which to so many people was one of the few great, hopeful signs in the post-conciliar period. 'We have conducted the debate with complete frankness,' he said, 'and given the other side the opportunity of witnessing what we were doing as much as they wanted, and of being drawn into it. I repeat, not for propaganda purposes but only to render a service. For the questions we have been discussing were not really ours only. No one is entitled to use the Lord's message as if it were his exclusive possession. We must always encounter it as a challenging message, and therefore one that is sometimes painful to us.

Thus we hope in this way to contribute something to the reconciliation of the Churches.'[6]

That is the spirit and the tone in which the author wishes to present what he has to say in this book, urging patient and persevering co-operation on the 'long march through the institutions'. The unforgettable John F. Kennedy described this effort of ours in relation to his own task in these words: 'All this will not be finished in the first 100 days. Nor will it be finished in the first 1,000 days, nor in the life of this Administration, nor even perhaps in our own lifetime on this planet. But let us begin. In your hands, my fellow citizens, more than mine, will rest the final success or failure of our course.'

Tübingen, Whitsun, 1970

Chapter One

INFALLIBLE TEACHING OFFICE?

I. PAST ERRORS

To non-Christians and Christians outside the Catholic Church the attribution of 'infallibility' to the Church's teaching office has always been unacceptable. Recently, however, it has to an astonishing extent become at least dubious within the Catholic Church itself. This is often a matter of feeling rather than of explicit attitude among clergy and laity; nevertheless the question is increasingly ventilated and discussed. It will therefore be subjected here to a considered theological enquiry, with a view to arriving at a definite answer.

It is easy to understand why the question obtrudes itself. The errors of the Church's teaching office have been numerous and grave; nowadays, when open discussion can no longer be forbidden, they cannot be denied even by the more conservative theologians and Church leaders. Among what might be called the classical errors now widely admitted are the excommunication of Photius, the Ecumenical Patriarch of Constantinople, and of the Greek Church, which formalized the now nearly thousand-year-old schism with the Eastern Church; the ban on lending money at interest imposed at the beginning of the modern age, a matter on which, after many compromises, the teaching office changed its mind, much too late; the condemnation of Galileo, and similar measures basically responsible for the estrangement between the Church and science that to this day has not yet been finally overcome; the condemnation of new forms of worship in the Rites controversy, which is one of the main reasons for the large-scale failure of the Catholic missions to India, China and Japan in modern times; the upholding by the use of all secular and spiritual means, including the use of excommunication, of the Pope's medieval temporal power until the time of the First Vatican Council, which to a large extent made the spiritual ministry of the papacy incredible; and finally, at the beginning of the twentieth century, the numerous condemnations of the application of the methods of critical and historical exegesis to the authorship of the books of the Bible, and of research into the sources of the Old and New Testaments and the historicity and literary genres of the Comma Johanneum and the Vulgate; as well as the condemnations in the dogmatic field, particularly in connection with so-called 'modernism' (study of the historical development of dogma); and in recent times in connection with Pius XII's encyclical *Humani Generis*, and the consequent disciplinary measures, and so on.

In every century the errors of the Church's teaching office have been numerous and indisputable; scrutiny of the Index of forbidden books yields abundant evidence of this. Yet over and over again it has found it difficult frankly and honestly to admit them. Generally, the correction of past mistakes has been only 'implicit', carried out in veiled fashion, lacking in courage and frankness, and lacking above all any open admission of having been at fault. It was feared that the admission of fallibility in certain important instances would be detrimental, if not fatal, to the claim to infallibility in others. For a long time Catholic apologetics was able very successfully to ward off the calling into question of infallibility by resorting to the basically simple expedient of arguing either that no error had been committed or – if in the last resort it could not be denied, reinterpreted, rendered innocuous or belittled – that it was an issue in which infallibility had not been at stake. In this way theology helped the hierarchy, and in return the hierarchy helped theology. Such theological manoeuvres often create a painful impression. As an example from the distant past we shall quote the case – discussed at Vatican I – of Pope Honorius, who was condemned as a heretic by an ecumenical council and by several subsequent popes. As a less remote example of a mistake, in an age when such theological manoeuvres are no longer possible, we may quote the recent decision on the immorality of birth control. We propose to begin our analysis with an examination of this highly illuminating test case in regard to the problem of infallibility.

Not only in scientific experiments, but in theology and in the Church also, unintended side-effects are often more important than the intended main effect. Many discoveries have come about by 'chance'. Pope Paul VI's encyclical on birth control, *Humanae Vitae*, did not make history because of its main purpose.

Public opinion polls in the most varied countries show that it did not succeed in stopping or even checking the use of 'artificial' methods of contraception. The arguments used obviously failed to convince the majority, even within the Catholic Church, and in the years that followed the use of the methods referred to increased rather than declined. Karl Rahner wrote at the time: 'From all that has been said so far, the sober conclusion must be drawn that the objective situation in relation to the mentality and practice of the majority of Catholics will not change after the encyclical.'[1] But its unforeseen and unintended side-effect was a widespread major examination of conscience about the meaning of the Church's authority – in particular, its teaching authority.

2. AUTHORITY QUESTIONED

The radical nature and the universality of this examination of conscience surprised even those who had previously been worried about the consequences of a possible negative papal decision on the subject. But is it not intelligible that there should have been such a reaction? In the first place, the issue is one to which neither navvy nor university professor, neither farmer nor civil servant, can remain indifferent; it affects New Yorkers and Romans, Indians and Canadians, alike; it affects everyone, and everyone feels it to be either a positive or a negative challenge. In the second place, it requires a definite, unequivocal answer, without beating about the bush. It all boils down to whether it is legitimate to take the Pill or not. Theologians skilled in the dialectics of the Catholic 'on the one hand, but also on the other' are ultimately compelled in this instance to come down from the fence and answer positively yes or no.

Pope Paul deserves respect for having had the courage to make an unpopular and unequivocal decision. For all the discussion about its purposes, the encyclical is written with Gallic clarity (the identity of its chief author is known). At worst an answer in the Roman manner might have been expected – the traditional 'no', with an expansible 'yes' tucked away in a subordinate clause. But fortunately there was none of this. All theological-political hermeneutic is excluded, misunderstandings are ruled out, and ways out – such as a broad interpretation of 'therapeutic treatment' with hormones, morally permissible according to the encyclical – are condemned as offences against scientific honesty. The encyclical is clear and unequivocal. It declares 'artificial' methods of contraception – by contrast with the 'natural' method of periodic abstention – to be impermissible because of natural law emanating from the Creator himself. Though the Pope is obviously striving to speak not harshly but pastorally, and though he recommends sympathy and compassion for the individual sinner, in reality this only makes it clearer that in his view guilt and sin are basically involved. So this time we are grateful for knowing quite clearly where we stand. In view of its very definite tone on the essential issue, it would be illusory to suppose that the document might be withdrawn or revised in the foreseeable future. The Church will have to learn to live with this encyclical.

But the novel feature of the whole debate is that it is centred, not so much on the encyclical's actual arguments as on its authority. In view of the purpose of the present work, there is no need for us to discuss the questionable points in the encyclical. The replies to it largely repeat the points made in the report of the progressive majority on the papal commission. They point out that the encyclical's arguments based on natural law are not convincing; that its concept of what is natural is naïve, static, narrow and completely unhistorical; that it ignores man's historicity, and that it dissects him in the light of an abstract conception of his nature; that the restriction of the concepts of nature and natural law to the physical and biological sphere is a regression to long obsolete Aristotelian-Stoic-medieval ideas; that the distinction between 'natural' and 'artificial' is arbitrary, and in connection with hormone preparations for inhibiting ovulation becomes a matter for the microscope and a question of milligrams. '*Abusus non tollit usum*', as the Romans said; the fact that abuse of a method is possible does not make its reasonable use illegitimate. The rhythm method of Ogino-Knaus, with its complicated system of taking temperatures and following the calendar, is anything but natural, and in some circumstances might actually be unnatural. The artificiality of a method is no argument against its permissibility (the Pope declared heart transplants to be permissible) and unconditional respect for nature results in a numinization of it that conflicts with the modern view of human responsibility, reducing personal life to a biological process and overlooking the vital difference between animal and biological and human and responsible sexuality. Moreover, technical methods of birth control are essential in view of the human situation as a whole (in particular the world's enormous over-population). The document moralizes about this situation, but fails to appreciate it properly and plays it down; the attitude to sexuality is still marked by the latent influence of the unchristian Manichaean heritage, and the whole document and its language displays a complete lack of concrete experience, and so on.

In these circumstances it is hardly surprising that there was widespread agreement with the Tübingen canonist Professor Johannes Neumann when he said: 'If, because of an antiquated outlook on life, an anachronistic theology and an unsatisfactory – because unscriptural – notion of faith, the so-called Church teaching office does not proclaim the gospel of the crucified and risen Christ but deludes itself that it is the "preceptor of the nations of the world" and puts forward a "doctrine" consisting of an inappropriate medley of Platonic, Aristotelian and Thomistic ideas, it is going beyond its brief and can claim neither obedience nor credibility. Good intentions no doubt played a part in the composition of this encyclical, but the deplorable thing about it is that – quite apart from the empirical sciences such as medicine and sociology – the philosophical and theological assumptions on which it was based had been invalidated before it was published.'[2] In an age that would like to quash the Galileo case there was now the danger of a new one. 'In view of this encyclical and its underlying philosophical assumptions and assumptions about natural law, if they can be called such, the idea of reopening the Galileo case with a view to rehabilitating him is grotesque. That shameful case arose out of the same way of thinking as this encyclical, but it is 350 years too late for the Church to rehabilitate Galileo. It is not that case that needs dealing with today, but the question of the total meaning of marriage and of accepted and responsible parenthood. That is the Galileo case of the present day – the question of the personal meaning of marriage – that needs to be decided and requires a helpful answer. Only thus, that is, by giving factually, situationally and humanly objective guidance in the spirit of Christ, can the Church expect to be listened to and be taken seriously again by Christians, especially Catholics, and also by all men of good will.'[3]

In comparison with the negativism of the encyclical on the point at issue and the weight of the criticisms that it met, the 'advances' attributed to it by apologetic-minded theologians and bishops fade into insignificance. Some of these 'advances' are to positions taken for granted by most people in the Church as, for instance, when Paul VI, in contrast to Pius XII, refrains from calling for complete continence, or when 'responsible parenthood' is made the starting-point of the discussion, or when the marital union is no longer, as in the Code of Canon Law, considered a remedy for concupiscence. But these 'advances' in changing the earlier stand of the Holy Office are used in part to intensify the negativism of the encyclical as, for instance, when sexual love is no longer subordinated to procreation as the primary end of marriage, but the 'inseparable connection' between the two is used as an argument for rejecting birth control. Thus the essential negativism of the encyclical makes it a bitter pill to swallow, even though it is offered with modern colouring and is sugar-coated. That is why there has been practically no progress in objective discussion of its subject-matter since its publication. At bottom both sides have merely been reiterating the familiar; minds had long since been made up and were obviously not changed by the encyclical and, as has been made clear by the positions adopted at various conferences, the camp of its unconditional supporters in the Catholic Church is crumbling away. It is depressing that a Catholic theologian should write: 'World opinion, in so far as it responds to the matters raised in the encyclical, will not be very interesting; there is no going back on knowledge once acquired; in this respect the Pope's arguments are not interesting even as a contribution to the discussion . . . There will have to be intensive study of the question of the papal teaching office. Thus theologians will now have to show how far the competence of the papal teaching office extends, and will have to make it clear that, when a pope's theoretically fallible doctrinal opinions are treated as infallible, authoritarian abuse of power begins; and thus Paul VI's portentous mistake on the birth control issue may possibly lead to the theological clarification of many questions about the papal primacy which have remained open since Vatican I.'⁴

3. THE QUESTION OF AUTHORITY

Thus what interests us in this context is not the birth control question, but that of the teaching office. Many doubts about its authority have been expressed since the publication of the encyclical, but the arguments used have often been only too superficial.

In the first place, there are those who claim that the Pope can make doctrinal decisions only on matters of dogma and not on specifically moral issues, and that birth control is a specifically moral issue. It is true that by far the greater part of both papal and conciliar decisions lie within the field of dogma, and that the birth control question comes into the field of moral theology. But if the Pope's competence is granted in the one field, why should it be denied him in the other? Can dogma and morals be separated? Does not dogma have moral consequences, and are there not dogmatic assumptions behind morality? Is not the Catholic morality of marriage in particular based on dogmatic assumptions?

Others claim that the Pope is competent only to interpret the moral demands of the Christian revelation and not to draw conclusions from any so-called natural law. It must be admitted that not a single argument from the gospel is produced in support of the negativism of the encyclical, and that in the document as a whole the Bible plays little more than a decorative role. But here too a further question arises. How are the demands of Christian revelation to be adequately distinguished from those of natural law (if we wish to work with that problematical expression)? Is there not 'natural law' in the Bible? Does not the Decalogue to a large extent consist of both in one? And could not the prohibition of birth control be linked – if necessary – with the dignity of marriage as this is asserted in Scripture?

There are others again who point out that, though since

Vatican II the Pope has been bound to govern the Church
collegially, he issued this encyclical on his own. That is correct,
and the authority of the encyclical is gravely compromised by
the fact that he made his decision against the overwhelming
majority of the commission of expert theologians, bishops,
physicians, demographers and other specialists that he had set
up himself; and that, though they spent years discussing and
working on the question, he neither made serious use of their
single official report nor seriously replied to it; and, furthermore,
that by a peremptory intervention he prevented the Council
from discussing and reaching a decision on the question, and
also, after some initial hesitation, avoided subsequent consultation of the world episcopate and even of the synod of
bishops. Finally, he made his decision while the Church was in
a state of doubt, and consequently it was promptly plunged into
a state of doubt all over again. As a result of his acting in this
way, he himself gravely jeopardized the credibility of the
encyclical from the outset. Nevertheless a question arises here
too. At the Council did not the episcopate more or less passively
and without serious reason – though admittedly hoping for a
positive outcome – allow the Pope simply to reserve to himself
the decision both on this question and on the similarly weighty
one of the reform of the Curia? Did this not permit him to reach
his decision on these matters 'on his own', in the absolutist style
customary since the High Middle Ages? (In point of fact a
super-commission had been secretly formed, the Curial com-
position of which guaranteed the desired result in advance.)
Were not the problematic decisions of Vatican I on papal
primacy simply repeated at Vatican II without the bishops'
safeguarding themselves and the Church against possible
absolutist abuse of papal power? Was not the Pope assured that
in principle he was entitled to act on his own? Was not the
question, raised in ancient and medieval times, whether even
the Roman Pontiff might not separate himself from the Church
and thus become a schismatic, considerately avoided in
conciliar discussion? Taking all these circumstances into
account, is one entitled to complain of illegitimate, uncollegial
procedure on the Pope's part? Do not much more fundamental
issues of Church government and the teaching office arise?

This discussion should therefore not be embarked on with an

inadequate theological armoury. The arguments quoted above are at best of secondary importance. There is also another frequently heard allegation that must be even more definitely rejected; the allegation, that is to say, that Paul VI is an arch-reactionary, and wanted a negative decision from the outset. This allegation is based on ignorance, if not on malice; it betrays a mistaken view of the former Cardinal Montini and his pastoral intentions. At least he wanted a positive answer; at all events it must be a responsible one. It does him honour that he took his responsibility so seriously and wrestled with the problem for years before making up his mind. True, he could have done so more cheaply and at less expense to himself and his authority. Had he been simply an arch-conservative by nature, he would have needed only to confirm the negative decision of Pius XI, or he could simply have kept silent. Instead, he repeatedly declared that the question must be examined, and left the possibility of a reorientation open. He insisted that the traditional teaching remained valid 'at least as long as we do not feel obliged in conscience to alter it' (address to the College of Cardinals, 23 June 1964).[5]

This certainly put him in a difficult position when the theologians drew his attention to the fact that a papal announcement of the mere possibility of a change, the appointment of a commission to investigate the whole question, and the intense theological debate that had broken out in the meantime, clearly demonstrated the doubtfulness of the obligation to observe the birth control ban, for the ancient Roman principle *lex dubia non obligat*, a doubtful law is not binding, holds good under Catholic general moral theology. Everywhere priests and the faithful began appealing to this principle. This led the Pope, in his address to the Italian National Congress for Gynaecology and Midwifery on 29 October 1966,[6] to deny that the teaching office of the Church was 'at present in a state of doubt' on what he admitted to be this 'far-reaching and delicate question'. It was not *in statu dubii*, but *in statu studii*, in other words, in a state, not of doubt, but of study. He has more than once been accused of falsehood on this account, as he was on account of his address to the assembly of German Catholics at Essen in 1968, when he claimed that 'the overwhelming majority of the Church' had given the encyclical their 'assent and obedience'.[7]

The 1966 statement was the immediate occasion for the departure from the Church of Britain's foremost Catholic theologian on the grounds of its general dishonesty (*Observer*, London, 1 January 1967).[8]

But to simplify the matter by representing it to be a question of personal morality is to do the Pope an injustice. It is not personal dishonesty, but a quite definite view of the teaching and teaching office of the Church that leads the Pope to act, as he stated in the same address, 'in consciousness of the obligations of our apostolic office'. It must be held in his favour that he made the exercise of his teaching office no easier by the intense personal concern with which he devoted himself to the question, as he movingly explained in his defence of the encyclical on 31 July 1968. Here too he honourably admitted his doubts: 'How often have we had the feeling of being almost overwhelmed by this mass of documents,' he said, 'how often, humanly speaking, have we felt the inadequacy of our poor person when faced with the formidable apostolic duty of having to announce a decision on this matter. How many times have we trembled in the face of the dilemma between an easy surrender to current views and a decision that modern society would find difficult to accept, and which might prove too arbitrary a burden for married life.'[9] Three years earlier, in his first interview as Pope, he had said with the same disarming frankness as he glanced at the many files on his desk: '*E più facile studiare che decidere*' ('It is easier to study than to decide').[10] In this he notably distinguished himself from a number of his predecessors who in theological matters always found it easier to decide than to study (for example, Pius IX in connection with the Syllabus, or Pius XII in connection with the encyclical *Humani Generis*).

But we must also ask whether the Pope's own resources are not over-extended when in the exercise of his pastoral office of proclamation (an office that, as John XXIII showed, can have a highly positive function in the Church) he exercises with the best will in the world the specifically theological function of the teaching office, undertaking to study notoriously controversial theological questions in order then to make a decision on behalf of the whole Church. At all events, we cannot help feeling what a tragedy it is that a pope who in his opening address to the second session of the Council wished to show himself to be a moderate progressive should have felt himself increasingly called on to act in a reactionary manner; that, though he made a variety of compromises of a personal and material nature in his desire to satisfy everyone in the Church, he became a partisan figure as rarely a pope before him has done; that, though he wanted to work for the unity of the Catholic Church and of Christianity, he exposed the Church to the greatest split of the century; and that, though he wanted to be the heir both of John XXIII and of Pius XII, his whole attitude put him in danger of squandering to an alarming extent the credit that John and the Council accumulated for the Catholic Church; for in Paul VI Pius, put on the same plane as John and destined for canonization, was bound to prove the stronger. It is sad to have to say this, for it need not have been so. As the French theologian Jean-Marie Paupert said: 'But the Pope has publicly and definitely put himself on the other side, the side of conserving superannuated structures. *Humanae Vitae* is only one element in this decision, to which it is by no means difficult to add others: the papal encyclical on the celibacy of the priesthood (June 1967); the declaration on the body of St Peter (June 1968); the Credo of Paul VI (30 June 1968), and the massive attacks on the Dutch catechism. Though it distresses me deeply, I must declare my belief that, in view of the encyclical *Humanae Vitae*, we can regard it as certain that the door that was opened for the first time by the Council has been shut again, even before the Church was able to tread the path to which it gave free access.'[11]

4. TEACHING OFFICE AND CONSCIENCE

It would betray a poor knowledge of the former Cardinal Montini if one failed to see that he is deeply affected by a great deal of all this, and that it makes his pontificate an almost intolerable burden to him. For all one's differences with him, the human being who bears this burden deserves genuine sympathy, and above all his moral conscientiousness deserves respect. Professor Alois Müller, the Fribourg pastoral theologian, well says: 'Respect for the Pope does not cease, but in fact begins with this new and difficult situation of the Church. But we must decline to allow this respect to take the form of immature obedience that conflicts with our own insight. We must take the Pope seriously in his need and in his limitations. We must bear responsibility in the Church, to prevent his responsibility from becoming too heavy. Even in opposition, we must do him the service of leading the Church to new knowledge which will again give him confidence in faith, together with his brothers in the episcopal office and the whole people of God.'[12]

The obverse side of respect for the Pope's moral conscientiousness is thus respect for the moral conscientiousness of all those who believe themselves unable to agree with him. This obverse side of the whole problem must be seen in all clarity, as Hanno Helbling says: 'If the Christian family is to achieve the responsible self-development that the Pope himself describes as the purpose of his guidance, it must be assured of freedom, not only from state compulsion, but also from ecclesiastical tutelage. So long as this freedom is lacking in things that play an essential part in shaping individual lives, so long as it is not the individual conscience that sets the standard for the life of married couples and their children, the dignity of the individual lacks the independence that alone enables it fully to develop. This does not mean that the Church should let things take their course when it sees the dangers involved. On the contrary, the cure of souls will have achieved its highest and certainly most demanding task when it can offer its aid on the basis of free consideration of individual problems and questions of conscience. But the Pope does not permit such a situation to arise; by his encyclical he subjects the pastor to strict regulation. We cannot deny that he possesses the courage to bind. But he cannot find the courage to loose.'[13]

In regard to the individual's freedom of conscience, here we need only reiterate the principle that it was necessary to state immediately after the publication of the encyclical; it is a principle on which a consensus of international theological opinion is increasingly taking shape. Those who, after serious and mature reflection, before themselves, their marriage partners and God, come to the conclusion that, for the maintenance of their love and the endurance and happiness of their marriage, they must act otherwise than in the way enjoined by the encyclical, are, by the traditional teaching of the popes, obliged to follow their conscience. When therefore they have acted in accordance with their conscience and to the best of their knowledge, they will not accuse themselves of sin, but will take part in the life of the Church and its sacraments with a quiet mind.

A reminder of the Catholic tradition should not be out of place here.[14] The classic theological and canonical view is that a Christian should not be deterred from following the dictates of his conscience even by the threat of excommunication. As a believing Christian anyone who found himself involved in such a tragic conflict would have in a spirit of faith to bear the excommunication, however hard his loyalty to the Church made this. The answer was given long ago by Innocent III, relying on the words of St Paul that are always rightly quoted in such cases: 'Every act done in bad faith is a sin' (Romans 14:23). 'What is not from faith is sin', said Innocent, 'and whatever is done contrary to conscience leads to hell . . . as in this matter no one must obey a judge against God, but rather humbly bear the excommunication.'[15] Sebastian Merkle, the Church historian, referring to these matters in an article on Savonarola, writes: 'St Thomas, the greatest doctor of the Order of Preachers, and with him a number of other scholastics, accordingly taught that an individual excommunicated for erroneous reasons ought rather to die under the interdict than obey superior orders he knew to be mistaken. "For that would be contrary to the truth (*contra veritatem vitae*) which is not to be sacrificed even on account of possible scandal." '[16] Even at the time of the Counter-Reformation, when there was much more rigidity on this question, Cardinal Bellarmine, for all his emphasis on papal authority, admitted that 'just as it would be legitimate for a man to resist the Pope if he physically assaulted him, so, if the Pope made an assault on souls, if he sowed confusion in the State, and particularly if he set out to destroy the Church, would passive resistance be legitimate, in the form of refraining from carrying out his orders, and also active resistance, by preventing him from carrying out his will.'[17]

But, for all the emphasis on freedom of conscience, one should not succumb to the facile conclusion that the whole thing is settled by reference to the subjective conscience. The whole objective problem must be cleared up.

5. THE CRUCIAL POINT

This gives even greater urgency to the question of how things could have come to this pass. We must ask what caused the Pope to come down on the conservative side in the encyclical (the same question might be asked in connection with the papal Credo). We must now take a closer look, particularly at the Pope's own utterances.

There is no historical precedent for an encyclical's rousing a positive storm of protest in the Catholic Church, and causing the Pope to feel called on to defend it publicly immediately after its publication. He produced no further objective arguments, but spoke only of the subjective motives behind his decision. 'The first feeling was of the very heavy responsibility we bore . . . We have never been more conscious of the burden of our office than on this occasion.'[18] The reason for this, he explains, was that 'bearing in mind the obligations and also the freedom of our apostolic office, we had to take into consideration, not only a centuries-old teaching tradition, but the teaching of modern times, that of our three immediate predecessors'.[19] Johannes Neumann says of this: 'An insuperable obstacle stood in the way of an objective decision by Rome in the form of Pius XI's encyclical *Casti Connubii* of 1930. The positions taken in that encyclical, which appealed to an immutable natural law, obviously prevented the present Pope from reaching a decision with the necessary openness and freedom of heart and mind.'[20]

The Pope, on his own showing, evidently did not more closely consider the original gospel message. Presumably he believed that no arguments against birth control were to be derived from it, particularly as nowadays the former stock biblical example of birth control, Onan, who refused the Israelite obligation to give children to his brother's widow, is universally regarded by theologians and popes as irrelevant to the present issue. The Pope drew no conclusions from the surprising silence of the original documents of faith, in which all other sins are uninhibitedly called by their right names. To him something else was evidently more important.

What tipped the scales in favour of his negative answer? 'Natural law', on which the whole argument is built? Yes, but at least since the Council sat, the 'natural law' on this point has been a matter of controversy throughout the Church and in the papal commission itself. Thus it was not 'natural law' as such, but a particular ecclesiastical interpretation of it that swung the balance. And which one? According to the Pope's own words that we quoted above, it was that stated in the traditional teaching of the Church and of the recent popes in particular. In this short encyclical there are about twenty-five references to the 'teaching of the Church' and the *magisterium* and only two to the gospel, and then in the form of the 'law of the gospel' (as if St Paul had not contrasted 'law' and 'gospel'). There are thirty references in one way or another to the 'law' that the Church upholds and proclaims. Freedom of will and civil freedom are mentioned, but not the freedom of the children of God (as if St Paul had not taught that Christ liberated us from the law into this freedom). There are forty quotations of papal utterances, and thirteen of statements made by the Second Vatican Council (by the Pope who forbade it to make a decision on this question), while Scripture is quoted sixteen times, chiefly in a moralizing context and never in support of the encyclical's main theme.

All these are clear signs that in this document the law counts for more than Christian freedom, the Church's teaching office for more than the gospel of Jesus Christ, papal tradition for more than Holy Scripture; they show the extent to which the teaching office of the Catholic Church still suffers from moralizing legalism, ideologizing disconnected from real life, and triumphalist papalism. Otherwise there would have been no need to exercise the most varied kinds of pressure, using the tried and trusted channels of the nunciatures and the religious orders, or the secret letter of Cardinal Secretary of State Cicognani to the bishops of the world (published in *The Times* of London on 4 September 1968), in which, in the ornate style used by totalitarian party headquarters to convey their nevertheless unmistakable meaning, subordinates were required to bring to bear all their spiritual power in order 'to put forward again in all its purity the constant teaching of the Church', in other words, impose it. The letter goes on: 'And now, he [the

Pope] turns to all priests, secular and religious, and especially
those with responsibility as general and provincial superiors of
religious orders, to exhort them to put forward to Christians this
delicate point of Church doctrine, to explain it and to vindicate
the profound reasons behind it. The Pope counts on them and
on their devotion to the chair of Peter, their love for the Church,
and their care for the true good of souls. Like them, he is
informed of the ideas and practices prevalent in contemporary
society, and he is well aware of the efforts that will be needed to
educate men's minds on this point. He knows what sacrifices –
sometimes heroic ones – are involved in the application of
Catholic principles on conjugal morality. It is his desire that the
bishops, the priests, the Christian centres participating in
various Catholic movements and organizations, become with
joyful submissiveness the apostles of the teaching of Holy
Mother Church and be able to find convincing language which
will ensure its acceptance ... Finally, it is essential, in the
confessional as well as by preaching, through the press and the
other means of social communication, that every pastoral
effort be made so that no doubt whatever remains among the
faithful or among outside opinion on the position of the Church
on this grave question.'[21] Is it surprising that many people
inside and outside the Catholic Church drew comparisons with
the situation in Czechoslovakia? Or that unenlightened bishops
in 'their devotion to the chair of Peter' felt encouraged publicly
to abuse theologians and suspend from their duties the most
zealous of their priests and thus bring about crises in their
churches?

With all respect to the traditional teaching of the Church
and the most recent popes, why was such immense effort
concentrated on this particular issue? Why was so much staked
on it? This brings us to the heart of the matter, the question of
error in the traditional teaching of the Church and of the most
recent popes. The Pope's own statements make this clear. He
wished to make 'a personal examination of this grave question
[birth control] ... above all, because certain criteria of
solutions had emerged [within the commission] that departed
from the moral teaching on marriage put forward with constant firmness by the teaching authority of the Church'.[22] That
explains it. The permissibility of birth control could have been

granted only subject to a condition totally unacceptable to Pope and Curia, namely the disavowal of the traditional teaching of the Church and of the last three popes in particular, the admission of an error in the teaching of the Church. But as it is, should it turn out that in spite of everything so much was staked on the wrong card, another, even grimmer, possibility appears on the horizon; the possibility, that is to say, that a successor of Paul VI may have to disavow four popes.

6. WHY THE POPE WAS NOT PERSUADED

The theologians of the progressive majority on the commission were in fact prepared to admit an error on the part of the teaching office. 'Not a few theologians and faithful fear that a change in the official teaching could damage the confidence of Catholics in the teaching authority of the Church. For they ask how the assistance of the Holy Spirit could permit such an error for so many centuries, and one that has had so many consequences, especially in recent centuries. But the criteria for discerning what the Spirit could or could not permit in the Church can scarcely be determined *a priori*. In point of fact we know that there have been errors in the teaching of the *magisterium* and of tradition. With regard to sexual relations, it should be noted that for so many centuries in the Church, with the active concurrence of the popes, it was all but unanimously taught that conjugal intercourse was illicit unless accompanied by the intention to procreate – or at least (because of I Corinthians 7) to offer an outlet for the other partner; and yet no theologians hold to this teaching today, nor is it the official position.'[23]

The only resolution of the progressive episcopal commission (adopted by nine votes to three with three abstentions) was not so clear on this point, but it was clear enough for the president of the commission, Cardinal Ottaviani, the leader of the small but valiant Curial minority, to refuse to submit it to the Pope, though after endless discussion it had been passed by a fair vote (only two out of fifteen bishops had answered the question whether birth control was intrinsically evil with an unequivocal yes). Cardinal Döpfner, the vice-president, was then asked to submit it, and did so. The Pope waited for several months and then, in spite of interventions by various cardinals and also by the German episcopate, came down on the side of Cardinal Ottaviani and the conservative minority. Undoubtedly this was a notable victory for Curial theology, assuming it does not turn out to have been a Pyrrhic victory.

The great question, though it is seldom asked, is why the progressive majority failed to persuade the Pope (on whose good intentions we have constantly insisted). Our answer is that (consisting largely as it did of moral theologians) it did not take sufficiently seriously the arguments of the conservative Roman minority, which (in relation to the birth control question) were in the last resort not moral theological but fundamental theological (in relation to the authority of the teaching office). This statement requires amplification. To justify a new moral theological position in the eyes of the teaching office of the Church, the progressive majority attached special weight to two points: 1. that a new historical situation justified a new position; and, 2. that the teaching contained in Pius XI's encyclical was not based on an *infallible* decision, which would put basic dogmatic difficulties in the way of adopting a new position. The conservative minority violently attacked both arguments, rightly, it seems to us. We rely on the report of the conservative theologians which was later put forward as the 'minority report' on the commission's official resolution. This report is very revealing and significant for the theological position of the conservative minority.

1. The progressives argued that a new historical situation justified the adoption of a new position. Since 1930 (the year of the encyclical *Casti Connubii*) great changes had taken place in the world, psychologically, sociologically and medically (not least because of the Pill).

The conservatives do not deny that changes have taken place, but reply that in terms of theological principle the situation remains unchanged. They have a convincing case. They point out that essentially the same arguments in favour of birth control were accepted by the Lambeth Conference of Anglican bishops in 1930 (the commission agreed unanimously that the present problem was not confined to the Pill), and that the encyclical *Casti Connubii* was written in reply to those arguments. In other words, the case that was being presented now was basically that which had been presented then and rejected by the Church's teaching office. The 'minority report' explains: 'For, as a matter of fact, the teaching of *Casti Connubii* was solemnly proposed in opposition to the doctrine of the Lambeth Conference of 1930, by the Church "to whom God had entrusted the defence of the integrity and purity of morals . . . in token of her divine ambassadorship . . . and through our mouth." . . . Some who fight for a change say that the teaching of the Church was not false for those times. Now, however, it must be changed because of changed historical conditions. But this seems to be something that one cannot propose, for the Anglican Church was teaching precisely that and for the very reasons which the Catholic Church solemnly denied, but which it would now admit. Certainly such a manner of speaking would be unintelligible to the people and would seem to be a specious pretext.'[24]

In other words, the theory of the development of dogma abundantly used and abused in Catholic theology since the nineteenth century – under the influence of Newman and the Tübingen Catholic school, especially Johann Adam Möhler – did not apply here. If the progressive theologians had been able to present Paul VI with a formula enabling a positive teaching today to seem merely to be a 'development' of the negative teaching of Pius XI in 1930, enabling him, that is to say, to state more plainly (explicitly) what Pius XI said unclearly (implicitly), we do not for a moment doubt that Paul would have decided in favour of birth control. For the continuity of Catholic teaching, and that of the last three popes in particular, would have been maintained. No error would have had to be admitted, but only incompleteness, provisionality, or something of the sort; and with this continuity the authority of the teaching office would have been assured or once again triumphantly confirmed.

But obviously this could not be done. Indeed, even with all the devices of theological dialectics it would be impossible to persuade anyone that a sanctioning of birth control by Paul VI in 1968 was implicitly if imperceptibly contained in the ban on it imposed by Pius XI in 1930. In short, if Paul sanctioned birth control, there would be no evolution, but simply contradiction between him and Pius XI, no continuity, but dis-

continuity; and, for the sake of the continuity of Catholic
teaching and the authority of the teaching office, that was
something that he was in no circumstances willing to concede.
But it must be admitted that the progressive majority on the
commission offered him no help in overcoming this obstacle,
which is a decisive one, at any rate from the point of view of
traditional Roman dogmatics. They offered him no help in the
second argument either.

2. The progressives declared Pius XI's *Casti Connubii* to be
in the last resort not an infallible doctrinal statement, and that
consequently an error of the teaching office could if necessary be
admitted without putting its authority in mortal peril. The
teaching office had, indeed, succumbed to error in the past,
even in the field of conjugal morality.

The conservatives do not dispute that the teaching office
committed errors, but they claim that the examples quoted
were of a different and essentially lesser nature. They say that in
the condemnation of Galileo a marginal (cosmological) issue
was at stake, and that the excommunication of the Eastern
Patriarch Photius, which was withdrawn nine hundred years
later by Paul VI, was merely an excess in a matter of procedure.
But a similar concession on the present issue would be equivalent
to admitting very grave error *in moribus*, in matters of morality.
'If contraception were declared not intrinsically evil, in
honesty it would have to be acknowledged that the Holy Spirit
in 1930 (*Casti Connubii*), in 1951 (address of Pius XII to mid-
wives) and 1958 (address to the Society of Haematologists in
the year of Pius XII's death), assisted the Protestant Churches,
and that for half a century did not protect Pius XI, Pius XII
and a large part of the Catholic hierarchy against a very grave
error, one most pernicious to souls; for it would have suggested
that they condemned most imprudently, under the pain of
eternal punishment, thousands upon thousands of human acts
which were now approved. Indeed, it can be neither denied nor
ignored that these acts would be approved for the same
fundamental reasons which Protestants alleged and which
they (popes and bishops) condemned or at least did not
approve.'[25]

Nor do the conservatives deny that Pius XI's was not
inherently an infallible doctrinal statement. But they claim that

this point is a diversion from the central issue, the immorality of contraception, as maintained and proclaimed – and this is the decisive point – by the united stand of the teaching office, popes and bishops, at any rate in recent decades, up to the (so 'confused' from the Roman point of view) times of Vatican II. The documentation produced by the conservative minority, who control the archives of the Holy Office (which are accessible to no one else), is in fact overwhelming. It consists of solemn statements by popes, bishops' conferences in every continent, many outstanding cardinals and bishops, and extracts from general theological teaching, compiled to show that, according to the universal consensus of the Church's teaching office at least in the present century (the use of spiritual means of compulsion for maintaining it is nothing new), the question at issue is a universal and binding doctrine of the Church, infraction of which is a grave sin: 'The question before us is that of the truth of the proposition that contraception is always a grave evil. The truth of this teaching derives from the fact that it has always and everywhere been put forward with such constancy, such universality, and such binding force, as something to be believed and followed by the faithful. Technical and juridical inquiry into the irreformability or infallibility of *Casti Connubii* (as if the true doctrine could be found and taught once this obstacle had been removed) is a diversion from the central issue and anticipates the answer.'[26]

In other words, the Curial group did not base their case on a particular encyclical or papal address; they did not appeal to what is known as the *extraordinary* teaching office (*magisterium extraordinarium*). They appealed to the ordinary consensus of Pope and bishops, that is, to what is known as the ordinary, everyday teaching office (*magisterium ordinarium*). There are many things (for example, the existence of God or the prohibition on killing the innocent) which have never been laid down by the *magisterium extraordinarium* of the Pope or of an ecumenical council, but which are nevertheless universally accepted as truths of the Catholic faith. In the language of the Roman textbooks, something can be *de fide catholica* – in other words, part of the Catholic faith – on the authority of the ordinary teaching office, without for that reason being *de fide definita*, that is, without having been laid down by a solemn

pronouncement of the extraordinary teaching office (a definition
by a pope or council).

Thus, even according to Roman theory, the prohibition of
contraception has not been laid down as an infallible article of
faith either by a pope or a council. Yet, because, as we have
just shown, it had always, or any rate for half a century before
Vatican II, been taught unanimously by the ordinary teaching
office of the Pope and bishops, it forms part of the universal,
infallible Catholic faith. In view of this it is comparatively
unimportant whether the intention was to proceed against the
progressives (who were such either on principle or on pragmati-
cal grounds) by 'endowing the papal statement with formal
infallibility' (as the group of authoritarian conservatives had in
mind) or to avoid a pronouncement *ex cathedra* (as was the
purpose of the pastorally-minded conservatives). This more
moderate group was 'very concerned to secure the continuity of
the teachings of Pius XII in order to "ensure the exercise of
authority in the Church" '. 'In their eyes, while unchangeable
principles must be maintained, there should be a search for
possible "openings". Hence a pronouncement *ex cathedra* should
be avoided, the therapeutic use of contraceptive methods should
not be forbidden (but left open to use as the occasion arose) and
the moral sanction should not be emphasized again.'[27] For the
rest, one can only be genuinely horrified at the dark, eerie
goings-on in the Vatican after the commission had finished its
work. There was 'a veritable labyrinth of editorial committees
and drafting of reports by individuals who not seldom had little
or no knowledge of each other's existence'.[28] One wonders what
was left of the Pope's freedom in all this. His position in the
whole picture reminds one of 'a spider in the net'.[29]

However that may be, we can now see plainly why the
progressive majority on the commission failed to persuade the
Pope. To judge from their own progressive report and the
progressive official report of the commission, they evidently
failed to grasp the full weight of the conservative case, which
was that the moral impermissibility of contraception had been
taken for granted for centuries, and then, against resistance in
our century up to the time of the Council (and the resulting
confusion), had been specifically taught by bishops everywhere
in the world, acting in moral unity and by common consent, as

Catholic morality to be observed on pain of eternal damnation. From the point of view of the ordinary *magisterium* of the Pope and the bishops, it was therefore *de facto* an infallible moral truth, even though it had not been defined as such.

This argument, after the obvious breakdown of the developmental theory, was bound ultimately to prevail with the Pope. He must have said to himself – rightly from this point of view – that he could not be expected to abandon as error a moral truth constantly and unanimously taught by the *magisterium ordinarium* and therefore in practice infallible. We can now well understand his continual references to the constant teaching of the Church and of his immediate predecessors in particular, and his sharp rejection of any deviation from this teaching. We can also now understand a number of other, minor details:

1. Why Cardinal Ottaviani refused even to submit to the Pope the report of the commission, which he must have regarded as heretical, and why opposition in the Curia evidently increased instead of declining.

2. Why the Vatican at first proposed, not an encyclical, but merely a 'declaration' (*declaratio*) on this teaching, for which there was unquestionable authority elsewhere.

3. Why Paul VI refrained from describing his encyclical as not infallible, but rather presented it as the teaching of Christ and declared himself and his encyclical to be 'like her [the Church's] divine founder, a "sign of contradiction" '.[30]

4. Why, as in the case of an infallible doctrinal statement, he called for complete and unconditional obedience, invoking the name of the Holy Spirit, to the teaching authority of the Church. 'That obedience, as you know well, obliges not only because of the reasons adduced, but rather because of the light of the Holy Spirit, which is given in a particular way to the pastors [note the plural, indicating the *magisterium* of the whole episcopate] of the Church in order that they may illustrate the truth. You know, too, that it is of the utmost importance, for peace of consciences and for the unity of the Christian people, that in the field of morals as well as in that of dogma, all should attend to the *magisterium* of the Church, and all should speak the same language. Hence, with all our heart we renew to you the heartfelt plea of the great Apostle Paul: "I appeal to you, brethren, by the name of our Lord Jesus Christ, that all o

you agree and that there be no dissensions among you, but that you be united in the same mind and the same judgment." To diminish in no way the saving teaching of Christ constitutes an eminent form of charity for souls.'[31] To priests the Pope said: 'We are full of confidence as we speak to you, beloved sons, because we hold it as certain that while the Holy Spirit of God is present to the *magisterium* proclaiming sound doctrine, he also illumines from within the hearts of the faithful and invites their assent.'[32] He concluded: 'Great indeed is the work of education, of progress and of love to which we call you, upon the foundation of the Church's teaching, of which the successor of Peter is, together with his brothers in the episcopate, the depositary and interpreter.'[33]

5. Why great displeasure was caused in certain Curial circles by Mgr Lambruschini, who said, in reply to a question at a press conference, that the encyclical was an authentic but not infallible document (according to the Roman view, the most that should have been said, to put it subtly, was that the document, though intrinsically fallible, was a statement of doctrine that derived its infallibility from elsewhere); and why this statement by Mgr Lambruschini, though it was undoubtedly more important than most of what he had to say, was not reported in the *Osservatore Romano*. (The incident is said to have been the reason why he was soon afterwards relieved of his duties and appointed Archbishop of Perugia.)

6. Why there appeared on the front page of the *Osservatore Romano* of 3 October 1968 a long article by the Pope's longstanding and closest theological friend, the Swiss neo-scholastic theologian Charles Journet, under the heading: 'It is absurd for a son of the Church to oppose the infallibility of his own personal conscience to the authority of the encyclical.' The Cardinal called on all the resources of the theology of Roman primacy to try to show that the Pope, loyal to the constant teaching of his predecessors, was exercising his ordinary supreme teaching authority basically in order to specify the meaning of the first article of the creed, on God the Creator, and thus close a controversy that cast doubt on a traditional teaching that had been approved for centuries by the teaching office. The arguments adduced in the encyclical led to but did not establish the conclusion, which was concerned with a fundamental point of

morality. Rather was the conclusion substantiated by the light of the Holy Spirit, with which the pastors of the Church were endowed in a special way in order to throw light on the truth. The Pope was doing this after subjecting to examination a tradition that was not only centuries old but was also new, having been that of his three predecessors. Cardinal Journet, quite logically, went so far as to envisage a possible future infallible decision: 'One thing is certain', he wrote. 'The ordinary teaching office of the Pope was here exercised in its plenitude. The theologian who reflects on the gravity of the matter, the exalted light into which it was brought for clarification, and finally the exactitude and certainty with which the answer was given, might even suppose – and this is our personal opinion – that he was confronted here with a point of moral doctrine which could be further defined and thus in the future might be confirmed by a consensus of divine faith.'[34] This is followed by a repetition of the dictum that it would be absurd, even in the absence of such a definition, for a son of the Church to set the infallibility of his own conscience against the authority of the encyclical.

7. Finally, we see why Cardinal Pericle Felici, who was the Curial general secretary of the Council and is now president of the commission for the reform of canon law, wrote an article in the *Osservatore Romano*, that was sensational only to non-Romans, in which he said with all desirable clarity and in reference to Cardinal Journet: 'In regard to the doctrine stated in the encyclical *Humanae Vitae* in a clear, evident and moreover official and authentic manner, no state of doubt can be based on the fact that the doctrine has not been defined *ex cathedra*. Since they are not faced with a definition *ex cathedra*, some indeed conclude that the teaching is not infallible, and thus that there is a possibility of change. In connection with this problem it must be borne in mind that a truth can be sure and certain, and therefore binding, even without the charism of an *ex cathedra* definition, as indeed is the case with the encyclical *Humanae Vitae*, in which the Pope as supreme teacher of the Church proclaims a truth that has constantly been taught by the Church's teaching office and corresponds to revealed doctrine.'[35] This is unequivocally the Roman doctrine of the infallibility of the *magisterium ordinarium* in all its continuity, coherence and firmness, though it does not necessarily follow

that it is Catholic doctrine. It must be taken into account if the crisis is to be properly understood.

Thus there is a dilemma here. The conservative minority had on its side the form of the doctrine (infallibility), but its substance (the permissibility of contraception) was against it, while the progressive majority had the substance (the permissibility of contraception) on its side, but the form (infallibility) against it. The Pope, in spite of all the objective arguments of the experts whom he had himself appointed, came down on the side of infallibility. But at what a cost! Unfortunately it must be said that the cost to the Church and the Pope and their credibility is incalculable. Time has now passed since the papal decision, but a large part of the Church and the episcopate is unable to accept it. The consensus on the question that the Pope hoped to achieve is further away than ever. On the contrary, he is in danger of isolating himself in the Curial ghetto from the most dynamic elements in the Church. This situation forces us to the conclusion that there can be no escape from the dilemma by insisting on the continuity, tradition, universality, authority and infallibility of the Church's teaching when the content of that teaching is no longer accepted, at any rate in our time, by the whole Church in a consensus of faith and the Pope is thus disavowed on the basis of his own principles.

But might there be an escape from the dilemma by taking the opposite course? How can one take a stand, with serious theology and a large part of the Church on one's side, for the permissibility of contraception without thereby abandoning the whole continuity of Catholic doctrine and the authority of a pastoral office of teaching and proclamation? Alternatively we might put the question in concrete form, and ask how the commission might have persuaded the Pope to come to the opposite conclusion. One thing is certain – it could have done so only if it had not evaded the formal problem of infallibility. It should have taken the bull by the horns; at the present day the problem of the infallibility of the Church's teaching office can no longer be assumed to have been finally settled.

But has the problem of infallibility really not been finally settled? Cannot the Pope rely for his view of infallibility on textbook theology, and also on Vatican I and II? That is the question to which we must now address ourselves.

Chapter Two

FIRM FOUNDATIONS?

I. THE TEXTBOOK ARGUMENTS

There was a time when Catholic theologians tried to dispose of difficult points of Church doctrine by interpreting them as broadly as possible. Propositions were stretched, bent and dialectically juggled with until they came to mean one thing or the other or sometimes the very opposite. This led to a basic ambiguity in many cases, or violence to and complete distortion of the original meaning, and thus to an unintended dishonesty of scholarship.[1] But these methods did not prevent the teaching office in case of need from having recourse to these propositions in all their original rigour, without taking any notice of the theologians' interpretative arts. At all events, if all that was to be found on infallibility in the textbooks on fundamental theology and dogmatics had been taken more seriously and criticized and corrected more seriously, we might have done better on the birth control issue we are using as our example. We shall now, even though it makes things no easier for us, do the opposite and take as seriously and literally as possible the declarations both of the theological textbooks and the councils without, however, concealing our critical questions.

All that is necessary to see that Paul VI is amply covered by textbook theology in his view of the binding nature of the Church's teaching tradition is to open at random any manual of dogmatics belonging to the Roman neo-scholastic school. The Pope is infallible when he speaks *ex cathedra*, and an ecumenical council is infallible when giving a binding definition of doctrine on faith or morals. Also the totality of bishops dispersed throughout the world – by contrast with the individual bishop – are infallible when, together with the Pope, they agree on a truth of faith or morals held by all the faithful. The textbooks describe as a dogma of faith (*de fide*) the following: 'The totality of bishops are infallible, when, either assembled in general council or scattered round the world, they put forward a doctrine of faith or morals as one to be held by all the faithful. (*De fide*.)'[2]

By contrast with the extraordinary teaching office of an ecumenical council or of a Pope speaking *ex cathedra*, what we are faced with here is the 'ordinary', everyday teaching office (*magisterium ordinarium*): 'The bishops exercise their infallible teaching power in an *ordinary* manner when they, in their dioceses, in moral unity with the Pope, unanimously promulgate the same teachings on faith and morals.'[3] And how can such agreement on a particular point of doctrine be established? 'The agreement of the bishops in doctrine may be determined from the catechisms issued by them, from their pastoral letters, from the prayer-books approved by them, and from the resolutions of particular synods. A morally general agreement suffices, but in this the express or tacit assent of the Pope, as the supreme head of the episcopate, is essential.'[4]

A truth of faith or morals is thus infallible by the mere fact of being promulgated as binding by the episcopate in universal agreement; it does not have to await promulgation as infallible truth. And who could deny that such a consensus on the birth control issue existed for centuries, and that from the beginning of this century the condemnation of it has been upheld by numerous episcopal conferences and individual bishops whenever controversy about it became acute outside the Catholic Church or isolated Catholic theologians diffidently tried to raise questions about it? Thus the conservative minority on the papal commission was able to point out that 'history provides the fullest evidence (cf. especially the excellent work of Professor John T. Noonan, *Contraception*, Harvard University Press, 1965) that the answer of the Church has always and everywhere been the same, from the beginning up to the present decade. One can find no period of history, no document of the Church, no theological school, scarcely one Catholic theologian, who ever denied that contraception was always seriously evil. The teaching of the Church in this matter is absolutely constant. Until the present century this teaching was peacefully possessed by all other Christians, whether Orthodox or Anglican or Protestant. The Orthodox retain this as common teaching today. The theological history of the use of matrimony is very complicated ... On the contrary, the theological history of contraception, comparatively speaking, is sufficiently simple, at least with regard to the central question: Is contraception always seriously evil? For in answer to this question there has never been any variation and scarcely any evolution in the teaching. The ways of formulating and explaining this teaching have evolved, but not the doctrine itself. Therefore it is not a question of a teaching proposed in 1930 which because of new physiological facts and new theological perspectives ought to be changed. It is a question rather of a teaching which until the present decade was constantly and authentically taught by the Church.'[5]

How is one to respond to this? There are only two alternatives. One either accepts it as infallible and unalterable doctrine, as the commission minority and the Pope did, and holds firm to it in spite of all difficulties and criticisms, if necessary to the point of *sacrificium intellectus*; or one questions the whole theory of infallibility. The progressive majority failed to gain acceptance for its views because it failed to see this dilemma as clearly as its Curial opponents did.

The chain of argument produced by neo-scholastic textbook theology in support of the very far-reaching propositions quoted above is as follows.[6] Infallibility is defined as the impossibility of falling into error. According to the Council of Trent (D 960) and Vatican I (D 1828), the bishops are the successors of the apostles. As such they are pastors and teachers of the faithful (D 1821) and thus also agents of the infallibility assured to the ecclesiastical teaching office; their active infallibility in teaching (*infallibilitas in docendo*) is the cause of the passive infallibility of the faithful in believing and assenting (*infallibilitas in credendo*). If we look further back for this infallibility assured to the ecclesiastical teaching office, we find on the one hand a reference to Vatican I (D 1839) and on the other a reference, though an indirect one, to Scripture. Because Christ promised to remain with the apostles (Matthew 28:20), or that his spirit, the spirit of truth would remain (John 14:16f), the purity and integrity of the proclamation of faith by the apostles and their successors is assured for ever (cf. Luke 10:16). If it is objected that there is nothing about infallibility in any of these texts, the answer is: 'This assumes [!] that the apostles and their successors in the promulgation of faith are removed from the danger of error.'[7] St Paul's reference to the Church as 'the pillar and bulwark of the truth' (1 Timothy 3:15) is dealt with in the same way. 'The infallibility of the promulgation of faith is a presupposition [!] of the unity and the indestructibility of the Church.'[8] Thus there is no more mention of infallibility, in the sense of the impossibility of falling into error, in the scriptural texts than there is in the rare quotations from the Fathers, Irenaeus, Tertullian (the heretic) or Cyprian (the opponent of the Bishop of Rome). Thus the whole question is whether the assumption made is the correct one or whether these same scriptural texts permit an alternative. For the moment we propose to defer further critical questioning along these lines, though we must not omit to mention how broadly papal and episcopal infallibility is interpreted by textbook theology: it extends not only to the formally revealed truths of Christian teaching on faith or morals, but also to all truths and matters closely connected with revealed doctrine, that is to say, theological conclusions, historical facts (*facta dogmatica*), truths of natural reason, and the canonization of saints. Since even the canonization of saints is claimed to be covered by infallibility, it is not surprising that infallibility can extend also to the birth control question.

Many readers will perhaps be tempted airily to dismiss all these textbook arguments as pre-conciliar. (Was the recent 'deposition' of saints supposed to be infallible too?) But the question is not so simple as that.

2. VATICAN II AND INFALLIBILITY

It has always been noticed that the spirit that blows in Chapter III of Vatican II's Constitution on the Church, *Lumen Gentium*, differs from that in the two that precede it.[9] In the chapters on the mystery of the Church and the people of God, the language is above all biblical, pastoral, ecumenical; in Chapter III it becomes juridical, institutional, disciplinary, Roman, though with an occasional touch of unction. This chapter, on 'the hierarchical structure of the Church, with special reference to the episcopate', begins with a massive endorsement of Vatican I and its declaration on the Pope's primacy and infallibility (Article XVIII). Vatican II, however, sought quite consciously and deliberately to create a counter-weight to Vatican I (which was never closed) and its emphasis on the papal prerogatives. It did this by a very detailed exposition of the position and functions of the episcopate (Articles XIX–XXVII), though it paid scant attention to the position of priests (Article XXVIII) and deacons (Article XXIX), not even providing a thorough exegetical-historical clarification of the advantage the bishop is supposed to have over the priest, apart from jurisdiction over a larger ecclesiastical area.

The exposition of the duties and functions of the episcopate begins with a section on the appointment of the twelve apostles (Article XIX) and on the bishops as their successors (Article XX). There follow three sections on the sacramental nature of a bishop's consecration (the fact that a bishop becomes a bishop by ordination seemed important to counterbalance the Roman claim to appoint bishops or at least confirm their appointment, Article XXI), on the episcopal college and the Pope as its head (here is the section on the collegiality and co-responsibility of bishops in the supreme government of the Church, which was fiercely opposed by the Curia, Article XXII), and on the mutual relations of bishops within the college (here there is a section on the local church that is fundamental to the new image of the Church, Article XXIII). Finally the office and function of bishops is described (Article XXIV) in threefold perspective: as teaching office (Article XXV), as sanctifying office (Article XXVI) and as governing office (Article XXVII).

For our purpose the vital section is that on the teaching office, particularly the second paragraph on the teaching office of the college of bishops. The latter paragraph, however, presupposes the observations of the former on the ordinary teaching office of the individual bishop, though significantly infallibility is not mentioned.[10] The whole article begins with the basic proposition that the bishop's pre-eminent task is the proclamation of the gospel. The reason given is that bishops are messengers of the faith, leading new disciples to Christ, genuine teachers equipped with Christ's authority. It is noticeable that all these propositions about the bishops (and the corresponding propositions about the Pope) are in the indicative (bishops are, proclaim, etc.) as if they were statements of self-evident reality, while those about the faithful that follow are severely framed in the imperative: 'The faithful are to accept their [bishop's] teaching and adhere to it with a religious assent of the soul. This religious submission of will and of mind must be shown in a

special way to the authentic teaching authority of the Roman
Pontiff, even when he is not speaking *ex cathedra*' (Article XXV).

On the one hand, it cannot be denied that a very big claim is
made here. Can religious submission of will and mind be due to
a pronouncement by an admittedly fallible bishop (on the
schools question, for instance, or some issue of that kind, which
he may declare to be a matter of faith or morals)? In the event
of such unguarded and unconditional utterances, what safe-
guards are there against the abuse of the episcopal teaching
authority, of which there have been innumerable examples?
Suggestions for amendments to the text were rejected as unnecessary by the theological commission of the Council, which
referred critics to the textbooks.

On the other hand, however, very little indeed is asserted. It
is assumed – and explicitly stated at the beginning of the next
section – that 'the individual bishops do not enjoy the prerogative of infalliblity' (Article XXV, 3), but the question arises:
Why not? As a successor to the apostles, who, according to this
theory, enjoyed infallibility as individuals, why is the individual
bishop not infallible too? Were some possible consequences of
this theory suddenly felt to be alarming? And if some, why not
others? There seems to be a lack of clarity here. But let us leave
this aside and come to the Council's key declaration on infallibility. Here it is verbatim: 'Although the individual bishops do
not enjoy the prerogative of infallibility, they can nevertheless
proclaim Christian doctrine infallibly. This is so, even when
they are dispersed around the world, provided that while maintaining the bond of unity among themselves and with Peter's
successor, and while teaching authentically on a matter of faith
or morals, they concur in a single viewpoint as the one which
must be held conclusively. This authority is even more clearly
verified when, gathered together in an ecumenical council, they
are the teachers and judges of faith and morals for the universal Church. Their definitions must be adhered to with the
submission of faith' (Article XXV, 3).

Does this not make the whole thing clear? Vatican II
completely adopted the teaching of textbook theology on
the infallibility of the episcopate as a whole, in regard to both
the extraordinary and the ordinary teaching office. In regard
to the ordinary teaching office of the bishops dispersed around

the world, the conditions are clearly indicated. Teaching is infallible:

1. when *communio*, a bond of unity and agreement, exists between the bishops themselves and between them and the Pope;

2. when the teaching is authentic, i.e. not private but official, and

3. is concerned with matters of faith or morals, in so far as these are put forward as

4. definitely to be held.

At this point we may ask whether the traditional teaching on the immorality of contraception does not meet all these conditions. It must again be borne in mind that such infallible teaching by the episcopate does not have to be put forward as infallible. Teaching is infallible if it is put forward by the episcopate as 'definitely to be held' (*definitive tenenda*), and this is unquestionably the case in regard to the issue of contraception, which has been constantly condemned, with reminders of eternal damnation. This is the case though the matters at issue are not *definitive credenda*, 'definitely to be believed', but only *definitive tenenda*, 'definitely to be held'. Karl Rahner rightly comments that '*tenenda* – instead of *credenda* – is the term used because, according to the general view, a definition by the Church is possible in matters that are not strictly matters of revealed truth, which can be believed only by "divine faith", *credenda* because of the direct authority of God's revelation.'[11]

This last specification is perhaps supremely important if we compare the definitive text of 1964 with the Council preparatory commission's first draft of 1962. What was stated at that time was in fact absolutely the same: the episcopal college is infallible, not only in ecumenical council, but also 'when individual bishops, each in his own diocese, together with the Roman Pontiff, as witnesses of the faith, share the same view (doctrine, statement, *sententia*) when transmitting revealed doctrine. Whatever therefore is held by the bishops everywhere in the world, together with the Pope himself, on matters of faith and morals, and taught by the ordinary teaching office, even if there is no solemn definition, must be maintained as irrevocably true and – if put forward as divinely revealed – must be believed by divine and Catholic faith.'[12]

In the final version, Paragraph 3 offers a definition of the practical extent of the infallible teaching authority of the episcopate (and of the Pope): 'This infallibility with which the divine Redeemer willed his Church to be endowed in defining a doctrine of faith or morals extends as far as extends the deposit of divine revelation, which must be religiously guarded and faithfully expounded' (Article XXV). To the uninitiated in Roman theology infallibility here might seem to be restricted to revealed truth, but this is not so. So far as the extent of infallibility is concerned, the concluding words, though they appear to be of secondary importance, are the most important of all. What is the meaning of 'religiously guarding' the deposit of divine revelation? 'By the words *sancte custodiendum* those truths which, even if they have not been formally (explicitly or implicitly) revealed, form part of the protection of the deposit of real revelation, are drawn into the jurisdiction of the teaching authority.'[13] And what cannot be regarded as forming part of the protection of the deposit of revelation? Thanks to such definitions, the Rome teaching office has never hesitated to take up an 'authentic' position on practically all questions of interest to it in any way, from the fields of exegesis or history to those of science, politics, economics, culture, education, and thus also birth control – and the boundaries of infallibility have become very fluid in the process. And what is meant by 'faithfully expounding' the deposit of revelation? 'The words "to be faithfully expounded" are a perfunctory indication that there is such a thing as the historical development of dogma itself, and not merely of theology.'[14] On the basis of this second qualification the Roman teaching office has regarded itself as entitled, 'authentically' permitted, to interpret all sorts of things about which there is not a word in Scripture or in early tradition, or even to define them infallibly, as in the case of the two new Marian dogmas.

Thus we see that this brief, sober statement is concerned, not with abstract theory, but with very concrete defence or justification of a very concrete practice. But a positive element in it may be that for once it refers to the infallibility with which the Redeemer willed to endow, not just the bishops or the Pope, but the *Church*. How do episcopal or papal infallibility fit in with that of the Church? Which is fundamental? And if we talk of the Church's, and not just of the bishops' infallibility, to what extent do all the elders and laity – who are the Church – share in that infallibility? Are they, as textbook theology has it, endowed only with a passive infallibility, in hearing, believing, and obeying? Or, as Vatican II seems to suggest, does the infallibility of the bishops actively produce the infallibility of the Church? Unfortunately nothing is said here on this highly important question. Instead, though Chapter III begins with a solemn endorsement of Vatican I and the papal infallibility that it defined, Article XXV, paragraph 3, is followed by a long section on papal infallibility. Adapting a well-known saying, we might well say of the Rome mentality, *de Romano Pontifice nunquam satis*. As if out of an unacknowledged fear, all the anti-Gallican points made by Vatican I are hammered home again. The only difference is that in one sentence infallibility is extended to the episcopal college, though with the qualification 'when that body exercises supreme teaching authority with the successor of Peter' (Article XXV, 3). The conflicts between Pope and episcopal college that have constantly arisen at dramatic moments in Church history are passed over in silence. Instead the last sentence of this section, again solemnly put in the indicative, speaks of never-failing assent, which is of special interest in view of the dissent roused by the encyclical *Humanae Vitae*: 'To the resultant definitions the assent of the Church can never be wanting, on account of the activity of the same Holy Spirit, whereby the whole flock of Christ is preserved and progresses in unity of faith' (Article XXV, 3). But, we feel forced to ask, when this assent is not forthcoming in a particular instance, what has gone wrong? The blame can hardly be attributed to the Holy Spirit.

Section 4 of the article briefly describes how infallible truth is discovered. This again is not put forward as an assumption, but as a simple, self-evident statement of fact. 'But when either the Roman Pontiff or the body of bishops together with him defines a judgment, they pronounce it in accord with revelation itself. All are obliged to maintain and be ruled by this revelation, which, as written or preserved by tradition, is transmitted in its entirety through the legitimate succession of bishops and especially through the care of the Roman Pontiff himself. Under the guiding light of the Spirit of truth, revelation is thus religiously preserved and faithfully expounded in the Church.' Does this not almost make it seem that the teaching office of the Pope and bishops is the ultimate, self-sufficient authority on what revelation is? Is this confirmation of the charge levelled by many at the Catholic Church and Catholic theology, that in it tradition gets the better of Scripture, and that the teaching office in turn gets the better of tradition, because it decides what the tradition is and hence also what Scripture is? Nevertheless, everyone – Pope and bishops apparently included – is called on to be ruled by revelation. The ambiguity arises from the awkward circumstance that four hundred years after the Council of Trent Vatican II did not feel in a position clearly to define the relationship between Scripture and tradition, which has been thoroughly investigated by theologians during the present century. From the viewpoint of history, the books of the New Testament (and the Old) are the only witness that is acknowledged and recognized by the Church as genuine, original tradition (that is, as 'canonical' Scripture), though not nearly the whole of them were written by the apostles. What original, divine tradition is there outside the New Testament? What purports to be such outside the New Testament (gospels, acts, letters of the apostles), though dating in part from the second century, was rejected by the early Church as apocryphal. Its inferiority to the canonical literature was easily discernible by the superficial reader then, and its uselessness as historical source material is universally recognized today. Thus the New Testament (and the Old) rightly remain definitive. All subsequent Church tradition consists of comment on or interpretation, application or transposition, of this original tradition, though this has been done with varying degrees of success. Thus it is Holy Scripture that is the vital, binding norm for the Christian Church of all times; the *norma normans* of a Church tradition that must also be taken seriously as *norma normata*. Thus, to put it figuratively, Scripture is, as it were, the mains tap which, if it were ever turned off, would mean that the whole house would be deprived of its water supply, cut off from the springs of Church tradition. Vatican II's only attempt to take this seriously, however, appears in the supplementary final chapter on the Bible in the life of the Church in the Constitution on Revelation. The Curial preparatory commission, completely under the influence of unhistorical Counter-Reformation views and the obvious interests of Church policy, upheld a two-source theory of Scripture *and* tradition. No more than a compromise was reached, unfortunately. The theological commission, under pressure from the Curial minority, ended by leaving open the question of the relationship between the two, hence the words in the text, 'written *or* (*vel*) handed on'. It was felt to be progress, though it was none, that, instead of separating Scripture and tradition, they were brought as close together as possible, made to flow from the same tap, rather like hot and cold water in a modern plumbing system. This of course enables the two to be mingled in any desired proportions, a very practical arrangement in everyday life, but a very harmful one in theology. For what Scripture does not supply is supplied by tradition, and the teaching office of the Church serves as the concrete, *proxime*, decisive voice of both. What the ultimate criterion of the teaching office is we do not know. Chapter II of the Constitution on Revelation, on the transmission of divine revelation, which the commission put forward explicitly as a compromise, covers up the problem with a quasi-trinitarian formula that rides smoothly over the bumps and a eulogy of harmony that sounds very well in Latin. The *norma normans* is pushed into the background by appealing to the ways of God. 'It is clear, therefore, that sacred tradition, sacred Scripture, and the teaching authority of the Church, in accord with God's most wise design, are so linked and joined together that one cannot stand without the others, and that all together and each in its own way under the action of the one Holy Spirit contribute effectively to the salvation of souls' (Article X). Vatican II suffered from first to last from the fact that the question of what really is the ultimate, supreme norm for the renewal of the Church was left undecided. Once again the beneficiaries were the group that for understandable reasons was able to obstruct a decision in favour of the New Testament – the Roman Curia, its teaching office and canon law.

The chapter on the Constitution of the Church goes on – again in the ambiguous indicative – to make a statement on the teaching office's human striving after knowledge: 'The Roman Pontiff and the bishops, in view of their office and the importance of the matter, strive painstakingly and by appropriate means to enquire properly into that revelation and to give apt expression to its contents' (Article XXV). Karl Rahner rightly observes: 'This sentence is phrased very briefly and formally, obviously for fear that more detailed statements about the ethical norms by which views are formed and the truth is established by the *magisterium* might be regarded as canon law, the carrying out of which might be subject to investigation by another authority.'[15] This raises the question whether the activity of the teaching office, which wishes to lay down the law on so much, is subject to any control, or to no control at all; whether in accordance with its own will and pleasure it is able to resort or refrain from resorting to 'appropriate means' (perhaps an excessively political expression when we recall certain repressive measures adopted in the past). Meanwhile Article XXV ends with a statement that will perhaps be disappointing to some, but will be consoling to others: 'But they [the Roman Pontiff and the bishops] do not receive a new public revelation as pertaining to the deposit of divine faith' (Article XXV, 4).

3. SOME QUESTIONS

As compared to the schema of the Curial preparatory commission on the Constitution of the Church, which devoted two whole chapters out of eleven to the teaching office and obedience and wanted specifically to forbid discussion by the theologians even of fallible doctrinal statements by the Church, the final version represents a gratifying improvement; and the discussion is broadened to include more important issues, in particular the idea of the Church as the people of God, the community of the faithful, in relation to the universal priesthood, and the charismatic dimension of the Church in relation to the local Church and ecclesiastical office as service.

But we have already pointed out that the Constitution on the Church, like that on Revelation, contains chapters and passages on very different theological levels. In particular Chapter III, on the hierarchical structure of the Church, in spite of the improvement we have just noted, is backward- rather than forward-looking. But it looks back to and relies on, not the New Testament, for instance – Article XXV contains only three biblical quotations, and these are not concerned with the main issues – but Vatican I, particularly the statements made by Bishop Gasser, the spokesman for the deputation on faith. On the basic theme of the infallibility of the episcopate dispersed around the world it quotes as its authority a declaration by Vatican I on the *magisterium ordinarium* (DS 3011) in which infallibility is not mentioned, as well as a note on a schema on the Church which was never adopted by Vatican I, but had been taken over from Cardinal Bellarmine and commented on by the Council theologian, Kleutgen.[16] Did Vatican II hope in this way to tame the Pope's infallibility by way of the infallibility of the episcopate? The documents cited, and also the quotation from the letter from the Syllabus Pope, Pius IX, to the Archbishop of Munich-Freising on the conference of German theologians (DS 2879), ought to have roused suspicions.

Both the Constitution itself and the documents make it clear that the question of the infallibility of the episcopate was neither seriously discussed nor seriously examined at Vatican II, which simply adopted the textbook theology position on the matter that also determined the position of Vatican I. But outstanding questions are not disposed of by being simply ignored; the result is merely that they pop up again with renewed vigour when everything seems to have been settled. If one takes one's stand on history, the questions posed by history are particularly dangerous. As an ancient saying pointedly put it, *facta infecta fieri nequeunt*, things that have happened cannot be undone. This is an exceedingly valuable principle, in jurisprudence in particular, and the opposite proposition can also be stated to the advantage of theology: *infecta facta fieri nequeunt*, things that have not happened cannot be made to have happened. But now let us leave aside both the numerous infelicities of Article XXV that we have already mentioned and the substantiation of papal infallibility by Vatican I on which the whole article is based. Vatican II with the best of intentions (the collegiality of the bishops and the Pope) asserted the infallibility of the universal episcopate as a counterweight, derived from textbook theology, to the infallibility of the Pope, but in doing so made some historical assumptions that can no longer be regarded as sound at the present day. The whole case for episcopal infallibility is based or the assumption that the bishops are in a definite, direct and exclusive way the successors of the apostles and that the latter claimed infallibility for themselves. This raises some historical questions.

1. It cannot be shown that the apostles claimed infallibility in the textbook sense (the impossibility of falling into error) either as a college or as individuals. There is no need to waste words here on the vital and universally acknowledged importance of the apostles in the foundation of the Church. But their connections with the number twelve ('the twelve apostles') is a later construction; even in the Acts of the Apostles the college of twelve – as representing the twelve tribes of Israel and as basic witnesses of the resurrection – slips completely into the background, and as such it dies out. What is vital is the apostolate (which is not restricted to the twelve); the apostles are the primary witnesses appointed by the Lord himself and as such are the preachers of the gospel and thus the founders and first leaders of the Church. But the real apostles are described neither as heroes nor as geniuses, but as weak and frail human beings who carried their treasures in earthly vessels (2 Corinthians 4:7) and could do nothing of themselves (John 15:5). The Synoptic Gospels illustrate more than is to the liking of many today the statements to this effect by Paul and John, who provide concrete evidence of the weakness and folly, the humanness and failings, of Jesus' chosen disciples, both before and after the Resurrection. In particular Peter, the first of the apostles, offers a prize example of how error, though it does not make the apostolic mission impossible, impedes it (each of the three classical passages on Peter's special importance is accompanied by the dark shadow of a particular failing). To the believer all this, so far from being scandalous, is consolatory. For it shows that the apostles were human and thus, as Paul shows plainly, needed the intercession, comfort and support of their fellow-Christians. The Church 'has the apostles (and the prophets) for its foundations' (Ephesians 2:20; cf. 1 Corinthians 12:28; Revelation 21:14), but there is no mention of any kind of personal or collegial infallibility or inability to fall into error.[17]

2. Similarly it is impossible to show that the bishops are in any direct and exclusive sense the successors of the apostles (or of the college of the twelve). Certainly there is nothing to object to in the bishops' regarding themselves as being in a special sense in the line of succession to the apostles in the exercise of their

ministry, in so far as they found or lead churches as the apostles did. But it is easy to go too far in the theoretical and practical interpretation of this proposition. For

a. As the direct primary witnesses and messengers of Christ the apostles are *a priori* irreplaceable and unrepresentable by any successors; it is they (and the prophets) and not the bishops who are and remain the founders of the Church.

b. The task and duty of the apostles, that is, apostolic mission and apostolic ministry, remain, even though there can be no new apostles. But the apostolic mission and apostolic ministry are primarily continued by the Church as a whole. Every Christian is a successor to the apostles in so far as he strives for harmony with the apostolic witness (succession in apostolic faith and confession) and for connection with the apostolic ministry (succession in apostolic service and life). In this sense the whole Church is and should be the apostolic Church.[18]

c. It is true that there was church leadership from the outset, whether through the apostles or through other charismatic ministries. Not divine intervention, however, but a long and complex historical development must be held responsible for the following facts:

(1) That as against the prophets, teachers and other charismatic ministries the *episkopoi* (presbyters) prevailed as the principal and ultimately the sole leaders of the congregations (from the 'collegiality' of all the faithful there emerged a collegiality of certain groups of ministries over against the congregation, resulting in the emergence of a distinction between 'clergy' and 'laity');

(2) That in relation to the majority of *episkopoi* (presbyters) in the congregation there gradually emerged the 'monarchical' episcopacy of a single individual (the collegiality of the various *episkopoi* or presbyters developed into the collegiality of one *episkopos* with his presbyterium and deacons, with the result that the distinction between clergy and laity was finally established);

(3) That as the Church spread from the towns to the country, the head of the congregation, the *episkopos*, became the head of a whole ecclesiastical area, i.e. a diocese, and so on, thus becoming a bishop in the modern sense of the word; his 'apostolic succession' was now formalized by the drawing up

of lists of succession; over and above the collegiality of *episkopoi* and presbyterium, the collegiality of individual 'monarchical' bishops with one another now grew in importance, and later their collegiality with the Bishop of Rome, though this occurred only in the West.[19]

3. On the basis of the above it seems impossible to show that bishops have any advantage over presbyters other than supervision of (jurisdiction over) a larger ecclesiastical area. While a canonical and disciplinary distinction between the two is possible and reasonable, a theological-dogmatic distinction between them is unjustified and impossible. *Episkopoi* and presbyters were originally either distinguished otherwise or not at all, as we have just shown. The tripartite division of offices (*episkopoi*, presbyters, deacons) is not to be found in the New Testament, but appears in Ignatius of Antioch; it is thus an historical development that first took place in the Syrian area. No difference in principle is discernible between the ordination of a bishop, on the sacramental nature of which there was, up to a point, so much discussion at Vatican II, and the ordination of presbyters. Nor is any difference discernible in regard to the authority transmitted by ordination. While the Council of Trent still ascribed authority to confirm and ordain exclusively to the bishop, under pain of excommunication (D 967), according to Vatican II the presbyter also can be the ordinary minister of confirmation (cf. Article XXVI) and the question of authority to ordain is explicitly left open.[20]

4. Taking into account the historical development we have briefly described, it is also impossible to show that the bishops are the sole (or sole 'authentic') teachers in the Church. According to the New Testament, all are called on to proclaim the word. And, though the leadership of the congregations that fell to the *episkopoi* and presbyters in the course of historical development had to be exercised primarily through the word, that certainly cannot mean the absorption by them of other charismata and ministries of proclamation. In 1 Corinthians 12, Paul specifically attacks tendencies to monopolization, and in addition to the apostles mentions two other groups, 'prophets' and 'teachers' (1 Corinthians 12:28), to whom in the Didache the *episkopoi* and deacons still seem to take second place in the celebration of the Eucharist. Besides the special succession to

the apostles there is also a special succession to the prophets and teachers. We shall not deal here with the meaning of this when it is translated into contemporary terms, but shall revert to it later in connection with the obscure concept of the teaching office.[21]

Many of those who recognize and consider these far-reaching questions will wonder whether they ever came into the purview of Vatican II. The answer is yes, it had at least a distant glimpse of them, but in practice ignored them. Nevertheless it amended the dogmatic definition of the Council of Trent that the 'divinely ordained hierarchy' consists of bishops, presbyters and deacons (D 966; cf. 960), so that now 'the ecclesiastical ministry [not 'the hierarchy', equivalent to 'sacred authority'] is exercised on different levels by [not 'consists of'] those who from antiquity [not by divine ordinance, i.e. from the very beginning] have been called [not *are* or *must be*] bishops, priests and deacons' (Article XXVIII). But, looked at as a whole, the vital Chapter III on 'the hierarchical structure of the Church' is oriented to the *status quo* and presents us merely with a theological-pastoral description of the present division of offices. Thus we miss an exegetically and historically solidly based and at the same time critically constructive account of the essential structure and historical development of the ministry of the Church from its beginnings. 'Whatever may be the historical origin of presbyters, deacons or other ministries and also the exact meaning of the terms used to describe them in the New Testament, it is asserted . . .': this note by the theological commission on the central statement from Article XXVIII[22] that we quoted above would make an appropriate sub-title for the whole of Chapter III.

But why were these truly important questions not discussed? There are a number of reasons: 1. Any council that sets out to practise theology in the proper sense of the term and not 'merely' proclamation is overtaxing itself.[23] 2. In particular, a conciliar commission necessarily overtaxes itself if it attempts to draft, not only important guiding lines for the modern understanding of the Church, but also a comprehensive constitution for the Church. 3. On the theological commission of Vatican II historical and critical exegesis, though vitally relevant to the questions raised above and many others as well, was in practice

represented hardly at all, or at any rate not in sufficient strength.
4. Like all council documents, that on the Constitution of the
Church in particular was a compromise between a basically
progressive conciliar majority and a reactionary Curial minority.
5. The Curial minority that controlled the Council machinery
ensured, with the Pope's aid, that revision of a schema drafted in
a post-Tridentine spirit would be possible only within very
definite limits, and that certain traditional views and formulations were taken over unexamined into the new draft and that
certain important questions and problems were not dealt with.
In these circumstances it turned out to be easier to introduce
'new' features into the Constitution than to subject to serious
examination what had long been dogmatically fixed. This
applied to questions concerning the episcopacy and infallibility.

Thus it is clear that, even if we take into account the positive
reorientation represented by the Constitution on the Church
and its fruitful new beginnings and, in spite of all our critical
questions, accept in theory and practice the historical legitimacy and pastoral utility of a presbyterial-episcopal Church
constitution,[24] we are nevertheless bound to point out that the
attribution of infallibility to the college of bishops, based on the
traditional, unhistorical theory of the bishops' direct and
exclusive apostolic succession, stands exegetically, historically
and theologically, on feet of clay. That is, unless the authority
for it is Vatican I, to which Vatican II constantly refers in its
Article XXV on the infallibility of Pope and bishops.

We shall therefore investigate Vatican I and its substantiation
of papal infallibility. A not unimportant question will serve as a
transition from the Second Vatican Council to the first. Would
the former have defined papal infallibility if it had not previously been defined by Vatican I? There are two reasons for
believing that it would almost certainly not have done so.

In the first place, Vatican II was averse to dogmatism. Under
the influence of John XXIII, who was neither a Pius IX nor a
Pius XII, its basic attitude, unlike that of the preparatory
commission, was not doctrinaire but pastoral. New dogmas were
unwanted on principle, and even formulations that sounded
dogmatic were eliminated. The Council aimed, not at fixation,
but at as much renewal as possible, both in practice and in
theory.

In the second place, it showed an aversion to centralism. Many bishops and theologians had had more than enough of the perpetual excessive demands of the central authority in Rome. Triumphalism, juridicism, centralism, were the targets in the pious struggle for more collegiality, more solidarity, more dialogue in the Church. Again it was John XXIII who had shown his brethren a new image of an unpretentious, ecumenically and humanly disposed Petrine ministry, and attached so little importance to the infallibility attributed to him that he once said, with a smile: 'I am not infallible; I am infallible only when I speak *ex cathedra*. But I shall never speak *ex cathedra.*' And he never did.

It is very remarkable that the Council, which in its Constitution on the Church had so much to say about the infallibility of the episcopate and also of the ecumenical council, followed in the footsteps of John XXIII by not once formally claiming it, this to the chagrin of many faithful to the heritage of Vatican I. Vatican II, indeed, was basically so little interested in infallibility that it never seriously discussed it. Will the Church perhaps ultimately manage without it? On a bright spring day one is apt to forget the murky autumn – until it returns. If we do not wish to be haunted for ever by the recurring problems of infallibility, Vatican II must not let us forget Vatican I. But, unfortunately for Christianity, there are in the post-conciliar period plenty of reasons for not doing so.

4. VATICAN I'S INTEREST IN INFALLIBILITY

If Vatican II was so surprisingly uninterested in infallible definitions, why was Vatican I so acutely concerned to secure an infallible definition of infallibility? It is not our intention here to write a history of Vatican I, or its debate on infallibility, or even to summarize it.[25] To do so thoroughly we should have to go very much further back.

We should have to describe how, in spite of all resistance and opposite trends, the policy and theology of the Church of the capital of the Roman Empire and of the two chief apostles, Peter and Paul, worked towards the development of a unified Church with a rigid juridical organization under a monarchical Roman universal episcopate. We should have to trace this

development from the time of the early Bishops of Rome, Victor
and Stephen, Damasus, Siricius, Innocence and, in particular,
Leo; we should have to note the new impulse given to the trend
in the ninth century by Nicholas and John VIII, and we should
have to show how from the time of the Gregorian reform in the
eleventh century it was deliberately and systematically worked
for under the influence of the forged Isidorian Decretals. We
should also have to show how, also at the time of the Gregorian
reform and essentially as a result of this process, the unity of the
Eastern and Western Churches was finally shattered, and how
the Church was now really centralized, juridicized and Roman-
ized, a process that reached it acme with the religious-political
universal monarchy of the popes in the thirteenth century; and
how the religious-political decline of the papacy became evident
with the Avignon exile and at the time of the Reformation
Councils, though the Renaissance popes continued to conduct
themselves in a more absolutist and unchurchly way than ever.
Finally, we should have to show how the unity of the Western
Church also ended by breaking on this absolutism, thus bringing
about a radical change in the state of Christendom, and how at
the time of the Counter-Reformation Rome did not dismantle
the bastions of her power in the remnant of her empire but
single-mindedly consolidated them, admittedly in a more
spiritual form, and continued to do so against all external and
internal opposition right through the period of the French
Revolution and into the nineteenth century.

If we showed all this, it would be evident why even twentieth-
century Catholic ecclesiastical historians exalt Vatican I (and
the 1918 Code of Canon Law) as the glorious peak of a thousand
– or, indeed, nearly two thousand – years' history of the Church
of Christ. There is no doubt of the ability of these historians to
demonstrate how much the Church policy and theology of
Rome, particularly since the age of the Migration of the
Peoples, did for the unity and freedom of the (Western) Church
as these things were understood in Rome. But these positive
aspects do not obliterate the negative aspects of that history,
their devastating consequences for the unity and credibility of
the Church as a whole. Less intelligible, however, is the fact that
Catholic historians and theologians showed so few doubts about
the legitimacy of the whole process and, more important, that

the majority at the First Vatican Council had no doubts about
it at all. Why?

We shall never understand the definition of papal infallibility
merely by analysing the text of the Council's Constitution in
Denzinger's *Enchridion*, or even by studying the Council documents in Mansi's great collection. The issue was largely decided
before the Council met. Would papal infallibility ever have been
defined in 1870 if the majority of the Council Fathers had not
grown up in the period of political restoration and the anti-
Enlightenment and anti-rationalist romanticism of the first
half of the century? In the age that followed the chaos and
excesses of the French Revolution and the Napoleonic period,
Europeans longed for peace and order, for the good old days,
and looked back longingly to the 'Christian Middle Ages'. Who
better than the Pope could offer a religious basis for the maintenance or restoration of the political and religious *status quo*?
Most of the leading Catholic churchmen in the different
countries were supporters of political and social reaction; some
were closely connected with the fashionable philosophical trend
of traditionalism (traditionalism was then an honourable term).
And would papal infalliblity have been defined in 1870 if in the
second half of the century the restoration had not been threatened to its foundations by the swift advance of liberalism (and its
enemy, socialism, which had so much in common with it) that
accompanied rapid industrialization? Did not liberalism, with
its faith in progress and economic, political, scientific and
cultural freedom, threaten to undermine all religious authority
and tradition? Clericalism provoked anti-clericalism, and
vice versa. The rationalism of the Enlightenment returned in the
form of anti-idealist and anti-romantic positivism and the
rising empirical sciences. The ecclesiastical authorities not only
supported the established political system but clung to the
traditional 'biblical' cosmology, and this drove many politicians
and scientists into violent aggressiveness towards all that had to
do with religion.

As a result of this historical constellation, or historical pre-
dicament, into which a Church leadership that had ceased to
understand the signs of the times and was always too late had
largely manoeuvred itself, it was almost inevitable that Vatican
I, in complete contrast to Vatican II, was conceived as a

Council, not of hope but of fear, not of internal reform and renewal but of reaction and encapsulation against the outside
world, not of *aggiornamento* but of polemical self-defensiveness.
Thus it met wholly in the spirit of the 1864 *Syllabus Errorum*, the
list of errors with which Pius IX had condemned practically all
modern developments under the heading of naturalism, socialism, indifferentism, Gallicanism, Freemasonry, and so on, thus
rousing tremendous indignation among progressive, educated
Europeans.

But these two more general factors are not sufficient to explain
Vatican I's desire for a definition of infallibility that – in complete contrast to previous conciliar definitions – was not called
for by any particular heresy, but was wanted by the Church
leadership itself. To understand what happened, at least two
further factors must be taken into account.

The infallibility of the Pope would not have been defined in
1870 if the most pressing question in the minds of Pope and
Curia had not been the so-called Roman question. Certainly
they had other anxieties too. In France there was political and
ideological strife between the pro-revolutionaries and the anti-
revolutionaries, between the Church hierarchy and the anti-
clericals, between republicans and supporters of Napoleon III,
who extended a protecting hand over the French Church
and – for the time being – the Papal States also; and in Germany there was theological strife between the university
theologians who were committed to contemporary scientific
methods and the neo-scholastic theologians and seminary
instructors trained in and backed by Rome, which led at the
Council itself to a polarization of Catholic theology between
that of the German universities (its leader, Ignaz Döllinger,
was not invited) and the neo-scholasticism of the Gregoriana,
the Jesuit university in Rome (represented by Perrone, Schrader,
Kleutgen). Nevertheless in Rome the Roman question over-
shadowed everything else; the question, that is to say, whether
the Papal States, which had been restored in 1849 but had been
reduced to Rome and its immediate neighbourhood by the
intervention of the Piedmontese government in 1860 and were
notorious everywhere for their monsignorial mismanagement
and social backwardness, would have to be given up, or whether
it would be possible to hold on to them permanently, with

nothing but French support to rely on, in the face of the Italian unification movement which wanted Rome for its capital. In the Vatican the situation was viewed with the most extreme anxiety. Almost the only ray of hope for those who, relying on Matthew 16:18, wanted at all costs to hold on to temporal power was the idea that no one would dare to take action against a pope whose infallibility had been solemnly proclaimed *urbi et orbi* in ecumenical council.

Nor would papal infallibility have been defined in 1870 if the reigning pope had not himself pressed for a definition of papal infallibility as his dearest wish; this he did more and more openly with the passage of time. On his election in 1846 he had been hailed as a liberal and a reformer, but after his political failures and exile in 1848, he grew more and more reactionary, both in politics and in theology. Without a trace of church- manly or theological critical self-reflection, he not only enumer- ated and condemned the so-called errors of his time and called for the subordination of the State and of science to the authority of the Catholic Church – which created difficulties for Vatican II on questions of religious freedom and freedom of conscience – but also obstructed the Italian national unity movement with his consistently maintained *non possumus*, accompanied by continually reiterated emotional protests that roused the ultra- montane press and many bishops and laymen, particularly in France, to a violent anti-Italian campaign. Though he thus unnecessarily caused Italian Catholics severe conflicts of con- science, he nevertheless gained tremendous sympathy for him- self and his office in the role of victim of unchristian forces. The dogmatic tie that bound Catholics to the Pope was thus charged with feeling, and a completely new phenomenon appeared in the form of emotional 'veneration of the Pope', which was rein- forced by the papal audiences and mass pilgrimages to Rome that now became customary. Pius IX was a friendly, very articulate, radiant personality, though he was dangerously emotional, had only a superficial training in theology, and was totally unfamiliar with modern scientific methods. Moreover, he was badly advised by zealous but mediocre, dogmatically minded associates who were out of touch with the world about them, and he regarded the Papal States crisis as an episode in the age-old struggle between God and Satan. He hoped to

resolve the crisis by mystical trust in the victory of divine providence. It is only in the light of this basic outlook of his that his
desire for a dogmatization of his own primacy and infallibility
can be understood. Only in the light of the veneration offered
him can we understand why such a responsive chord was
struck among wide circles of clergy and laity by the definition of
infallibility; the same phenomenon also explains why the
process of indoctrination and administrative centralization in
the Church that was rapidly and systematically pushed forward
by Rome after the middle of the century, following some initial
nervous hesitation, no longer met with opposition. Not only was
the Syllabus issued, German theologians condemned, and all
works of Gallican or Febronian tendency put on the Index, but
Rome increasingly influenced the appointment of bishops, papal
nuncios increasingly intervened in domestic ecclesiastical
affairs, bishops were called on to strengthen their contacts with
Rome, priests who propagated Roman ideas, often in opposition
to their own bishops, were promoted, and the faithful were
increasingly instructed in the doctrine of papal primacy.

Thus the way was well prepared when, to strengthen his
position and align the Church in battle array under Roman
command, Pius IX surprised the world by summoning an
ecumenical council to meet after an interval of three hundred
years in Rome – by that time no other meeting-place was
conceivable. However, the ultramontane press, again encouraged by the Curia, worked itself up to such a pitch in its
campaign for the Romanization of the whole Church in
doctrine, liturgy, discipline and customs that it almost over-
reached itself, and led immediately before the Council to a
revival among many bishops, theologians and laymen in Germany and France of the 'Gallicanism' that was supposedly dead,
with the result that the Council proceedings did not pass off as
swiftly and smoothly as the organizers and their most zealous
partisans had hoped.

Meanwhile it remains to be pointed out that in this survey of
the problematical background of the definition of infallibility
we are concerned, not just with its prehistory but with its
actual history. It will not do openly and critically to reveal that
background, as Catholic historians do today, while refraining
from any critical reflection on the definition itself. The historical

problem that is disclosed here is not concerned just with the 'opportuneness' of the definition of infallibility, as has often been stated in the past, depriving the question of its sting; it is also concerned with its truth.

5. THE DEFINITION OF PAPAL INFALLIBILITY

We shall now turn our attention to the actual definition of infallibility and its validation by Vatican I, on which all that was laid down on the subject by Vatican II was in fact based. The debates at Vatican I, fascinating as the often painful story is, are of interest to us here only in so far as they reveal the motivations behind and the significance of the definition itself.[26]

A. The definition of papal infallibility presupposes the definition of papal primacy. Both were included in the dogmatic Constitution *Pastor Aeternus* of 18 July 1870; the order of the original schema on the Church was boldy reversed, the chapters on the Pope being put first in spite of minority opposition. The Pope's primacy was validated in three stages, as Petrine, perpetual, and Roman. The mood that led to the definition of primacy and infallibility is made clear in the introduction: 'With daily increasing hatred, on all sides, the gates of hell are rising, to overturn the Church, if it were possible, against its divinely established foundation. Therefore we judge it necessary for the protection, safety and increase of the Catholic flock, with the approval of the sacred council, to propose the doctrine of the institution, perpetuity and nature of the sacred apostolic primacy, in which the strength and solidity of the whole Church consists, to be believed and held by all the faithful, according to the ancient and constant faith of the universal Church and to proscribe and condemn the contrary errors so pernicious to the Lord's flock' (D 1821).

Chapter I deals with the establishment of the apostolic primacy in Peter. Relying on John 1:42, Matthew 16:16 ff., and John 21:15 ff., it declares that anyone who says that 'blessed Peter the Apostle is not constituted by Christ our Lord as prince of all the apostles and visible head of the whole Church militant, or that he received directly and immediately from the same Lord Jesus Christ a primacy only of honour and not of true and proper jurisdiction' (D 1823) is excluded from the Church.

Chapter II deals with the continuation of the Petrine primacy in the Bishops of Rome. Relying on a speech by the Roman legate at the Council of Ephesus in 431 and a still later sermon by Leo the Great, as well as a sentence each from Irenaeus and Ambrose which, however, are not about the Bishop but about the Church of Rome, it states that anyone who says that 'it is not by the institution of Christ our Lord himself or by divine law that blessed Peter has perpetual successors in the primacy over the universal Church, or that the Roman Pontiff is not the successor of blessed Peter in the same primacy' (DS 3058) is excluded from the Church.

Chapter III defines the content and nature of the primacy of the Bishop of Rome. After a general appeal to early Roman and conciliar witnesses and after repeating a passage from the Decree for the Greeks issued by the Council of Florence in 1439, there is a more precise account of the papal primacy of jurisdiction and statements about the subordinate jurisdiction of the bishops, the Pope's free and direct communication with all the faithful, and the permanent possibility of appealing to his final and inappellable judgment. Finally it declares that anyone is excluded from the Church who says that 'the Roman Pontiff has the office only of inspection and direction, but not full and supreme power of jurisdiction over the universal Church, not only in matters pertaining to faith and morals, but also in those pertaining to the discipline and government of the Church spread throughout the whole world; or that he has only a principal part and not the whole plenitude of this supreme power; or that this power of his is not ordinary and immediate, both over all and individual Churches and likewise over all and individual pastors and faithful' (D 1381).

There is no need to go into great detail about this, especially as our subject is not papal primacy, but infallibility. It will be sufficient to point out the following:

1. Though the composition of the Vatican I deputation on faith was completely one-sided and wholly under the influence of the Curia and it rejected the inclusion in the Constitution of any statement implying limits to the papal primacy because of its fear of Gallicanism, the proceedings make it clear that its spokesman at the Council admitted the existence of such limits, to which the Pope was morally bound; the limits set in general

by Christ and the apostles, by natural and divine law, and in particular those arising from the existence of bishops and their ordinary exercise of office, as well as those applying to the Pope's exercise of his office, in so far as this must not be arbitrary or immoderate and must be directed towards the building up of the Church and not its destruction.[27]

2. The history of the Church, of theology and of canon law, make it clear that all the implications of the question of papal primacy can be seen only if the problem of a possible schismatic or heretical pope is taken into account; the possibility, that is, of a pope's excluding himself by his own actions from communion with the Church, for example, by the tyrannous exercise of power or otherwise, thus depriving himself of his office and creating circumstances that might conceivably call for his trial by a representative organ of the Church (council, episcopal synod, college of cardinals).[28] This problem has been discussed and its existence accepted since the Middle Ages, but it was tendentiously ignored by Vaticans I and II.

3. The whole of the Vatican I argument for the existence of a Petrine primacy of jurisdiction, and *a fortiori* a continuation of the Petrine primacy, and above all its continuation in the Bishop of Rome, runs into grave difficulties from the standpoint of contemporary exegesis and history (as it did to an extent to the exegesis and history of the time), and no Catholic theologian has yet been able to dispose of these difficulties. They make any attempt to demonstrate a historical succession of the Bishops of Rome in a Petrine primacy a highly questionable enterprise.[29]

4. It does not follow from this that the primacy of an individual in the Church is contrary to Scripture. Indeed, it might well be in accordance with Scripture, that is, in so far as it was a spiritual (possibly charismatic) succession to the Petrine mission, the Petrine witness and the Petrine spirit; succession, that is to say, to a really living primacy of service that would be more than a mere primacy of honour or of jurisdiction—a pastoral primacy in the spirit of the gospel, in accordance with Matthew 16:18; Luke 22:32 and John 21:15–17, and following the pattern, not of Leo the Great, Innocent III, Pius IX or Pius XII, but of Gregory the Great and John XXIII.[30]

B. In comparison with the definition of papal primacy, which was deliberately left unqualified, the definition of papal infallibility was laid down subject to the clearest qualifications. This could be counted a success for the ultimately defeated opposition at the Council. There is no doubt that the formula finally agreed on in a chapter supplementary to the three chapters on the primacy – to which the original Constitution on the Church was reduced – fell far short of the original ideas probably of the Pope himself and certainly of the extreme ultramontanists. Let us begin by noting some characteristic statements by the leading propagandists for the definition of infallibility, who had a tremendous influence on the clergy and the Catholic laity.

To W. G. Ward, the editor of the *Dublin Review*, who was a convert and the champion of infallibility in the British Isles, 'all direct doctrinal instruction in all encyclicals, in all letters to individual bishops and allocutions published by the Popes, are *ex cathedra* pronouncements and *ipso facto* infallible'.[31] The layman Louis Veuillot, editor of *l'Univers* and a nimble, not very scrupulous, but highly influential propagandist for papal infallibility in France, wrote: 'We all know only one thing for certain, that is, that no man knows anything except the man with whom God is always, the man who carries out God's idea. We must unswervingly follow his inspired directions.' During the Council he wrote: 'Does or does not the Church believe that its head is directly inspired by God, that is, is infallible in his decisions on faith and morals?'[32] In *l'Univers* he did not shrink from addressing hymns such as '*Veni Sancte Spiritus*' to Pius IX personally or from changing the wording of '*Rerum* Deus *tenax vigor*' into '*Rerum* Pius *tenax vigor*'. Even the Rome Jesuit organ, edited by theologians, *La Civiltà Cattolica*, printed such statements as 'the infallibility of the Pope is the infallibility of Jesus Christ himself' and 'when the Pope thinks, it is God who thinks in him'.[33] A famous or notorious article that appeared in the journal in the guise of 'French correspondence' on 6 February 1869 caused a sensation by proposing that the 'dogmatic infallibility of the Pope' (as well as the Assumption of Mary), should be defined at the Council by unanimous acclamation.[34]

Some strange attitudes to the Pope were to be found among those present at the Council. Some spoke of him as 'Vice-God of mankind', and Bishop Mermillod, the auxiliary Bishop of Geneva, spoke of the 'threefold incarnation' of the Son of God:

in the Virgin's womb, in the Eucharist and in the old man in the Vatican.[35] What carried greater weight was the fact that Archbishop Manning, the Archbishop of Westminster, who prided himself on being the only convert at the Council, was the powerful leader and whip of the pro-infallibility majority and did not shrink from intrigue in promoting its cause, had in 1865 suggested a formula that spoke without qualification of the infallibility of every papal utterance on faith and morals: 'A public utterance by the Supreme Pontiff on faith, morals or what are known as dogmatic facts, or on truths connected with questions of faith or morals, is infallible.'[36]

The form of words in the supplementary Chapter IV on the infallible teaching office of the Roman Pontiff in the Constitution *Pastor Aeternus* of 18 July 1870 in which papal infallibility is defined as God-given dogma should be considered in the light of all the above statements. Again the following significant explanation is given: 'But since, particularly at this time when the salutary efficacy of the Apostolic office is needed more than ever, there are not a few who impugn his authority, we think it absolutely necessary solemnly to assert the prerogative which the only-begotten Son of God deigned to link with the supreme pastoral office' (D 1838). The definition of papal infallibility, laid down, according to the text, by the Pope himself 'in agreement with the sacred council', follows: 'The Roman Pontiff when he speaks *ex cathedra*, that is, when, exercising the office of pastor and teacher of all Christians, he defines with his supreme apostolic authority a doctrine concerning faith or morals to be held by the universal Church, through the divine assistance promised to him in blessed Peter, is possessed of that infallibility with which the divine Redeemer willed his Church to be endowed in defining faith and morals: and therefore such definitions of the Roman Pontiff are irreformable of themselves (and not from the consent of the Church)' (D 1839).

This form of words, perhaps the eighth or the ninth since the original draft of the supplementary chapter, was clear and unambiguous to supporters and opponents alike. The nearly four-hour-long address by Bishop Vinzenz Gasser, the spokesman for the deputation on faith, which is generally accepted as the official commentary on the definition of infallibility,[37] should be read in conjunction with it. When, then, is the Roman

Pontiff infallible? When he speaks *ex cathedra*, that is, in the exercise of his supreme teaching authority. For this, according to the formula, the following conditions must be fulfilled:

1. To define, that is, give a final decision in declaratory form, the Roman Pontiff must be speaking, not as a private individual or even merely in his capacity as Pope, but as the supreme pastor and teacher of Christendom by virtue of his supreme apostolic authority; only then is he the subject, or perhaps better, the organ of Church infallibility.

2. Not any kind of teaching, but only doctrines on matters of faith or morals can be the object of an infallible definition which, however, can cover, not only formally revealed truths (*credenda*), but also all truths connected with them (which are therefore *tenenda*).

3. The Roman Pontiff speaks infallibly, not by virtue of any new revelation or inspiration (which are confined to Scripture), but by virtue of divine aid (*assistentia*): thus the aid of the Holy Spirit of which papal infallibility is the result is not continuous, but is operative only from case to case. It merely protects from error, and is therefore referred to as 'negative'.

4. What is assumed here is not an infallibility granted exclusively to the Roman Pontiff, but the infallibility of the Church with which the Redeemer himself wished his Church to be endowed in final decisions on matters of faith and morals; the (primary?) subject of infallibility is here the Church, of which the Pope is the organ.

The definition is followed by the statement that 'if – which may God avert – anyone should presume to contradict this definition of ours, let him be anathema' (D 1840). As we know, this had concrete results. It led to the excommunication of Ignaz Döllinger, the leading Catholic theologian in Germany (and perhaps in Europe); and it also led to a new schism, the formation of the dissident Old Catholic or Christian Catholic Church in Germany, Austria, Switzerland and the Netherlands. Was that really necessary? An even greater schism might well have taken place. For the sake of this definition the Pope and the Council majority were prepared to accept the consequences, whatever they might be. In this respect, including the treatment of the (in this instance conservative) minority, Vatican II took a different course.

6. POPE VERSUS CHURCH?

The Vatican I formula left open the question of the basic relationship of the Church and that of the Pope, and subsequently, up to Vatican II and beyond, there have been discussions as to whether there are two subjects of infallibility or only one: the Pope alone, or the Pope together with the episcopate or the council, as the case may be. But this is an argument about non-essentials. Bishop Gasser, the spokesman for the deputation on faith, had no hesitation in rejecting views that made it seem 'as if all the infallibility of the Church were seated in the Pope or were derived from him and communicated to the Church'.[38] But he and the pragmatic Roman-minded majority were interested less in such abstract, theoretical questions than in the real, practical outcome, which was that the Pope, of his own volition and without necessarily consulting the Church or the episcopate, could at any time claim to be speaking in the name of the infallibility of the Church when he announced a final decision made by himself on any theoretical or practical question important to the Church. So that not the slightest loophole might be left for any kind of Gallican way out, a sentence was added to the definition at the last moment – at the instigation, it is supposed, of Archbishop Manning and Bishop Senestrey of Regensburg – saying that: 'Therefore such definitions of the Roman Pontiff are irreformable (*irreformabiles*) of themselves, and not from the consent of the Church (*non autem ex consensu Ecclesiae*), (D 1839). This phrase might be capable of misconstruction by some, but to all connoisseurs in the matter the meaning is only too plain. It states quite unequivocally that no previous, contemporaneous or subsequent consent of the Church is necessary for an infallible definition by the Pope to be completely valid, and in particular that no consultation of, co-operation with or ratification by the episcopate is necessary, as the 'Gallicans' and a number of the minority members of the Council had believed. The meaning of this additional clause was well understood. It was the final tip of the balance that led to the premature departure from Rome of the most outstanding representatives of the minority, including, in addition to the Archbishops of Milan and St Louis, Missouri, the representatives of the most important metropolitan sees in France, Germany and Austria-Hungary, whose successors were to provide the nucleus of the progressive majority at Vatican II which, for all its struggle for collegiality and for giving the Pope his place among the people of God, merely repeated the notorious phrase *non autem ex consensu Ecclesiae* without amending it. But did this solve all problems? Neither the pro-infallibility party nor the anti-infallibility Gallicans can have gone to the heart of the matter.

In the report of the deputation on faith, Bishop Gasser among many other things made two important points in regard to papal infallibility that seemed to go much further to meet the minority than the definition itself.

In the first place, he explained that no absolute infallibility was claimed for the Pope. 'I answer and confess frankly that in no case is papal infallibility absolute, because absolute infallibility belongs only to God, the primary and ultimate truth, who can never and nowhere deceive or be deceived.'[39] In contrast to this, the Pope's infallibility is granted to him for definite ends and is limited in three ways: *restricta est ratione subiecti . . . ratione obiecti . . . ratione actus . . .*[40]

At the same time he explained that the Pope is not to be separated from the Church. 'Therefore we do not separate the Pope from his ordained connection with the Church. For he is infallible only when in his office as teacher of all Christians, that is, representing the universal Church, he judges and defines what is to be believed or rejected by all.'[41] 'He can no more be separated from the Church than the foundations can be separated from the building they are meant to support.'[42] The infallibility of the Pope is based on the pastoral ministry to the universal Church, for 'outside this relationship to the universal Church, Peter does not in his successors possess this charism of truth by the certain promise of Christ'.[43]

So some things can be quoted from Vatican I that would have pleased the majority at Vatican II, and some progressive theologians erected great edifices on them. But all this scarcely affects the basic problem, which is that of papal absolutism as it has developed since the eleventh century and as it was exercised in the Middle Ages and the Renaissance and has continued to be exercised in modern times, also at the expense of the Church and the unity of Christendom. For all its solemn and pious talk and decisions on collegiality, Vatican II did not succeed in making headway against this papal absolutism. But the progressive majority at Vatican II could have been used in a much more decent and democratic and yet no less effective fashion than that in which the very unscrupulous (conservative) majority, or their whips, exploited the situation at Vatican I; the post-conciliar Church now has to bear the consequences of the lazy compromise with the Curial minority. The fact that infalliblity on the lines of Vatican I was now formally extended to the episcopate represents no real counterweight (being completely dependent on the Pope), and actually complicates the problem, as we saw in connection with the *magisterium ordinarium*. None of the decisions of Vatican II in any way prevents the Pope from single-handedly issuing infallible proclamations, or of course very fallible ones, whenever and on whatever subject he chooses, which is exactly what Vatican I wanted and decided. For if we look without wishful thinking (most of it, indeed, unfulfilled) at what Vatican I decided and Vatican II half-heartedly confirmed, it is evident in relation to *Humanae Vitae* and other matters that Paul VI had not only textbook theology and Vatican II, but also Vatican I, of course, completely on his side. He could, indeed, have acted with even greater insouciance, even less consideration for the episcopate, theology, Council commissions and public opinion in the Church. For what does the sober, dogmatically and juridically assured reality look like?[44] Vatican I declared that the Pope should use his infallible teaching office for the building up and for the good of the universal Church.[45] But he and he alone (together, of course, with his court) can decide from case to case what is for the good of the Church. Vatican I itself declared that the Pope must act with due care and reflection.[46] But no one in the Church can prevent him from acting wilfully and arbitrarily. Again, Vatican I declared that to assist him in correctly establishing and stating the truth the Pope must make use of the appropriate means (councils, synods, advice from bishops, cardinals, theologians, etc.) before issuing a definition (or other doctrinal pronouncements).[47] But he alone, free of any controls or checks, decides whether, when and what use will be made of these 'means', depending on the importance of the matter.

Again according to Vatican I, the co-operation of the episcopate in a definition is not excluded (and good use was made of this, when there was assurance of its backing, in 1854 and again in 1950).[48] But the Pope alone decides whether or not to resort to such consultation or to accept the resulting advice.

Presumably even the Roi Soleil would have had no objections to such theoretical and abstract restrictions of his power. There is no disguising the fact that according to Vatican I (and II) no one can prevent the Pope from acting arbitrarily and autocratically in matters of doctrine, whether fallible or infallible. He is of course bound by revelation and the beliefs of the Church, as is always zealously pointed out. But he himself decides, with the means that seem appropriate to him, what the meaning of this revelation is and what the true beliefs of the Church are. This applies to all matters of faith and morals and to everything that in the Rome view comes under that heading; and we know from recent Church history how much that is. But that is what Vatican I laid down. If he wishes to, he can act as he chooses even without the Church. To the pro-infallibility majority this was the all-important point. It was the rock on which all reasonable compromise foundered, and it had to be established unconditionally. The phrase 'and not from the consent of the Church' was added to make assurance doubly sure. Here, as Bishop Gasser correctly stated, lay the parting of the ways. The consent of the Church could be described as 'opportune' or even 'relatively necessary', or in any way one chose other than 'absolutely necessary'. 'It is on this point of strict or absolute necessity that the whole difference between us lies, and not on that of opportuneness or relative necessity, which must be left completely to the judgment of the Roman Pontiff who weighs up the circumstances.'[49]

Nor did Vatican II in any way alter the fact that in the last resort the Pope has on his side both dogma and law (in this instance, in the good Roman fashion, one and the same thing); and that is what the Romans are concerned with here, dogma and law, not morals and conscience, which are the Pope's private affair. As Bishop Gasser said, returning the soft answer to various members of the Council who wanted further conditions for the exercise of the infallible teaching authority to be stated ('good faith', 'care', etc.), such conditions would certainly be binding on the Pope's conscience, but for that reason had no place in a definition. 'They are to be ascribed more to the moral than the dogmatic sphere', he said.[50] Presumably he would have commented similarly on only too abstract speeches about dialogue and collegiality, at any rate so long as more specific and concrete proposals were not made. There were some in Rome who did not shrink from saying that, even if the Pope sinned in the act of defining (for example, if he were actuated by wrong motives), he and his definition would still be right. Thus his sin, being a question of morals and conscience, would concern only his confessor, while his definition concerned the Church. The Roi Soleil also had a confessor for matters of morals and conscience without his absolutism being in the least hampered thereby.

The Pope and the Curia are very well able to ignore abstract conciliar declarations about collegiality and the like, as was shown after Vatican II, not only by the high-handed papal encyclicals and decrees, but also by the first two 'collegial' bishops' synods, which were in fact completely manipulated by the Curia and consequently were totally ineffective; and this was shown in still more dangerous form by the Roman secret draft for a 'basic law of the Catholic Church' (*lex fundamentalis Ecclesiae*), which was interlarded with Vatican II phraseology but was conceived in a completely absolutist spirit and would finally bury all the progress made at Vatican II if it were ever accepted. Can anything be done about all this? If it is desired to meet the Romans on equal terms, collegiality in the Church will have to be given the same solid juridical base, with the aid of all the devices of ecclesiastical law, that the Romans have taken care for centuries to give the papal primacy. This is hardly possible without modifying what was laid down at Vatican I. But that is the only way in which the absolute monarch – the only representative of the *ancien régime* who survived the French Revolution – might be turned into a constitutional monarch and the Roman Empire into something in the nature of a Catholic Commonwealth.

In this connection the still possible contingency of a conflict between Pope and Church, and the possibility, a constant subject of discussion in Catholic tradition, of an heretical or schismatic pope, can no longer be evaded, as it was, whether out of ignorance or anxiety or cowardice, at both Vatican I and Vatican II. For the considerations we have noted in connection with the primacy of papal jurisdiction are just as applicable in matters of doctrine, and there have been enough popes from antiquity to modern times whom the Church has subsequently disavowed. We must therefore ask in principle (and Vatican I itself suggests the question) whether the Pope, who can perhaps act *without* the Church, can act *against* it. If he can define without the *consensus Ecclesiae*, could he – in an infallible pronouncement, perfectly possible to the Roman extremists, on the immorality of birth control, for instance – define *against* the *consensus Ecclesiae*? Even Vatican I did not dare suggest anything like this, though there are Roman theologians who, if the Pope were in opposition to the whole Church, would attribute orthodoxy to the former and heterodoxy to the latter. According to the classical Catholic tradition even of the Middle Ages and the Counter-Reformation, it is certain that a pope who tried to excommunicate the whole Church, or made a definition against the consensus of the Church, would have to be dealt with, if not as a heretic, at least as a schismatic, because 'he does not maintain the unity and connection with the whole body of the Church that he must maintain'.[51]

7. SOME CRITICAL QUESTIONS

What we have said so far, however, is not sufficient, for more fundamental questions arise. Since, according to the Roman theory, the Pope's primacy of teaching follows from his primacy of jurisdiction, the same unresolved difficulties that apply to the latter apply to the former.[52] These concern Peter's primacy of teaching, even more the continuation of such teaching, and most of all its continuation in the Roman Pontiffs. It might have been expected that the Vatican I Constitution on Papal Infallibility would be helpful here. But neither the chapters on primacy nor that on infallibility provide a justification of this far-reaching definition sufficient at any rate for the present state of theology. The theologians certainly cannot be satisfied with the juridical information that the decree is valid quite apart from its substantiation. Since – as Vatican I itself declared – neither Pope or Council are granted new revelation or inspiration, and since Vatican I described its infallible definition as divinely revealed dogma, the justification, on the Council's own showing, must be discoverable in the witness to that revelation. The Council therefore cites such witness. But here we are plunged into even greater difficulties, if that is possible, than those we encountered in connection with the primacy. Stating this frankly and honestly can be only of assistance to the Church at the present day.

A. The first thing that strikes us is that, apart from an indirect reference to Matthew 16:18, there is only one quotation from Scripture in the whole chapter on infallibility. This is: 'I have prayed for you, Simon, that your faith may not fail, and once you have recovered, you in your turn must strengthen your brothers' (Luke 22:32.)

Let it be said straight away that Christians outside the Catholic Church would also rejoice if anyone in Christendom undertook this Petrine ministry in an evangelic spirit and posture, strengthening, consoling and encouraging his brothers by virtue of his strong faith. That is what John XXIII did – inevitably one continually returns to him, because his is the only indubitable example in recent times – but, as we said, without any appeal to infallibility, the use of which, indeed, he specifically renounced. Hence the question is not that of the Petrine ministry, as represented in the living succession to the faith of the brethren, but of the historical, legal succession of a papal teaching office with a claim to infallibility. To show this, the following points would have to be demonstrated; hitherto all scholastic speculation and logical argumentation have failed to establish them.

1. That Luke 22:32 (as well as Matthew 16:18 and John 21:15) refer to a teaching office. But infallibility is not mentioned. A man whose faith does not 'cease' (that is the literal translation) is not necessarily immune from error in detail; and an individual who is by no means infallible (for example, Peter) can in fact strengthen his brothers in faith.

2. That in these passages it is not just Peter who is addressed, but his successors also. But successors are not mentioned.

3. That the Bishop of Rome is such a successor. In relation to the question of the infallible teaching office, this creates much

greater difficulties than it does in relation to the question of primacy of jurisdiction.

It would be interesting to see a serious attempt to reply to these points; I have been able to find none in the Roman text-books. It seems, however, that no Catholic theologian has yet succeeded in convincing Christians outside the Catholic Church in the matter. Since Vatican II it has not been legitimate to attribute mere ignorance or ill-will to such Christians, and experience shows that it is better not to ask average Catholics, or often average Catholic theologians, to comment on them.[53] Still less encouraging is the fashion in which Scripture is treated in the latest Catholic commentaries (though most of them are still pre-conciliar) by exegetists who are regarded as critical. J. Schmid,[54] for instance, writing on Luke 22:32, says quite positively that 'Jesus' words do not look beyond the situation immediately after the Passion or outside the group of the disciples'. This interpretation, of course, flatly contradicts that of Vatican I. However, the Catholic author continues: 'But as soon as this passage is connected' – whether by him or not is a question on which he prudently does not commit him-self – 'with Matthew 16:18' – by what right and on the basis of what hermeneutical principles is not stated – 'and it is acknow-ledged' – apparently less an act of intellectual insight than of faith – 'that Peter is here promised an office that holds good not merely for him personally and his time' – which is just as questionable in relation to Matthew 16:18 as it is in relation to Luke 22:32 – 'it must [!] also be acknowledged that the task of giving the "brothers" support in faith also holds good for all those in whom Peter lives on as head of the Church'. If such 'exegetical' arguments are regarded as acceptable, it will be noted without surprise that the exegetist incorporates in brackets as dogmatic substantiation of his argument: 'Vatican Council, Session 4, Chapter 4.'

But only the naïve reader will have overlooked the fact that, apart from all its other peculiarities, the argument has broken down, for 'Vatican Council, Session 4, Chapter 4' relies pre-cisely on what does not follow from this remarkable exegesis, namely on the proposition that Luke 22:32 is concerned, not only with stability in faith, but with infallible definitions.

It may be recalled in this connection that that key text to

modern Roman Pontiffs, Matthew 16:18 f., which now adorns Saint Peter's in big black letters on a golden background, is not once quoted in full in the whole of Christian literature of the first two centuries, but is quoted for the first time in the second century by Tertullian, and then with reference, not to Rome, but to Peter; that not till the middle of the third century did a bishop of Rome – Stephen II, an early example of Roman authoritarianism who worked above all with the weapon of excommunication and abused the great St Cyprian as a pseudo-apostle and pseudo-Christian – claim the better tradition by appealing to the pre-eminence of Peter; that it was not till the fourth century that Matthew 16:18 f. was quoted (notably by the Roman Bishops Damasus and Leo) in support of a claim to primacy, though without any formal claim to infallibility; and, finally, that in the whole of the Eastern exegesis of Matthew 16:18 until the eighth century and beyond at most a personal primacy of Peter was thought of, without any idea of Roman primacy being seriously entertained. And neither in East or West was any claim to the Bishop of Rome's infallibility ever made in connection with Matthew 16:18 f. or Luke 22:32.

B. This explains why the Vatican I definition of infallibility is supported by such meagre references to tradition. At the beginning of the chapter on infallibility the Roman Pontiff's primacy of teaching (as part of the primacy of jurisdiction) is asserted in general terms. 'This the Holy See has always held, the perpetual usage of the Church confirms and the ecumenical councils have declared' (D 1832). It must be pointed out here, if we are to avoid arguing in a circle, that no Church tradition should be accepted uncritically, but must be subjected to examination in the light of the original Christian message; we must ask, that is to say, whether it represents a development in accordance with the gospel, contrary to the gospel, or outside the gospel (*secundum, contra, praeter evangelium*). Its existence in practice, and often also its juridical validity, in no way legitimize it theologically from the gospel point of view. But there are some doubts about the Bishop of Rome's infallible teaching primacy even from the point of view of its existence in practice.

No one of course wishes to dispute the fact that the role of the Roman Church was meritorious in many respects. The Church of the imperial city, as ancient as it was powerful, distinguished

itself by its widespread work of love and bore witness to its faith
in a variety of persecutions, and was rightly regarded as a bulwark of orthodoxy. It proved itself in the struggle against
Gnostics, Marcionites and Montanists, the idea of the apostolic
succession and tradition took root in Rome at an early stage,
and it exercised an important influence in regard both to the
baptismal creed and the New Testament canon. In matters of
doctrine the Roman Church wisely adopted a central, media-
tory position, in which it later enjoyed the support of Alexandria
in particular. We need not look further for an explanation of
the fact that the reputation it enjoyed was transferred to its
Bishop.

Nevertheless there was no question of his or his Church's
enjoying any primacy of teaching or infallibility. The Roman
claim became questionable as soon as it began to be imposed in
an authoritarian fashion, and it was interpreted more and more
legalistically as time went on, without respect for the individuality or independence of the other Churches in doctrine, liturgy or
organization; for example, when in the league of episcopal
Churches towards the end of the second century Bishop Victor
of Rome (against the opposition of the Western bishops,
including St Irenaeus, and the Eastern bishops also) excommunicated the whole of Asia Minor in order to enforce a new
Roman date for Easter; or when, in the middle of the third
century, Bishop Stephen (against the opposition of St Cyprian,
the Churches of Africa and the great Churches of the East)
wished to excommunicate large areas of the Church because of
their different attitude to the baptism of heretics. Neither Victor
nor Stephen succeed in establishing their primacy in the
succession to Peter. Not till the age of Constantine – and
notably the Western rump synod of Sardica (Sofia) in 343 – did
a monarchical structure begin to be established in the Western
Church under Roman influence, as when Bishop Damasus
first claimed the title of *Sedes Apostolica* exclusively for the Roman
See; when Bishop Siricius (a contemporary of the far more
important Bishop Ambrose of Milan) first called himself 'Pope',
peremptorily began calling his own statutes 'apostolic', adopted
the imperial style, and vigorously extended his powers in all
directions; and when Bishop Innocent I insisted on all important matters being laid before the Bishop of Rome for decision

after they had been discussed by a synod and tried to establish liturgical centralization with the aid of historical fictions, and so on. The further expansion of the power of the Roman *Sancta Sedes* – particularly in connection with the Papal States and the forged 'Donation of Constantine' and the similarly monstrous but influential forgery of the Isidorian Decretals, and finally with the Gregorian Reform – is a familiar story.

Only after the Gregorian Reform in the High Middle Ages did the Roman power begin to exercise a rigidly juridical and centralist influence on doctrine. Rome had certainly exercised weighty influence in the Arian struggle, and at Chalcedon Leo won a great victory. But the most important bishops and theologians of the Western Church at that time, St Ambrose and St Augustine, so far from deducing any prerogative for the Bishop of Rome as Peter's successor from Matthew 16:18, kept completely to the line of St Cyprian. When the Bishops of Rome from Damasus to Leo tried to establish legal justification for claiming Roman jurisdiction over other Churches, their claims remained largely unaccepted and unrealized. That great Roman and great jurist Leo, who was the first to adorn himself with the title of the pagan high priest *Pontifex Maximus*, and to demand that the ecumenical council should obey and actually subordinate itself to him on the basis of the Petrine text, had to reconcile himself to the Council of Chalcedon's granting the same position of supremacy to his great opponent in Constantinople, the Patriarch of the Eastern Church. And though the ecumenical councils, at which, with the exception of Chalcedon, the Bishops of Rome exercised scarcely any influence, made no doctrinal decisions without or against the Pope – the Patriarch of the Western Church and the first Patriarch of the Imperial Church – they nevertheless made their decisions by virtue of their own authority, for they were neither summoned nor led by him, nor were their decisions necessarily confirmed by him. How little the Roman claim to orthodoxy was interpreted as 'infallibility' was strikingly shown by the excommunication by the fifth ecumenical council at Constantinople in 553 of Pope Vigilius, who thereupon gave in; even more striking was the famous condemnation of Pope Honorius I by the sixth ecumenical council at Constantinople in 681, which was repeated by the Trullan synod of 692 and by the seventh and eighth ecumenical councils and was, moreover, accepted by Honorius's successor, Leo II, and again confirmed by subsequent popes.

Until the twelfth century the Roman Church was not regarded as possessing teaching authority properly so-called, as has recently been shown by Yves Congar in his admirable work on the ecclesiology of the High Middle Ages in which he summarizes all the historical research on the subject. 'The teaching work that the Pope was specifically granted was more of a religious nature, due to Rome as the place of the martyrdom of St Peter and St Paul. Peter was the faith, Paul the proclaimer of the faith. It was gladly agreed that the Roman Church had never erred in faith. It was a model, being the Church of Peter, the first to profess his faith in Christ and thus set an example. . . . But this was not an admission of what we wrongly call papal infallibility, or, more exactly, the infallibility of the judgments that he can make in his final authority as universal and supreme pastor. Doctrinal pronouncements by popes were sometimes disputed.'[55] Congar relies here on the work of J. Langen, who assembled facts and documents to show that the Pope was not regarded as infallible from the seventh century to the twelfth.[56]

The great change, however, came about in conjunction with the Gregorian Reform, when the condemnations of popes we mentioned above had been forgotten. The papal teaching authority was now buttressed by the monstrous ninth-century forgery of the Decretals of the Pseudo-Isidore (115 forged documents attributed to the early bishops of Rome from Clement of Rome onwards, and 125 documents with interpolations).[57] They destroyed all feeling for the historical development of institutions, and created the impression that the Church had been governed in detail since the earliest times by papal decree, and the resulting image of the Church and Church law was based entirely on Roman authority. On questions of doctrine the assertions in the forged documents that were of the greatest importance were that the holding of councils, including provincial councils, was linked with the papal authority and that all important Church affairs were subject to papal decision. The Pope, by virtue of his own authority, was the norm for the whole Church. 'Pseudo-Isidore ascribes to the Pope's teaching office and disciplinary authority an autonomous character which is not bound by the norms of tradition. It ascribes to

Pope Lucius, a contemporary of St Cyprian, the declaration that the Roman Church, "mother of all the Churches of Christ", has never erred.'[58]

It was on such and similar statements that Gregory VII relied in the second half of the eleventh century for his monarchical conception of the Church, which in fact represented a new Church constitution; and in the first half of the thirteenth century Gratian, the founder of canon law, wrote his law-book, which laid the foundation for all that was to follow in later times, including the 1918 Code of Canon Law, quoting 324 passages from popes of the first four centuries, of which 313 are demonstrably forged. Henceforward Matthew 16:18 was applied in Rome to the Roman Church and the Roman Pontiff in this absolute, monarchical sense, with all the juridical consequences that the great papal legislators of the twelfth and thirteenth centuries were able to deduce from this primacy and enforce in exceedingly practical fashion with the aid of papal synods, papal legates, and mendicant orders similarly independent of local Church leaders (bishops and parish priests). Both the Western and the Eastern Empires were weak during this period, and as a result of these developments the Eastern Church had turned away completely from Rome, and the schism with the East became final. Now there were no more obstacles in the way of the development of the papal teaching authority. True, in his *Dictatus Papae* Gregory VII asserted only that the Roman *Church* could never fall into error in faith, and his claim that the Pope possessed a personal sanctity by reason of the merits of Peter transmitted to him was never established; it could, presumably, only too easily have been used to question a pope's legitimacy. Also even the Curially minded canonists argued that a pope could lapse into heresy and be tried by the Church. Nevertheless in the thirteenth century papal power not only attained its peak in world politics and canon law, but also established itself in theology in spite of the latter's reservations.

It was St Thomas Aquinas, himself a member of a centrally controlled mendicant order, who in the second half of the thirteenth century incorporated the new political-juridical development into the dogmatic system. That must be admitted, in spite of his indisputable services to theology as a whole. In his *Contra errores Graecorum*, which was commissioned by the Curia for Pope

Urban IV in his negotiations for union with the Greek Emperor
Michael VIII Palaiologos, he confronted the weak Greeks with
an exorbitant argument for the Roman prerogatives, which in
turn reacted on the West. On the supreme question of the
Trinity he 'demonstrated' to the Greeks in several chapters
towards the end of a work that positively teems with quotations
from forged documents 'that the Pope of Rome is the first and
greatest of all bishops', 'that he presides over the whole Church
of Christ', 'that he has plenitude of power in the Church', 'that
the Pope of Rome is the successor of Peter in the power con-
ferred by Christ on the latter'.[59] In regard to the papal teaching
authority he shows 'that the Pope decides what is part of faith'.
All these chapters culminate in the assertion, apparently first
dogmatically formulated by Thomas and then abruptly defined
by Boniface VIII in the Bull *Unam Sanctam*, 'that to be subject
to the Roman Pontiff is necessary for salvation'.[60] In this article,
which is of fundamental importance for the papal teaching
authority, Aquinas again relies on forged quotations from
Cyril's *Liber Thesaurorum*, which he took from an anonymous
Libellus de processione Spiritus Sancti: 'It is understandable that
Thomas should have quoted from the *Libellus* those passages
that were adapted to establishing his propositions on the
primacy; from what has been said, however, it is clear that
these are mostly propositions that were either forgeries or
interpolated through forgeries.'[61]

These propositions based on forgeries were then taken over by
St Thomas into his *Summa Theologiae*, where they really began to
make history. In our present context the article of vital importance is on whether it is the Pope's business to lay down the
creed.[62] Thomas begins as usual by stating the opposite proposition, pointing out with complete historical correctness that
'the publication of a profession of faith takes place in general
council'. To this he replies with a proposition that he documents
only from a passage in the Decretals which is again based on the
above-mentioned forgeries of Pseudo-Isidore, and in no way
corresponds to the historical truth:[63] 'But such a council can be
called only by authority of the Pope. Thus the publication of a
profession of faith pertains to the papal authority.' Then comes
Thomas's full answer: 'A new publication of a profession
of faith is necessary to avoid errors that are arising. The publi-

cation therefore comes under the authority which has to define formally what matters are of faith, so that they may be held by all with unshakable faith. But this belongs to the authority of the Supreme Pontiff, to whom the Church's greater and more difficult questions are referred.' (Here again there follows a passage from the Decretals based on Pseudo-Isidore). 'Hence too our Lord says to Peter (Luke 22:32), since he had appointed him Supreme Pontiff: "I have prayed for you, Simon . . ." And the reason for this is that there must be one faith of the whole Church according to 1 Corinthians 1:10: "All say the same thing, let there be no divisions among you." This could not be maintained unless a question arising on faith were decided by him who presides over the whole Church, so that his judgment may be firmly held by the whole Church. Hence a new publication of a profession of faith pertains solely to the authority of the Supreme Pontiff: as also everything else that pertains to the whole Church, such as convoking a general council and other things of the same kind.'

There is no doubt that St Thomas Aquinas, basing himself in good faith on the forgeries, as we may assume, thus laid the foundations for the Vatican I doctrine of infallibility. Not that it established itself so quickly. Soon afterwards the Avignon exile, the Western schism, with its two and then three contending popes, and finally the conciliar period, made exaggerations of the papal teaching authority look just as Utopian as exaggerations of the papal jurisdiction over the world-wide Church. After the Council of Constance, however, Cardinal Torquemada revived the papal ecclesiology we have just described on Thomistic foundations (though he admitted the possibility of a heretical pope), and he was followed later, when the Curia had again to a large extent gained the upper hand, by Luther's contemporaries, Cardinals Cajetan and Jacobazzi. But in the fifteenth century, and at the time of the Reformation – this must be pointed out if Luther is to be understood – there was no unanimity of view in the Church about the papal primacy (and its relationship to the council) or the papal teaching authority. Even the Council of Trent, fearing a revival of conciliarism, did not dare make any decisions on these matters. But Cardinal Bellarmine reverted to the line of St Thomas Aquinas, Torquemada and Cajetan, and then in the nineteenth century, when the time had grown ripe for a definition of papal infallibility, became a crown witness for it, jointly with St Thomas. Incidentally, we may note that the condemnation of Pope Honorius by several councils and popes was unknown to St Thomas. After it became known, Torquemada brazenly declared it to have been an error of the Greeks, and in the Reformation period A. Pighi and Bellarmine even more brazenly declared it to be a forgery of the council documents (which resulted in a sharp protest by Melchior Cano, the theologian of the Council of Trent). Finally the historicity of the condemnation of Honorius was acknowledged by the pro-infallibility party at Vatican I but, by virtue of what had now become a customary anachronistic way out, was interpreted as not having been a declaration *ex cathedra*.[64]

In the light of this brief outline of the history of papal infallibility, we can understand why Vatican I was content to validate the definition with the brief generalizations that 'this the Holy See has always held' and 'this the perpetual usage of the Church confirms'. The historical reality in the matter looks different. Papal exaggeration of the teaching authority in theory and practice can quote proved forgeries and decretals based on them in its favour, as well as theological arguments based on those decretals, but it cannot rely on Scripture or on the common ecumenical tradition of the Church of the first millennium. It bears a substantial share of the responsibility for the maintenance of the schism with the Eastern Churches, which have never accepted it, and with the Churches of the Reformation, which rebelled against it in the name of the freedom of the gospel and of Christian man.[65]

If still further illustration is required of the questionable nature of the development we have described, let us consider the conciliar texts quoted in support of papal infallibility in Chapter IV of the Constitution *Pastor Aeternus*. None of these three surprisingly extensive texts stems from a general recognized council. Vatican I certainly cannot be blamed for not quoting the Council of Chalcedon, with its famous Canon 28, which granted New Rome (Constantinople) the same prerogatives as Rome itself; for here we hear the voice of a different, non-Roman tradition. (Heinrich Denzinger, usually so meticulous in tracking down quotations on primacy and infallibility often of very secondary importance, as in so many other instances passes over in silence this canon of an ecumenical council that does not fit into his system.) Against the background of the whole historical development of the second millennium, what do the quotations from the Council of Lyons (1274) and Florence (1439) prove? They were acknowledgments of Roman primacy, composed by Romans, which they were trying – though they ultimately failed – to impose on the Greeks, who were hard-pressed by the Turks. Nevertheless, in spite of all the emphasis on the Roman teaching authority, neither the Lyons nor the Florentine texts contain anything about infallibility. The same applies to the Fourth Council of Constantinople (869–70), which is the first to be cited by Vatican I. It says nothing about either infallibility or the Bishop of Rome, but speaks only about the Roman See. Nor is this council included among the generally recognized councils. On the contrary, as it was held during the quarrel between the Patriarch Ignatios and the Patriarch Photius, it was formally annulled some years later, its original documents were lost, and in all the Byzantine collections it is completely ignored. It carried no weight in the West either, until the second half of the eleventh century, when it began to be referred to as the Eighth Ecumenical Council, again, significantly though, in connection with the Gregorian Reform and the final breach with Constantinople.[66]

C. The case for the dogma of infallibility based on Scripture and tradition is plainly as meagre as it is brittle. When we look at it, we may well wonder how it was possible for the overwhelming majority of bishops to give their assent to its definition. We have also examined their motives. Many extra-theological motives undoubtedly played their part. We mentioned the mentality of most of the bishops, which bore the imprint of the restoration, romanticism and traditionalism, and, connected with these things, an aversion to modern liberal and democratic ideas, which caused them to favour a strengthened hierarchical order based entirely on the Pope. We spoke of the new type of sentimental veneration for Pius IX, which could deny him nothing he seriously wanted and saw in the definition of his prerogatives a compensation for the obloquy to which he had been subjected. More could also be said about the desire of

many bishops finally to liquidate 'Gallicanism', which was felt
to be a weakening of the Catholic united front, and also of the
pressure of the Curia, which undoubtedly played a ˏpart,
especially in the case of those bishops who were financially
dependent on it. But all this is still insufficient to explain the
real motivation.

What, then, was the decisive factor that led to the definition
of papal infallibility? It was simply that most of the bishops
took it for granted before it was defined. For the most part they
came from the traditionally Catholic countries; to these were
added Eastern prelates trained in Rome and nearly all the
missionary bishops, as well as some from countries where the
struggle against liberalism or Protestantism was especially
acute. They gave little thought to the enormous exegetical,
historical and systematic difficulties in the way of a definition,
and to all of them the whole thing seemed as clear as daylight
from the outset, as R. Aubert, who carefully analysed the
different factors at work, correctly states. 'Even if these prelates
did not approve of all the centralizing tendencies of the Curia,
they had no objection to the Council's solemnly recognizing the
infallibility of the Pope, which had long been recognized, at any
rate in practice, by the whole of their flock and their clergy and
seemed to them to be an established theological truth. On the
other hand, they regarded the Gallican and Febronian theses as
a regression to outworn theories, while the validity of the old
tradition was attested by several passages in Scripture, the
import of which seemed to them to be perfectly clear and
unambiguous, as well as by all the great scholastic teachers
from St Thomas to Bellarmine. Hence it seemed to them to be a
perfectly normal and natural step to take advantage of the
opportunity provided by the Council to make short work of the
revival of what, in their view, were totally unfruitful discussions of the subject.'[67]

On the other hand, we must not overlook the fact that a
variety of motives were at work in the minds of the minority,
and that the true situation was not clear to them either. The
minority consisted chiefly of German, Austro-Hungarian, and
about thirty French, twenty Italian and some Eastern bishops.
Their education and training and the political situation in their
countries played a part with them too; they feared that a

renewed condemnation of modern ideas would lead to reactions by their governments. But pastoral and ecumenical factors were more important. They feared a schism – unfortunately with very good reason, as things turned out – a jeopardizing of ecumenical efforts, or a revival of aggressivity on the part of Protestant circles, as the case may be. But the chief factors were theological, as again is very clearly shown by Aubert, though we cannot refrain from pointing out that he makes the usual unconsidered use of depreciatory theological labels (here indicated by question-marks) that obscure the fact that some of the oldest and best Catholic traditions lay behind a number of these trends. 'In the first place there were the theological considerations', he writes. 'There was a Gallican [?] or semi-Gallican [?] view of the teaching office in the Church that contested the claim that the Pope in certain definite instances could decide questions of doctrine independently of any episcopal assent; there was the influence of the Bossuet tradition; a tendency to episcopalism[?] that derived from the Febronian[?] theologians of the eighteenth century; there were historical difficulties, such as the condemnation of Pope Honorius in 681, an archaising [?] view of theology that looked too exclusively [?] to the sources and in the process lost a sense for the reality of dogmatic development[?]. All these things led them to the conclusion that the Pope did not enjoy the prerogative of papal infallibility or that the question had not been sufficiently investigated, and that it was therefore premature to try to decide it at the present time. But a still more frequent theological motive seems to have been a very legitimate, though sometimes rather exaggerated [?] concern to safeguard the second element that, according to divine law, formed part of the Church hierarchy, the episcopate.'[68]

And yet Aubert, with many other authors, is not completely wrong in resorting to labels such as Gallicanism, semi-Gallicanism, Febronianism, and so on. For it cannot be overlooked that the minority too remained largely congealed in an out-of-date posture. This was due not least to the fact that, as a result of the diversity of the motives and positions of those who constituted it, it concentrated on the question that provided the broadest base for the opposition to the definition of infallibility, that of its opportuneness. The question of its opportuneness thrust the

essential question too much into the background, and going to
the heart of the issue was avoided. But one thing must have
become clear in the course of this chapter; that is, that the
traditional doctrine of infallibility in the Church, for all the
precision of its description in the theological textbooks and at
Vatican I and II, rests on foundations that cannot be regarded
as secure and unassailable from the viewpoint of present-day
theology and perhaps could not be so regarded even at that time.

Chapter Three

THE CENTRAL PROBLEM

I. TOWARDS A POSITIVE ANSWER

If the case for the neo-scholastic theory of infallibility is so weak, and its development, in relation both to the Pope (Vatican I) and to the episcopate (Vatican II), raises so many unsolved and perhaps insoluble problems, might not the best and simplest course perhaps be simply to drop it? We can anticipate the question that will come in reply. But what, it will be asked, would then become of the biblical promises on which the doctrine of infallibility relies, promises which, according to the original Christian witness, were given to the Church, a body that differs from any purely worldly community or institution, and which have come down to us in a variety of forms: the promises that the Lord will remain with his disciples until the end of the world, that the gates of hell will not overcome the Church, that the Spirit of truth will lead the disciples into all truth, that the Church is the pillar and the ground of all truth?

In this chapter we shall try to avoid hasty conclusions, either to the right or to the left, but instead to narrow the question down as far as possible and pin-point the basic difficulties. We shall do this on the basis of the argument developed in the previous chapters, taking into account the most recent publications, particularly those issued in connection with the 1970 centenary of Vatican I and its definition of papal infallibility. It will be seen that, though a great deal that is good and true has been said about it, the central problem has still not been seen sufficiently plainly. What is the central problem of Church infallibility if we set aside the inadequate, questionable and brittle arguments we dealt with in the last chapter? Before giving a positive answer, let us first clear away some misconceptions.

a. *Lack of Freedom at Vatican I?*

1. Today, at a century's distance, Catholic authors state frankly that the majority at the Council were biased by the

mentality of the political and religious restoration, by anti-
enlightenment traditionalism and by papal absolutism. They
also speak of the oppressive atmosphere of the Council in
comparison with that of Vatican II and of the authoritarian
influence exercised on.it by Pius IX. Here is what some recent
authors have to say in the matter.

On the ideological blinkers of Vatican I, Victor Conzemius,
the Luxembourg Church historian and editor of the correspondence between Ignaz von Döllinger and Lord Acton, writes
as follows: 'In the age of restoration the papacy became the
indispensable support of backward-looking, legitimist-mon-
archist thinking. Moreover, new possibilities presented themselves for the development of the Pope's spiritual authority. For
the national Churches of France, Austria, Germany and Italy
were largely relieved of worldly tasks as a result of secularization. By depending on Rome they tried to buttress themselves
against national politics which sought partly to eliminate the
Church from public life, partly bureaucratically to tame its
newly won freedom; and Rome gave dependable support both
to national Churches struggling for their freedom and to the
missionary Churches that were rapidly developing in the nineteenth century in America and Asia. In return, these Churches
became more closely tied to Rome. Also, for a time Rome gave
real elbow-room to Catholic progressive forces that agitated
against state tutelage of the Church in the police states of the
restoration period. The papacy was extraordinarily favoured by
an ideological trend the direct upshot of which was a reinforcement of its moral prestige. Two Frenchmen, de Maistre
and Lamennais, both "converts" who found their way back to
the Church after many years' estrangement, were harbingers of
this movement. To them the Catholic Church was the foundation pier on which the European social order was based; any
attack on it was an attack on the foundations of society.'[1]

The following summary of the ideas of these two fathers of
papal ultramontanism, which in the second half of the century
were propagated with all the resources at its command by
Rome itself among laity and clergy, is important for the
historical understanding of this ideology. 'Typical of de
Maistre is the logical chain of argument by which he sought to
win King Charles X of France for his ideas: "No public

morality and no national character without religion, no European religion without Christianity, no Christianity without Catholicism, no Catholicism without the Pope, no Pope without the supremacy to which he is entitled." Lapidary phrases, such as "there is no Christianity without the Roman Pontiff", flowed from his pen. He did not back these assertions with arguments, but simply kept on dogmatically hammering away at the parallel between ecclesiastical and secular society. "There can be no human society without government, no government without sovereignty and no sovereignty without infallibility." He brings about a kind of cosmic identification of Church and society, both of which are subject to the same laws, the same ethos. He has a kind of obsessive compulsion to proclaim the principle of authority. Taking refuge in authority, which he transformed into a kind of mythical oracle, seemed to him to be the only way out of the social crisis of his time. It is as well to remember that this Savoyard count wrote as a very conscious opponent of the French Revolution while living under the feudal and authoritarian régime in Russia, where he was Minister to the Court of the Tsars. His ideas, which were regarded with reserve in Rome itself, immediately gained him a following. Lamennais, a great sower of ideas with a future, became their popularizer. He smoothed away their rough edges, related them directly to the life of the Church, and thus gave them a very great comprehensibility.'[2]

In the doom-laden atmosphere of the years before the loss of the Papal States, large sums of money flowed into the Roman coffers from all over Europe when 'Peter's pence' were revived as a voluntary offering for Pope and Curia, and young Catholics, from Holland in particular, competed with each other to enlist in the papal army, and Pius IX became the symbol of the Catholic will to survive. 'This was the climate in which a state of mind developed that made a reinforcement of papal authority seem the alpha and omega of Church wisdom. From the viewpoint of the history of ideas, it is interesting to note that at a time when personal authority was gradually giving way to material authority, the Church not only held fast to personal authority but reconsecrated it with dogmatic trimmings. This state of mind was consolidated by the general attack on Christianity.'[3]

Of the atmosphere that prevailed at the Council, Hubert Jedin, the conciliar historian, writes that 'it was full of tension. But it was not the glad, hopeful tension in which the "ecumenical" council was awaited after Pope John's first announcement; fears outweighed hopes, particularly in the intellectually leading circles of the German-speaking countries and France. Shortly before Pope Pius IX had declared war in the Syllabus on modern ideas and theories about the State.'[4] The dogmatician Walter Kasper indicates even more plainly the effects of this atmosphere, which differed so much from that of Vatican II, on the Council's definition of infallibility. 'The differences between the two Councils', he writes, 'were reflected in the very different atmospheres of the two. At Vatican I scheming or actually fanatical tendencies led to some highly exaggerated and ill-considered statements about papal primacy and infallibility. This caused a considerable minority of bishops who were highly qualified in the matter to be simply ignored. Most of them left Rome, filled with bitterness, before the Council officially ended. Thus problems were created for the domestic life of the Church, for the symbiosis of the separated Churches, and for the Church's relations with the modern world that could not be eliminated even by Vatican II. The papal primacy that Vatican I defined as the centre, sign and principle of unity became in practice a cause of separation between the Churches and the occasion of many psychological schisms within the Church. Thus the problems raised by Vatican I have by no means been settled.'[5]

Finally, this is what Kasper has to say on Pius IX's influence on Vatican I: 'The Council of the last century was called by Pius IX to condemn the errors of modern times, just as the Council of Trent was called to repel the false doctrines of the sixteenth-century Reformers. The object was to present the infallible authority of the Pope as the remedy for the crisis of modern society that was already beginning to take shape. In contrast to this, John XXIII, in his memorable opening address of 11 October 1962, rejected the prophets of doom who believed that all developments in society and the Church were for the worse and that the world was on the brink of disaster. He advised the Church in present-day circumstances to resort, not to severity, but to compassion, and to open the windows wide on to the outside world.'⁶ Of the actual proceedings at Vatican I Jedin writes: 'It must be acknowledged that in the highly dramatic struggle about the formulation of the definition of infallibility Pius IX did not maintain the reserve that his successor made it his business to maintain during the Second Vatican Council in relation to the debate on Chapter III of the Constitution on the Church. The removal of the chapter on the Pope from the general draft on the Church in March 1870 was due to him. On the basis of his personal ideas on the amplification of infallibility, he tried to influence members of the Council in favour of his view during the debate, and after Cardinal Guidi of Bologna, for instance, had made a proposal conciliatory to the minority in the General Congregation of 18 June, he rebuked him bitterly the same evening and, obviously in an outburst of anger, allowed himself to be carried away to the extent of uttering the notorious phrase, which went the rounds at the Council next morning: "Tradition? I am tradition." '⁷

As we pointed out in the previous chapter, an allowance must be made for all this in judging the Council and its definitions, which can be understood only in the light of this ideological conditioning and atmosphere.

2. Nevertheless, the frequently made assertion that the Council was not free cannot be maintained. In spite of the often shocking manipulation of the Council by the Curia, the Pope and the leaders of the majority, there was freedom of speech (there was often more plain speaking than at Vatican II) and freedom of voting. The decisive factor was that there was no need to bring pressure to bear on the majority, for the definition was in complete harmony with its ideas.

Of the assertion that the Council was unfree, Conzemius says: 'It is not correct. It is true that the Council leaders in their devotion to the Curia sometimes exercised undue pressure, and that in occasional outbursts of his easily unbridled temperament the Pope revealed his partisanship only too much. Nevertheless the right to the free expression of opinion was not thereby curtailed, and the Council's freedom was basically unaffected. The majority of the bishops had no need to be called to order by the Curia for, as we have described, they thought in categories that led directly to a strengthening of the papal prerogatives. Nor were the resolute champions of this trend Italians or Spaniards;

they were northerners: Archbishop Manning of Westminster; Bishop Senestrey of Regensburg; Mermillod, Auxiliary Bishop of Geneva.'[8] As the Catholic publicist Walter Dirks well says: 'The majority of the Fathers – and the same plainly held good for the general body of laity – did not just yield to the pressure of a tough and single-minded Pope, but shared his most important assumption about the establishment of dogma, namely that the Christian Church – the heretical Reform Churches did not count – had always believed in the infallible teaching authority of Peter's successor. Dogmas, in their view, did not create "new" truths, but "defined" more exactly what everyone had always believed.'[9]

b. *The Question of Primacy*

1. Agreement on the Petrine ministry in the Church and the question of primacy is not inherently impossible, as is shown, for instance, by the latest and very illuminating dialogue with the Old Catholic Church, which broke away from the Catholic Church as a result of the Vatican I definition.

In the Declaration of Utrecht of 24 September 1889 the international conference of Old Catholic bishops, in spite of their 'rejection of the Vatican decree of 18 July 1870 on infallibility and the universal episcopate', had no objection to acknowledging an 'historical primacy as *primus inter pares* such as had been attributed to the Bishop of Rome by a number of ecumenical councils and the Fathers of the early Church with the assent of the whole Church of the first millennium'.[10] The seven theses announced on 13 September 1969[11] by a conference of Old Catholic theologians, with the simultaneous assent of the international conference of Old Catholic bishops, reiterated the Utrecht Declaration (thesis No. 1) and accepted the 'special position of Peter' in the New Testament as having 'significative importance for the Church', so that 'the tasks entrusted to Peter might be expressed in the structure of the Church' (theses Nos. 2–4). Without 'entering the field of dogmatic conclusions' (cf. thesis No. 6), it could be stated that 'the function that had accrued to Rome in the history of the Church accorded with acceptance of that mission', though this was 'often very much obscured' (thesis No. 5). In thesis No. 7 the conclusion was drawn that 'in accordance with the function that Peter fulfilled according to the witness of Scripture, the Petrine office should be defined as service to Christ, to his Church and to the world through the obligation (not the legal entitlement) in all situations requiring a decision to take an initiative to make it possible for the totality of the Church to decide, express its faith and visibly manifest its unity'.

These gratifyingly unpolemical and promising theses, as explained by Werner Küppers, the leading Old Catholic theologian,[12] were regarded by Heinrich Bacht, the very capable Catholic who was his opposite number in discussions with him, as offering 'real chances for an understanding'.[13] In the light of his own studies,[14] the present author can only agree. He can likewise only agree with Bacht when he writes: 'Contemporary Catholic theology is aware of the "hierarchy of truths" (Decree on Ecumenism No. 11); but in this hierarchy, the question of papal primacy clearly takes a secondary place. Catholic theology is similarly aware that elements of very diverse origin and worth have converged into the complex phenomenon of the papacy and that their disentanglement is an urgent task. It is also aware that by no means all the papal prerogatives mentioned at Vatican I are divine law; and that as a consequence of the theology that led to Vatican I the papal function was set in undue relief against the totality of the Church and that it is therefore an urgent task to restore the question of the primacy to its proper place in the whole teaching of the Church. Moreover the "disarming" of the one-sided juridical concept of the Church's structures had begun long before Vatican II. Similarly, Catholic quarters are very well aware of the fact that in the shadow of the Gregorian reform the development of doctrine on the Constitution of the Church was marked by a one-sided concentration on the question of "power" and "authority". On top of all this, there is critical dissociation from all sorts of "inadequacies" and limitations at Vatican I (unfair agitation by the pro-infallibility party, lack of ecumenical responsibility, unnecessary exacerbation of feeling as a result of the use of the anathema ...).'[15] Bacht concludes with an appeal for understanding: 'May those who have responsibility read the signs of the times.'[16]

2. But settlement of the primacy question does not involve

settlement of the question of infallibility; on the contrary, it is at this point that it arises.

It is a striking fact that the word 'infallibility' occurs neither in the seven Old Catholic theses, nor in Küppers' interpretation, nor in Bacht's reply. This is hardly fortuitous. For a reference to the infallibility question we must look to the Old Catholic thesis No. 6, which says: 'In spite of the numerous disastrous developments of the past that led to various schisms, including that of Utrecht, an authoritarian way of thinking based on an axiomatic preconception that cannot be validated from Scripture or tradition was proclaimed as dogma by the First Vatican Council'. Also Küppers must have had the infallibility question in mind when he noted in the theses a 'complete reserve in regard to the "dogmatic conclusions" usually dominant in questions relating to the papacy'. 'This reserve', he writes, 'is based on the insight that a common basis for dogmatic discussion is still lacking in this field.'[17]

Thus it is clear that to the Old Catholics – to say nothing of the Orthodox and Protestant Churches – an eventual settlement of the question of the primacy does not imply a settlement of that of infallibility. The latter represents the most serious stumbling-block in the path of ecumenical understanding.

c. *The Rights of Conscience?*

1. Even in relation to dogma the rights of conscience remain. There is no need to repeat here what we said in Chapter I with reference to our treatment of the subject in our *Structures of the Church*. Fortunately the encyclical *Humanae Vitae* has greatly helped Catholics in the post-conciliar period to go ahead with the urgently necessary task of forming their consciences even in relation to solemn papal doctrinal statements.

In testimony to the importance of freedom as a factor in faith, let us quote W. Kasper's plain speaking on the matter in his reflections on 'The Church's Road from Vatican I to Vatican II': 'Only when it [the Church] preserves its own freedom can it serve the freedom of others', he writes. 'Its authority therefore must be the authority of freedom. For faith is essentially an act of free assent; as an act that is also wholly and entirely human, it does not exclude intellectual responsibility, but includes it. No one can or is permitted to delegate this responsibility in "blind" obedience, as it were, to the official Church and its teaching office. An obedience of faith that ran counter to one's own insight would be an immoral act.'[18] Similarly Walter Dirks writes: 'The Pauline doctrine, reinforced by St Thomas Aquinas, that whatever does not come "from the conscience", from conviction, is sin holds good for Catholics too. A basic assumption of the Catholic Church is the free and voluntary acceptance and maintenance of faith.'[19]

2. But that does not settle the question either of papal or of episcopal infallibility. True, it has become usual, particularly in recent times, to have recourse to conscience, and in general to find mitigating circumstances in subjective factors, when moral theology gets one no further on practical issues. Thus many a hard yoke imposed by conventional Catholic sexual morality could be made at any rate subjectively tolerable (lack of knowledge or lack of free will excuses from grave sin in masturbation or birth control). Such recourse to subjectivity was and remains justified as defence for the conscience and pastoral aid against an authoritarian teaching office that does everything in its power to prevent discussion. But it is no excuse or pretext for not tackling the actual problems theologically. Advice given in the confessional is no substitute for serious theological criticism. This applies especially to the question of infallibility. Individual Christians, theologians, bishops and bishops' conferences have rightly made use of the appeal to conscience in relation to the encyclical *Humanae Vitae*, for instance. But neither theologians nor Church leaders are thereby excused from getting to grips with the question, and in this concrete instance, apart from all questions of moral theology, this involves the question of the authority of the teaching office. Irrespective of the rights of conscience, is the claim of the teaching office to (ordinary or extraordinary papal or episcopal) infallibility valid or not? If this question had been tackled with sufficient seriousness at an earlier stage, many would have been spared grave conflicts of conscience.

d. *Opportuneness, Conditions and Limits of the Definition of Infallibility*

1. Even if we share the view of the minority at Vatican I that the definition of infallibility was inopportune, once it had been defined the prerequisite for any objective discussion of it

was a clear understanding of its modalities and limitations.

In the last chapter, as we had already done just before Vatican II, we once more briefly summarized the whole question, both by an analysis of the definition itself and by recapitulating the most important statements by the commission on faith. On the occasion of the centenary of Vatican I, Johann Finsterhölzl, in an article promisingly entitled 'Reflections on the Declaration of Papal Infallibility at Vatican I',[20] correctly pointed out that the Council defined less than the supporters of the definition wanted it to define and its opponents feared it would. His observations, based on Bishop Gasser's report, on the scope, the nature and the form of infallibility, and its agents, all point 'to the existence of a trend, more distinct than actually appeared in practice, to regard the Pope as the organ of the Church and his infallibility as the completion of the Church's infallibility'. 'The Council', he wrote, 'all too anxiously neglected to emphasize that the Pope himself is primarily part of the believing Church, which stands over against the demands of the word of God and its traditional interpretation. "Assent" to a dogmatic definition, so far from being debarred, is actually required.'[21]

2. But the problem of Church infallibility is not resolved by settling the limits of papal infallibility and allotting the Pope his due place in the Church. W. Dirks, for instance, in an article splendidly entitled 'The Dogma of the Fallible Popes', pointed out that the 'new' element in the Vatican definition was 'the restriction, the very exact and precise fixing of the limits and conditions' of papal infallibility. Then, relying on the fact that it was invoked only twice in a century (the proclamation of the doctrine of the Immaculate Conception in 1854 and that of the Assumption in 1950), he concluded 'that in practice the fallibility of the Pope was dogmatized in 1870. All theories of graduated authority do not alter the fact that the many encyclicals, sometimes of very authoritarian popes can be described as fallible. in the strict sense of post-1870 dogma. The Pope of *Humanae Vitae* has made it necessary to say this very forcefully.'[22] It must, however, be pointed out: 1. that in point of fact fallibility, perhaps unfortunately, has not been dogmatized; 2. that the definition of a single infallible dogma, or even the possibility of such infallible definition, is sufficient to raise the

question of infallibility in all its acuteness; and 3. that the encyclical *Humanae Vitae* in particular shows that because of the infallibility of the ordinary teaching office the restriction of papal infallibility does not go as far as some would like to believe.

J. Finsterhölzl is right when he says that 'the truth bestowed on the Church lives essentially on the truth of God, who himself as truth turns to her'.[23] But in deriving from this the 'infallibility of the Church, which the First Vatican Council says is expressed in solemn definitions by the papal teaching office' he short-circuits the vital question whether it is the truth of God that 'pre-eminently attains its historical realization' in such definitions and how this can be shown. When he says that in the Constitution on the Church, Article XXV, Vatican II provided 'a precise interpretation' of the nature and scope of infallibility, he overlooks the fact that, as we have shown, it said no more and no less than Vatican I said about its nature and scope, though it formally extended infallibility to the episcopate. He relies on the statement by Bishop Gasser that we quoted ourselves for the assertion that 'any attempt based on the doctrine of infallibility to ascribe divine attributes to a human being, that is, the Pope, is thus excluded',[24] though in a 'pre-conciliar' book he could have read the following: 'These intra-Catholic debates are often a diversion from the real difficulty of the question of freedom from error, and lead to a great over-estimation of the significance for ecumenical discussion of the theological points of which we have been speaking. Let us have no illusions on the matter. Whether the Pope alone is free of error or is so only in conjunction with the episcopate, whether or not he needs the aid of others before he can act infallibly, whether infallibility extends only to matters of faith and morals or to a wider field, whether or not the Pope needs the assent of the Church in order to define infallibly, and so on, all these are very secondary questions to an Evangelical Christian. To state it more specifically, it is sufficient if at any moment in the millennial history of the Church a single pope, speaking as *a priori* infallible, was able to proclaim a single doctrine with absolute certainty as binding on the Church. Can any human being who is not God be free from falling into error? What holds good for a single man holds good for a number, and also for an ecumenical council. In this respect the freedom from error of a council raises exactly the same problem as the infallibility of a pope.'[25]

We may conclude from these considerations that if, even with the aid of higher post-conciliar apologetics and dialectics, we concentrate only on the interpretation of Vatican definitions, we shall get no further in the discussion. Also it would become tedious and boring. Instead, the background of the definitions themselves must be subjected to critical examination. On the one hand the validity of the case made for them must be looked at, as was done in the previous chapter; and on the other hand we must look at the validity of their basic assumptions, as we shall do in the present chapter. Vatican I, together with Vatican II, imposes this course on us.

e. *The Term 'Infallibility'?*

1. The susceptibility to misconstruction of the term 'infallibility' is today widely admitted. Bishop Gasser, the spokesman for the Vatican I commission, himself remarked that the word *infallibilitas* was liable to be misunderstood, 'because, for instance, in German it could easily be confused with faultlessness, sinlessness, stainlessness'.[26] The finer points of Vatican theology have in fact never been clearly appreciated either by the non-Catholic or the Catholic public.

In regard to the two terms 'infallibility' and 'irreformability' Heinrich Fries recently wrote: 'Both words are not immune to misunderstanding, and one wonders why they continue to be used, although associations are connected with them that are not meant. "Infallibility" is connected with the idea of an absolute *non plus ultra*: in fact, it means that in a decision of faith in which the truth of Jesus Christ is involved the Church does not fall into error. *Irreformabilis* is connected with the idea of absolute fixity of a proposition, both its substance and its form of expression, but that again is not meant. *Irreformabilis* indeed means that the possibility of an error of faith is excluded from the definition, but leaves open the possibility of another, more complete version, which would not of course mean that it ceased to be binding, but opened the way to a deeper understanding of the content of a dogma and subordinated it to the word of God. But who can see all this in the word *irreformabilis?*'[27]

2. But the problem is not solved by a better translation of *infallibilitas*. As Vatican I interpreted *infallibilitas* in general as *immunitas ab errore*,[28] I previously suggested replacing 'infallibility' by 'freedom from error', which does not have the slight moral flavour of 'faultlessness' – though frankly admitting that 'theologically not much is clarified thereby'.[29]

Later, making a more accurate and perhaps more felicitous use of the root of the word *infallibilitas* (*fallere* means to let slip, take a false step, to lead astray, to delude, to deceive), I translated it by 'undeceivingness' (*Untrüglichkeit*), which certainly has a more general meaning. *Infallibilitas* can then be understood as sharing in the truth of God who, according to Vatican I, 'can neither deceive nor be deceived' (*'Deus revelans, qui nec falli nec fallere potest'*, D 1789). *Infallibilitas* would then mean freedom from deception and error.[30]

But that does not solve the problem either. For Vatican I did not just attribute inerrancy to the Church in general; *immunitas ab errore* was attributed also to the Pope, not only *de facto* but *de jure*. Not only does the Pope not err in practice when speaking *ex cathedra*, but *a priori* he cannot do so. That is a crux that cannot be overlooked or ignored. On the contrary, it is a challenge to reflection.

f. *The Truth, Mandate and Authority of the Church*

1. The truth of the Church cannot be equated with the truth of God. At this point we are faced with the ecumenical implications of our question, which are of course always present, and we shall examine them from both points of view.

In the view of the Evangelical systematic theologian Karl Gerhard Steck, it is clear after a hundred years 'that the two confessions were never so estranged from each other as they were at the time of Vatican I',[31] at which he sees the conflict of Church and doctrine begun by Luther still at work. 'Each confession emphasized one authority at the expense of the other. To put it in a nutshell, on the Reformation and Protestant side it was doctrine – in other words, Holy Scripture – that was the overriding principle, while on the Roman Catholic side it was the Church. This was very emphatically reiterated in the pronouncements of 1870 and the consolidation of papal authority.'[32] Nor was the conflict 'in any way modified or eliminated by the doctrinal pronouncements of Vatican II'.[33]

The Protestant applauds the fact that Vatican I, like Luther, 'in the last resort based the assent of Christian faith on acknowledgment of the truth of God', but deplores that this was supplemented by 'other reasons, obligations or pronouncements' – namely, those of the Church.[34] The Catholic theologian must agree with his Evangelical colleague's protest against the equation of the truth of the Church with that of God, with the result that the ambiguous historical reality of the Church is set up as a manifest sign of the credibility of the Christian truth, that faith is linked with the self-confident judgment of the Church even in regard to disciplinary matters governing entering or leaving the Church, and that souls and interpretation of the Bible are subjected to ecclesiastical control.

2. The Church, however, has full power authoritatively to attest the truth of God. It is certainly a large undertaking 'to base the certainty and binding character of faith solely on the authority of God's revelation'.[35] But is God's revelation and the word of revelation to be found in Scripture in a form that differs from that of the human word of believing witnesses and congregations? Thus it seems that the truth of God, which 'will be attested and prevail at all times', needs the testimony of the Church as the community of the faithful, and that there can be no objection to 'the authority of the Church' in the true sense of the term, for it is primarily attested by Scripture itself.

In spite of his attack on the authority in the Church, Steck finds himself forced to admit that 'the word of God is not as clear as Luther and his followers believed; Protestantism lacks the unity that would be desirable; without doctrinal authority the community neither of the New Testament nor of later Christendom is conceivable or real. The Reformers themselves certainly did not want the Church to become a debating hall for all possible types of belief'.[36] To the Catholic theologian all this, seen in its unpleasing reality, provides historical evidence for believing that the alternative to the Roman authoritarian, doctrinal system certainly cannot be a Protestantism that protests against all authority in the Church (in Protestantism it is to a large extent non-existent in any case). At the end of his paper the Evangelical theologian indirectly admits that 'reliance on the authority of the gospel' does not exclude 'possession of authority by the Church' but may actually justify it. This again means that exclusive reliance on the former will not do, but that we must acknowledge the corollary – the obviously subordinate corollary – implicit in that reliance.

It follows from all this that it is not the authority of the Church (understood in its proper sense) and its truth that constitute the problem. That is a Protestant fallacy. The real problem is that presented by an authoritarian Church authority, an autonomously wielded ecclesiastical supreme power, revealed truth of which the Church has taken possession, all concentrated in Luther's mind in the claim to infallibility in doctrinal pronouncements. In this respect one might have expected more searching questions from an Evangelical theologian, for example, about the 'charism of truth and never failing faith' postulated for Peter and his successors (D 1837) that is scarcely intelligible in the light of the Pauline doctrine of charisms and in relation to which we can only express surprise that it has worked only twice in a century; or about the eschatological finality and victoriousness of the truth of God, which is all too hastily claimed by modern Catholic theology for the infallibility of certain teachings of the Church, without the eschatologically provisional and fragmentary nature of the truth of the Church, even to the point of error and sin, being taken seriously.

We can now conclude this section. It has certainly become clear that the more closely we come to grips with the problem, the less we linger over secondary matters, and the more we renounce easy ways out and hasty solutions, the more hope there is of getting to its heart and arriving at a well-based answer. As we wish no longer to postpone our attempt at an answer, where does the central problem lie?

2. SHARED ASSUMPTIONS

It can be stated in this way. Is the *infallibilitas* of the Church based on infallible propositions? We deliberately use the Latin *infallibilitas* because of the indefiniteness of its meaning. It should not be assumed that the concept has been clarified or that that statement of the problem is meaningful. We shall show this in the further course of our discussion.

a. *The Faith of the Church is Dependent on Propositions of Faith*

It can be assumed here without much beating about the bush
that Christian faith is not dumb faith. The Christian knows what
he believes and professes what he knows. There is no faith
without content, whatever this may be, and no Christian *fides
qua creditur* that is not in some way also *fides quae creditur*. This
knowing and professing faith is dependent for expression on
words and propositions of faith. And in so far as the Christian
faith is in fact never merely the faith of abstract individuals, but
is faith within or in relation to a community of the faithful, inter-
communication within that community depends on language,
which is made up of words and sentences. Thus it depends on
sentences expressing faith.

But there is more to the statement than this generalization. It
means that a community of believers is based on, or to put it
more pragmatically, has shown that it is based on such common
propositions of faith. Thus we speak of the beliefs of the Church
(as a community of believers) based on propositions of faith
(common articles or formulations of faith). This can be explained in three ways, the first two of which should be recognized as
true, the third as false.

1. The faith of the Church relies on confessions of faith in
Christ in which that faith is comprehensively stated in summary
or recapitulatory or symbolic form. That, at all events, was the
state of affairs at the outset, as is shown by the New Testament.
This is not the place to consider in detail whether particular
statements are instances of the proclamation of the word rather
than of response to it; whether or not they are chiefly rooted in
the act of worship, catechesis or the Church order; whether they
are more liturgical, kerygmatic, catechetical, juridical, or
edifying; whether they should be properly described as acclama-
tory (such as amen, hallelujah, hosanna, maranatha, meaning
'Our Lord is present', or abba, meaning 'Father, Lord Jesus'),
or doxological, expressing praise and gratitude, mentioning God
and later Christ, and subsequently developing into hymnic
form; or are words of blessing, on the pattern of Jewish saluta-
tions and glorifications, or form part of the sacramental heritage
(fixed liturgical formulae for baptism or Holy Communion), or
are confessions of faith in the strict sense. The transitions are

essentially fluid, particularly those from acclamation to doxology and confessions of faith properly so called, and again, there may be a special connection between these last and baptismal instruction and baptismal liturgy.[37] At all events, it cannot be disputed that such brief formulas of faith, centring on the Christ event, were current in the New Testament communities. The shortest of these are the numerous monomial expressions that link the name of Jesus with a definite honorific title drawn from the Jewish or Hellenist world, such as 'Jesus is the Messiah', 'Jesus is the Lord', 'Jesus is the Son of God' (among the earliest and most familiar is 1 Corinthians 12:3). At the same time we also find in the New Testament binomial credal forms relating to God and Christ (e.g., 1 Corinthians 8:6), and more extensive short professions of faith in general, particularly in regard to the death and resurrection of Christ (e.g., 1 Corinthians 15:3-5; Romans 1:3 f.), and finally, confessions of faith in triadic form isolated in liturgical fragments (Matthew 28:19; 2 Corinthians 13:13).

It is not to be overlooked that such early (New Testament and post-New Testament) brief formulas of faith have survived in the Churches until the present day. Nor can it be denied that such brief formulas, old or new, can have a meaning at the present day, perhaps that which they had originally in connection with baptism, catechesis, or other events in the life of the ecclesial community. The original formulas of faith and the profession of faith were certainly not just fragments of a single creed. For all their concentration on the Christ event, on the significance of Jesus for the community of believers, they are too diverse for that in content and form, varying with this or that honorific title and in accordance with the subject-matter. Also, to make possible new professions of faith that will be perhaps more intelligible to a new age – which does not necessarily mean doing away with the old – for the 'edification' of the community and perhaps also for the sake of ecumenical understanding between the separated Churches, it must not be forgotten that these original professions of faith were not statements of dogma in the modern sense. They were not statements of doctrinal law, but spontaneous, diverse, utterances that were not intended to be fixed, unquestionable and unalterable definitive and obligatory propositions that excluded new or different formulations. Faith was not based on such forms of words, but expressed itself by means of them. They were not the statutory basis of the Christian community, but the free expression of its faith.

2. The faith of the Church is marked by polemical demarcations from the unchristian, that is, by self-defensive, defining statements (definitions of faith or dogmas of faith). There have always been such statements, in so far as the positive profession of faith was immediately given a defensive or polemical note by confrontation with disbelief or superstition – statements such as Jesus is the Messiah, the Lord, the Son of God. When Paul, for instance, says: 'No one can say Jesus is Lord unless he is under the influence of the Holy Spirit', he goes on in the same breath to make a negative demarcation. 'For that reason I want you to understand that no one can be speaking under the influence of the Holy Spirit and say, Curse Jesus' (1 Corinthians 12:3). No doubt negative exclamations such as 'anathema' went hand in hand with positive ones, just as curses went with blessings in the Old Testament (cf. 1 Corinthians 16:22; 5:4–5). As in the course of time it became more necessary to mark off the gospel from false doctrine, this became the occasion for statements of doctrine in negative form (as is especially plain in 1 John 2:22; 4:2–3). Persecution very often provided the challenge from which the profession of faith resulted. It is important to note that Paul in particular was obviously not primarily concerned with dogmas, positive or negative, but with the acceptance or denial of Jesus, with statements of belief, not belief in statements. To this extent we must be on our guard against trying to find 'dogmas', a 'dogmatic heritage', 'statements of dogma' ,everywhere in the New Testament.

Nevertheless it is intelligible that in the period that immediately followed the apostolic period, when the Christian communities could no longer appeal to the original witnesses, tradition acquired much greater importance. This applied both to the apostolic writings (or those believed to be apostolic) and the Church's ministry, and naturally also to the original professions of faith. This helped to prevent the youthful Church from losing contact with its origins and dissolving into the all-absorbing world of syncretic Hellenism. Statements of faith, defensively marking off Christians from the non-Christian world, thus became much more binding, and in cases of conflict assumed the nature of a definitive and obligatory formula for the believing community, that is, a dogma, which did not, however, necessarily mean that it was *a priori* free from error, not open to amendment, infallible and unchangeable.

It cannot be assumed that the Church at the present day has no need of such defensive formulas to mark itself off from non-Christian belief, disbelief or superstition. Under a totalitarian régime such as that of the Nazis, when a group in the Church may identify itself with the political authorities, there may be no alternative to such a demarcating profession of faith (such as the Barmen Declaration of 1934). Such a situation constitutes a *status confessionis*, which does not permit endless discussions and hair-splitting, but calls for a positive yes or no (for example, to Christ or to the 'Führer'). But the existence of such a *status confessionis* must not be too readily assumed. Three conditions must be fulfilled:

a. A *causa major* must be at stake in one way or another involving the life or death of the Church (*articulus stantis et cadentis Ecclesiae*).

b. The alternatives (discussion, exhortation, challenge, etc.) must have been exhausted, so that nothing remains *in extremis* but a dissociation in faith.

c. A definition must never be regarded as a final damnation of men – which God alone can pronounce – but as a temporary measure with a view to the restoration of the peace of the Church; a measure that must not automatically be extended to the guiltless dependants of those concerned.[38]

The conclusion from all this is that these defensive-defining propositions, even if they have a definitive and obligatory – and, to that extent, dogmatic – character in a particular situation, do not constitute rulings valid for all eternity, but pragmatic forms of words arising out of specific situations.[39]

3. The Christian religion does not depend on the deliberate development of dogma, the stating of interpretative propositions. This follows from what we have just said. The Church is continually called on to proclaim the gospel afresh in a continually changing situation; only in exceptional circumstances is it called to make dogmatic definitions. There is no New

Testament justification for the deliberate production of dogmas in other circumstances. The early Church of both East and West, the Orthodox Churches of ancient and modern times, the medieval Western Church, the Reformation Churches and the Counter-Reformation Church alike, did not define what they could have defined, but only what they had to define, 'yielding to necessity, not to their own impulse'. They did not define the maximum possible just for the pleasure of defining, but the necessaiy minimum under external pressure. Seen in the light of this nearly two-thousand-year-old common Christian tradition, which is supported by the New Testament itself, quite apart from the question of their truth, it must be regarded as an aberration when a Church, without being compelled to do so, produces dogmas, whether for reasons of Church or theological policy (the two Vatican dogmas about the Pope) or for reasons of piety and propaganda (the two Vatican dogmas about Mary). The aberration is the greater when it deepens the division of Christendom.

It is maintained that the deliberate development of dogma results in the growth and development of faith, that it is a 'living tradition'. The reply to such arguments is:

a. Definition does not result in the growth and development of faith. Many will doubt whether the ultimate effect of the four exceptional dogmas has been an increase in faith, especially since the waning of extreme Marian and papal piety and concentration on the 'hierarchy of truths'. It is as true as it has always been that even justified definitions can have negative as well as positive consequences for the faith, such as doctrinaire rigidity, new and graver misunderstandings, orthodox arrogance, theological unteachability and increasing ignorance on the part of the *beati possidentes*.

b. It has been the common view of all the Christian Churches at all times that faith grows and develops by the sound proclamation of the gospel, the correct administration of the sacraments, prayer, love, suffering, the individual's acquisition of knowledge. It is only since the nineteenth century that Roman theologians, misunderstanding the idea of development introduced into Catholic theology by the great Tübingen theologians (especially Johann Adam Möhler) on the one hand and by Cardinal Newman on the other, interpreted it intellectually and legalistically and, instead of the tried and tested methods of interpreting the faith, encouraged dogmatic interpretation and binding definitions. This though they could have read St Thomas Aquinas and noted that the truth of faith is sufficiently interpreted (*sufficienter explicata*) by the proclamation of Christ and the apostles, so that there is no need of any *explicatio*, interpretation, 'though *explanatio*, explanation, may be necessary because of errors that arise'.[40] Fortunately the Roman addiction to dogmatic definitions that continued to manifest itself in the preparatory work for Vatican II was checked by John XXIII and the Council itself.

b. *That Faith is Dependent on Infallible Propositions is Unproven*

By infallible statements we mean, as Vatican I did, those that on the basis of a divine promise must be regarded as carrying an assurance of inherent freedom from error: statements, propositions, definitions, formulations and forms of words that are not only *de facto* not erroneous, but in principle cannot be erroneous.

It is clear from what we said above that is is possible to accept the meaningfulness, utility and in certain circumstances the necessity of summary statements of faith (professions of faith or symbols), or of delimiting statements of faith (definitions or dogmas), without necessarily accepting infallible and immutable propositions of faith. In other words, the binding nature of statements of faith does not mean necessarily accepting their infallibility.

The question of course arises whether the Christian message itself does not require at any rate some doctrines to be regarded as not only binding but also infallible. This cannot be simply assumed, however, but has to be demonstrated. Even a Council, when it wishes to assert the infallibility of a doctrine, has to state the reasons for it, both for itself and for others. Our examination of Vatican I and II showed that:

1. The existence of propositions that are infallible in principle was not convincingly demonstrated either by Vatican I or by Vatican II. In its statements on infallibility Vatican II obviously relied completely on Vatican I, and when with the aid of an unhistorical conception of an exclusive apostolic episcopal succession it sought to broaden the approach of Vatican I it was

on very shaky ground.[41] Vatican I cited no scriptural testimony showing the necessity for infallible propositions and no
evidence of a universal ecumenical tradition that would justify
them.[42]

2. Neo-scholastic textbook theology is also unable to demonstrate from Scripture or the oldest ecumenical tradition either
the necessity or the reality or even merely the possibility of
propositions that are *a priori* infallible. It merely asserts that the
promises that according to Scripture were given to the Church
necessarily assume the existence of infallible propositions, but
fails to exclude the alternative possibility, namely that the
promises given to the Church hold good in the absence of such
infallible propositions.[43]

3. This possiblity, that the promises given to the Church (and
to Peter) might hold without the assumption of *a priori* infallible
propositions, was not discussed at Vatican I or at Vatican II,
as is evident from the silence on the matter both of the Constitution *Pastor Aeternus* and the proceedings of the Council (particularly the Gasser report). Just as the Council of Trent assumed
the validity of the Ptolemaic universe, so did Vatican I assume
a particular conception of truth, taking for granted the by no
means so self-evident proposition that the promises given to the
Church or the Church's 'infallibility' were inconceivable in the
absence of infallible propositions. Did the Council err? It
would be better to say that it was blind to the basic problem.
Instead of coming to grips with it, it passed it by. Why?

a. Instead of considering the question of the infallibility of
the Church (which it assumed), it dealt with the infallibility of
the Pope.

b. In dealing with the latter it concentrated attention first on
the pastoral, ecumenical and political opportuneness of a
definition, then on the conditions and limitations of papal
infallibility, and finally on the question of papal infallibility
with or without the assent of the Church.

c. Both supporters and opponents, the majority and the
minority, assumed that the promises given to the Church were
related to infallible propositions. Not all the opponents of the
definition were 'inopportunists', as earlier Catholic historiogra-
phers suggested in order to play down the controversy, who
regarded the definition as a statement of the truth but con-

sidered it merely to be 'inappropriate'. In fact there was a clash of different ecclesiological conceptions in regard to the relationship between Pope and Church (the episcopate). But whether they regarded the definition of papal infallibility as inopportune (as all its opponents did), or as opportune (as the majority did); whether they required the Church's assent for an utterance by the Pope to be infallible, or the assent of the episcopate (which was the position of the moderate 'Gallican' opposition), or regarded such assent as unnecessary (as the majority did); whether they accepted the infallibility of ecumenical councils but not that of the Roman Pontiff (as did the radical opponents of the definition, such as Döllinger and a number of minority bishops), or accepted the infallibility of ecumenical councils and that of the Roman Pontiff (as did the majority); they all, without exception, assumed that the promises given to the Church or the 'infallibility' of the Church depended on infallible propositions (whether of the ecumenical council or of the Pope, with or without the assent of the Church).

Looked at from this point of view, the majority and the minority were closer to each other than they might seem. 'A cross-section through the discussion shows that opponents and supporters often used the same arguments. On the one side they declared that something must be done to reinforce the Pope's authority and make the papacy a lighthouse for the rescue of shipwrecked human society. No, the opposition replied, a rigid papacy on the lines of an absolute monarchy would repel both separated Christians and unbelievers. Thus behind these arguments were preconceived ideas that bore the strong imprint of divergent views of Church and society; by comparison, the really theological objections to the doctrine receded into the background. Everything suggests that an accommodation between the two parties would have been possible if the text of the infallibility decree had laid greater emphasis on the link between the Pope and the universal Church.'[44]

The universal Church. To reach real clarification and agreement, both sides would have had to tackle the question of the infallibility of the universal Church, and thus that of infallibility in the Church in general, which both wrongly, or rather naïvely, assumed to have been cleared up. Because the way to it was blocked by secondary theological questions and questions of

Church policy by which they were fascinated, the Council fathers did not discuss this fundamental question. Was that too much to expect? Is this an anachronistic criticism? Not at all. Certainly it would have meant the taking up by Vatican I of questions raised by the sixteenth-century Reformers that the Council of Trent did not solve or even discuss. That at any rate was inconceivable at Vatican I.

To the majority of the Council anything that smacked of Protestantism was inherently undiscussable. The proem to the revised schema 'On the Catholic Faith' laid before the Council by the deputation on faith ascribed to Protestantism all the errors of the day: rationalism, pantheism, materialism and atheism. When Bishop Strossmayer, in a speech that became famous,[45] pointed out that these errors had existed long before Protestantism, that many distinguished Protestants fought against them, and that in the Protestant world, in Germany, Britain and America, there were many who loved the Lord Jesus Christ and deserved to have applied to them the words of St Augustine, 'they err indeed, but they err in good faith', there was increased murmuring in the assembly in St Peter's. When Bishop Strossmayer nevertheless continued with a quotation from St Augustine: 'They are heretics, but no one takes them for heretics', he was interrupted by Cardinal De Angelis, one of the presidents of the Council, and asked to refrain from words that caused scandal. When the bishop again continued, Cardinal Capalti, the other president of the Council, intervened to say that, as they were not talking about Protestants as individuals, it was not an offence against charity to say that the monstrosities of modern error derived from Protestantism. A heated exchange followed between Capalti and Strossmayer, leading to a veritable storm of indignation when Strossmayer, in the face of the rising murmur from all sides, said: 'I ascribe this to the lamentable circumstances of this Council'. When he raised the issue of 'moral unanimity', which he regarded as essential for Council decisions (a question by the minority bishops on this subject had been left unanswered for a month), he was positively shouted down. Many of the Council fathers were almost beside themselves with indignation (*obstrepunt, vix non fremunt*) and called on him to step down. There were more confused exchanges and mutual protests, and when Strossmayer eventually protestingly set about stepping down, the infuriated Fathers left their seats, muttering all sorts of things, such as: 'These people won't have the Pope's infallibility; this man is infallible himself.' Some said: 'He is Lucifer, anathema, anathema.' And others: 'He is another Luther, let him be cast out.' All called on him to step down. He repeated: 'I protest, I protest', and stepped down.

Commentators like to point out that this was the only real 'scene' at the Council. Nevertheless, it is very revealing, both of the Council's mood and of the attitude of the majority towards Protestantism (and infallibility). In the definitive draft of the proem the assertion of a direct link between Protestantism and the errors of modern times was modified and some insulting expressions (such as *impio ausu, opinionum monstra, impiissima doctrina, mysterium iniquitatis, impia pestis*) were omitted. But nothing good was said of Protestants (even as individuals), and the Counter-Reformation version of history was substantially maintained: 'For everyone knows that the heresies rejected by the Tridentine Fathers gradually broke up into many sects, because the rejection of the Church's divine teaching office meant handing over matters concerning religion to the judgment of each and every individual, and, while in their disunity they were disputing among themselves, for many all faith in Christ was finally shattered.' And so on and so forth, culminating in a reference to 'the abyss of pantheism, materialism and atheism . . .'[46] As if naked, systematic materialism and atheism had not made it first breakthrough in Catholic France.

There is no need to say more about the ecumenical aspect of Vatican I. There was even less inclination than there was at the Council of Trent to go seriously into the serious questions in regard to the claims of the teaching office raised by the Reformation. At Vatican II this readiness was present, at any rate in principle, and in some matters it made itself felt; in the proclamation of the importance of the Bible in the worship, theology and whole life of the Church, for instance; in the introduction of a simplified and more compact popular Mass in the vernacular; the upward revaluation, both in theory and in practice, of the laity as the people of God and the universal priesthood; a certain decentralization and adaptation of the Church to the various nationalities; the acknowledgment of a

Catholic share in the responsibility for schisms; the recognition of other Christian communities as ecclesial communities or Churches; the encouragement of an ecumenical attitude and practical co-operation with other Christians; and a readiness to make concessions, to the Orthodox Churches in particular, in regard to mixed marriages and intercommunion. But, together with many other questions raised by the Reformation, the question of infallibility that was raised in radical form by the Reformers was not tackled. Needless to say, what neither Vatican I nor Vatican II saw as a problem was not resolved by either. That is no reason why theology should wait for Vatican III. For Vatican II made it plain to see that the Holy Spirit does not function as a *deux ex machina* at councils. Problems for which there has been no theological preparation are generally not settled at councils.

Chapter Four

ATTEMPT AT AN ANSWER

I. THE PROBLEM OF PROPOSITIONS IN GENERAL

We are not so bold as to claim to give *the* answer. The question is too complex and the implications too many. But, in the present situation of the Church, it is essential to make a sober and resolute attempt to find *an* answer, concentrating not so much on drawing all the consequences as on establishing the right approach. So there will be no *ex cathedra* pronouncements about infallibility – a single infallible pope is preferable to many infallible theologian popes – but there will be discussion in a spirit of theological and pastoral responsibility.

Articles of faith are propositions. The formulas in which faith is expressed, whether professions of faith or definitions of faith, are propositions, simple or complex, and are subject to the laws that govern the making of propositions. Nor are articles of faith ever the word of God direct; at best they are the word of God attested and transmitted by human words; God's word is apprehended and transmitted in the form of human propositions. As such, statements of belief and doctrine are subject to the problems presented by human propositions in general. It would certainly be most interesting to deal with our special question in the light of modern linguistic philosophy (as represented by M. Heidegger, H. G. Gadamar, H. Lipps, B. Liebrucks, K. Jaspers, M. Merleau-Ponty, L. Wittgenstein, G. Frege, C. W. Morris. H. Lefèbvre and N. Chomsky). But any development of the subject on those lines would not only upset the relatively rapid pace and changes of tempo of this necessarily concise work, but would also give undue weight to what is only a subsidiary argument. Our main theme is infallibility, which is normally not a problem for philosophers, though in practice – dare we say so? – philosophers sometimes like making pronouncements *ex cathedra*.

Our aim in this part of the book is a very modest one. With the aid of some brief, but basic and hardly disputable observations, it will be made clear that propositions – of which the faith of the Church has to make use – constitute a difficult problem. From this it will be seen that a Church that summarizes or defines its faith in propositions, and perhaps has to do so, cannot evade the problems inherent in propositions.[1]

1. Propositions always fall short of reality; that is fundamental. Neither by a word nor a sentence nor combination of sentences can I ever capture reality complete. There is always a difference between what I want to say and what I say, between my intention and my spoken words. Language is both rich and poor. Its fundamental inadequacy has continually exercised the great tradition of linguistic philosophy, from Heraclitus, Plato and Aristotle by way of St Augustine and St Thomas Aquinas down to the modern age.

To take an example from theology. What would be said if the Church defined the certainly fundamental proposition that God exists? Everything – and yet so little as to amount to practically nothing at all by comparison with what there is to be said about it.

2. Propositions are susceptible to misunderstanding. Whatever I say is susceptible to misunderstanding, and not only due to ill will. Words have different, often iridescent and fluid meanings. And if I define their meaning, my definitions too have again different meanings and the variable factor in these meanings is often impossible to pin down. Even if I express myself completely unequivocally and try to make myself so intelligible to the other party that he is bound to understand me, what is unthought and unsaid but is perhaps thought or not thought by him still leaves plenty of room for all sorts of misunderstandings and non-understandings, perhaps the worst of which is when one does not understand or no longer understands oneself. Linguistic analysis and linguistic criticism continually try to show what language in practice can and cannot do.

To revert to our theological example, 'God exists'. 'God' is perhaps the noblest, the most ambitious word in human language, and what word has been more understood *and* misunderstood? 'Exists', 'is', is perhaps the most universal, comprehensive word in human language – and how its meaning varies. Philosophers dispute the meaning of 'being' just about as much as theologians dispute the meaning of the word 'God'.

3. Sentences, propositions, are translatable only up to a point.

The high C can be played on any musical instrument, but sounds differently on the violin and on the cello; the sounding board is different. In language it is more than merely *le ton qui fait la musique*. For some words there seems to be no translation; they are taken over into other languages untranslated. A play on words can rarely be preserved in translation, and many words can be translated only non-literally, and paraphrase has to take the place of translation. This is where the difficulties lie in the path of the ever-recurrent idea of a universal language (from R. Lull and Leibnitz up to modern theoretical and practical attempts on the lines of Esperanto). Here too lie the limitations of a dead language for which a universality is claimed that is bought largely at the price of intelligibility (the translation into the vernacular of the Latin liturgy shows up the inadequacies of translation).

And even our simple example of a theological proposition, 'God exists', which is translatable without difficulty into the languages familiar to us, continually presents completely unexpected difficulties when it comes to translating it into Asian or African languages that lie outside the Euro-American cultural area, where the corresponding words are differently cathected and defy the demands of translation.

4. Sentences are in a state of perpetual motion. My language is not mine alone. Language exists in dialogue, communication. Words are not handed on like bricks, for the simple reason that they are not matter, but mind. Language is not a static structure, but a dynamic event, embedded in the flux of the whole history of man and the world. A language that does not change turns into a dead language. In a living language words and sentences continually get and give new impulses. In a new situation words and sentences can completely change their meaning and, vice versa, can themselves completely change a situation, for there are words that make history. Language, then, is always on the way to reality, a basic phenomenon of man's historicity.

The sentence 'God exists' itself has a history. It meant one thing to a Greek of the age of Pericles, another to a Jew of the Maccabean period, and something else again to an early Hellenist Christian, or a Christian Frank, or a medieval scholastic, or a romantic neo-scholastic of the nineteenth century, or

Luther, or a representative of Lutheran orthodoxy, or a twen-
tieth-century Lutheran, etc., etc.

5. Sentences are susceptible to ideology. Words and sentences are at our service. They can be used, abused and
exploited, for advertising and propaganda, and also for pious
purposes. They are then subjected to a yoke that it is almost
impossible for them to shake off, for they are wholly and exclusively taken over by a particular idea, a particular ideology,
a particular system, with the result that they may end up by
saying the opposite of what they originally meant (e.g.,
'democracy', 'freedom', 'order'); they get distorted or become
unusable, turn into empty shells. Language can degenerate and
decay.

The sentence 'God exists' is itself susceptible to ideology.
With its aid, or in the form of *Gott mit uns* ('God with us') wars
have been waged, the poor have been consoled for their poverty,
the innocent have been tricked and slaughtered. It can be
misused both by right and left. Conservative ideologists of the
status quo are just as capable of distorting it as the fanatical
ideologists of revolution. Often it would have been better to
leave God out of it.

These five observations should be sufficient for our purpose,
to demonstrate the problematic nature of sentences and propositions. But, to eliminate misunderstandings as far as possible,
we do not mean that sentences or propositions are incapable of
stating the truth, that all propositions are equally true and
false, that they cannot be measured against the reality to which
they claim to refer, that understanding is impossible. All we
mean is that propositions are not as clear as they seem to be, that
on the contrary, a considerable degree of ambiguity is inherent
in them, that they can consequently be understood differently
by different people, and that with the best will in the world all
misunderstandings and misuse of them cannot be avoided.

In this respect it is plain to see how problematic it is in the
theological field when the Church tries, or in some circumstances is forced, to recapitulate or define its faith in definite
propositions. The frontiers of a binding, abbreviative or
defensive statement or of a dogmatic pronouncement intended
for eternity cannot be foreseen and are not transgressed with
impunity.

Many scholastic theologians of the age of Vatican I or II will object that nevertheless there are propositions, including propositions of faith, inherently clear enough to exclude the possibility of any misunderstandings, nearly as clear, in fact, as the proposition that twice two are four. So far as twice two are four, that is, mathematics, are concerned, this criticism carries some weight. It cannot be denied that mathematical propositions are least exposed to the difficulties we have described, but only so long as one does not pursue one's enquiries into the foundations of mathematics, which are as disputed as some of its applications, for example, in statistics ('with figures you can prove anything'). But it is intelligible that mathematics (and the exact experimental sciences based on it) should have had a special fascination for philosophers and theologians in their striving for clarity; and this phenomenon is in fact connected with our question about the definition of infallibility.

2. RATIONALIST ORIGIN OF THE THEORY OF CLEAR PROPOSITIONS AS THE IDEAL OF KNOWLEDGE

There is no doubt that there was a much stronger tendency at Vatican I than there was at the Council of Trent, for instance, to reply to specific attacks and over and above that – as exemplified by the previous, comprehensive *Syllabus errorum* and the encyclical associated with it – to aim at the most thorough possible clarification of the official teaching of the Church. Vatican I's Constitution on the Catholic Faith shows this trend, though, with the Constitution on the Pope, which was the smallest part of the projected Constitution on the Church, it was the only schema that was adopted. But how many schemata were prepared by the Curial commission and passed by the central commission as ripe for discussion before the Council began? No fewer than forty-six, of which only seven came up for discussion, though, with the two exceptions we mentioned, they were not adopted. In connection with this aim of a comprehensive clarification of the faith a notable feature was the pressure exercised by the Curia for a universal catechism binding on the whole Church, which led to long discussion at the Council. Another feature to be noted in connection with Vatican I is the adoption of Thomism (a system in fact very different

from St Thomas's own) as the standard Catholic theology, a
process that began under Leo XIII and ended with the reign of
Thomism becoming absolute. The Thomist encyclical *Aeterni
Patris* (1879) and the declaration that St Thomas was an
authentic doctor of the Church were followed by the new critical
edition of his works instigated by Leo XIII (published from
1882 onwards) and the promulgation in 1914 of twenty-four
Thomistic (not necessarily Thomasine) basic philosophical (!)
propositions by the Roman Congregation of Studies, which was
fortunately immediately plunged into the maelstrom of rivalries
between the schools of the various orders; and finally, as the
culmination of the process, and as a belated *quid pro quo* from the
Roman canonists to the theologians who were entitled to the
chief credit for the introduction of the new canon law into
Catholic dogmatics, there came the instruction in the 1918
Code of Canon Law that philosophy and theology in Catholic
seminaries must be taught 'according to the method, doctrine
and principles of St Thomas Aquinas' (can. 1366, § 2).

Nor is there any doubt that the Curial preparatory commissions of Vatican II worked largely in the same direction.
What Vatican I had failed to do was now to be made good (let
us recall the 'successful' Roman diocesan synod just before
Vatican II); a far-reaching systematic clarification of dogmatic
and moral theology from the foundations upwards was aimed
at, and schemata were drafted accordingly. Eminent members
of the theological preparatory commission were heard to say
before the Council met that now at last it would be possible to
clarify hitherto unclarified questions, ranging from the doctrine
of creation to eschatology, so that certainty would at last prevail in the Catholic Church about what had to be believed (by
which the clear textbook propositions of neo-scholasticism were
undoubtedly meant).

This enterprise again failed completely, even more completely than it had done before, and neo-scholasticism in general
and neo-Thomism in particular suffered a setback from which
they are not likely to recover quickly. But, for our present purposes, this trend towards clear propositions and systematic
clarification is worthy of brief examination. It would be
interesting also to go into the question of the extent to which
Greek intellectualism was taken over by medieval scholasticism

and superseded by it, at any rate in certain respects, and also the extent to which neo-scholasticism carried on the intellectualism of medieval scholasticism and in certain respects superseded it in turn. But, just as we previously renounced taking a deep plunge into linguistic philosophy, so shall we now refrain from a similar plunge into the history of philosophy. But we shall make a brief excursion into it in order to throw light on a trend of development that shows that the mentality of Vatican I and neo-scholasticism is not completely described by the attribution to it of restorationism, romanticism and traditionalism. It has often been overlooked in studies of the subject that quite a strong dose of rationalism is also present.

Between scholasticism and neo-scholasticism, between St Thomas and neo-Thomism, there stands – Descartes. Descartes marked a break, and not only because after him the philosophical tradition of the Middle Ages was largely forgotten. It was he and not St Thomas Aquinas who established clarity as the ideal of knowledge. Unlike the latter, he ignored the problems of linguistics, and we shall quote here the famous call for clear and distinct knowledge in his *Principia Philosophiae*: 'Many men throughout the whole of their lives apprehend nothing whatever so correctly as to be capable of forming a sure judgment about it. For not just clarity but also distinctness is required for the apprehension (*perceptio*) on which a sure and indubitable judgment can be based. I call clear (*clara*) the apprehension that is present and apparent to the apprehending mind, just as that is called clear which is present to the seeing eye and stimulates the latter strongly and obviously enough. I call distinct (*distincta*) the apprehension that, at the level of clarity that must be posited, is so separated and and different (*seiuncta et praecisa*) from everything else that it contains within itself nothing but clear characteristics.'[2]

To ordinary common sense this seems obvious, just as does the older theory of knowledge taken over by Descartes that naïvely regards knowledge as a reflection or copy of reality. But this is by no means clear and obvious. It has since been pointed out that the clarity of objects posited by Descartes is simply unattainable. The demand for such clarity in fact assumes that objects themselves are adapted to meet it, that they are inherently immobile and static, so that the eye can seize and hold them, as static as only numbers and geometrical diagrams are.

But that is precisely how Descartes regarded the world of the senses and the spatial world, from which he believed the eye should derive certainty and hence the ideal of clarity. To him that world was simply extension (*res extensa*, by contrast with the world of thought), and was thus identical with the subject-matter of geometry; and the clarity of mathematics and geometry was his model in his grand design of a universal method; the ideal of mathematical certainty was to be extended to all branches of knowledge, the criterion of the truth was to be clear and distinct insight, and truth was identified with certitude.

A big price, however, has to be paid for such a process. The required standard of clarity is attainable only if the object of apprehension is forced into shape (objects can, after all, be turned into geometrical figures). Leibnitz and Kant, however, pointed out that knowledge is richer than that, that clarity cannot be so clearly divided from unclarity, and that actually there is a continuous transition from obscurity to clarity, with an infinitude of levels and gradations in between.

Descartes's thought was based on a naïve view of subject and object; he considered the dynamics neither of the object nor of the subject. It was chiefly Hegel who drew attention to the dubiousness of a static approach that separated subject and object in this way, and instead put forward a dialectical approach to the problem of the apprehension of truth that sought to do justice to the dynamism of both object and subject, which could not be separated in apprehension.[3] The object of my apprehension is not something that passes by me as on a vehicle, but is itself inherently mobile and therefore quite unlike the Cartesian geometrized object. Nor am I myself, the subject of the apprehension, immobile, or static like a camera on a tripod; on the contrary, in the act of apprehension I move in harmony with the moving object.

The only kind of apprehension or knowledge adequate to this dynamism of subject and object takes part in the whole movement and does not depend on apparently obvious fixed definitions and clear propositions. That is what rationalism does, and that is why it never comes face to face with living reality in the whole of its mobility, concreteness and abundance. Thus Hegel was not riding a hobby or playing a game with the number three when his circling thought so often proceeded, both in small matters and in great, in steps of three (or triangles growing out of triangles). Underlying this was the since unforgotten basic insight that I cannot really tell the truth with a single sentence, but basically need three, to give definiteness and precision to what I have said, to deny it and to integrate it into a further assertion. Our train of thought could be: 'That's what it's like'; 'No, it's not just like that'; 'Ah, but *this* is what it's like'. And so the process can go on. The truth lies, not in the individual steps, propositions and elements, but in the whole.

But it is time to conclude this brief excursion into the history of philosophy. It was obviously impossible for theology uncritically to accept Descartes's mathematical conception of knowledge. It was subsequently influenced rather by Leibnitz and Christian Wolff, who of course shared Descartes's rationalism. Wolff, who also was both philosopher and mathematician and practised philosophy *more mathematico*, was a friend of Jesuits, and his clear, rich and comprehensive rationalist system on the one hand absorbed many insights of scholasticism and on the other transmitted many rationalist impulses to neo-scholasticism. This holds good even though it is not possible to establish the existence of a direct line leading from eighteenth-century Jesuits to the nineteenth-century Jesuits whose theology dominated Vatican I – the Roman school that included G. Perrone, who played an important part both in the preparation of the definition of the Immaculate Conception and at Vatican I, and his pupils and colleagues J. Kleutgen, C. Schrader and J. B. Franzelin. In this connection it is not unimportant to note that L. Taparelli (died 1862) and M. Liberatore (died 1892), who were the real inspirers of Italian neo-Thomism, which began earlier than its German counterpart, were partly influenced by rationalism.

There is need for further research in this field. In our present context it is sufficient to note that neo-scholasticism (and with it Vatican I) was, in contrast to scholasticism in its prime, marked by the very spirit of rationalism against which it violently protested. That is the only explanation of the great concern for clear and unequivocal propositions, for the maximum possible definition of the official teaching of the Church, and for a system that would be as 'closed' as possible. The leading philosophy of the time, however, had advanced far beyond naïve rationalism of this kind. The period that followed, and Vatican II in particular, showed how clear, unequivocal and unproblematic these clear and distinct definitions were to be. Often, when examining the propositions stated by Vatican I, and in particular those of the Constitution on the Catholic Faith, one has the impression that one is looking at a photograph of a noble animal in motion, but caught by the photographer at an unlucky moment. Is this supposed to be our faith? is the question that then arises. To which the only possible answer, in accordance with Hegel, is presumably yes and no.

Here, too, we must particularize, to avoid unnecessary misunderstandings. Our criticism of clarity as the ideal of knowledge is not directed against the idea of attaining a well-considered, critical clarity without which theology would succumb to confusion and destruction. In theology, as in other fields, Teutonic profundity, for instance, can only gain from Latin clarity and vice versa, particularly as these two characteristics are not distributed in strict accordance with nationality. Theology therefore will aspire to clarity, even though it cannot expect to achieve the kind of clarity that is characteristic of mathematics and the cognate sciences, at any rate so long as the latter restrict themselves to their immediate field of study without asking about what lies behind them.

But there is a difference between theology's striving for clarity in its propositions and claiming to have attained definitive clarity in those propositions. There is a difference between trying to grapple with the heart of one's subject at every point and letting it fossilize in clear propositions. There is a difference between clearly indicating obscurities and difficulties, i.e., clearly stating what is unclear, and refusing to admit the existence of obscurities and difficulties and thus trying unclearly to push the unclear away. There is a difference between a theology that in all its struggle for truth remains always open to greater truth, and a theology that shuts truth and itself in the golden cage of a closed system. There is, in short, a difference between a theology that is committed to the clarity of reason and a theology that is tied to the pseudo-clarity of rationalism. In this sense neo-scholasticism cannot be totally acquitted of rationalism, and the last two councils had to pay for it.

So much for the problem of so-called clear propositions. At this stage the question presents itself to us more urgently than ever: What would be the state of a Church that based its faith entirely on a number of clear propositions? The theologian in particular should remind himself and others that clarity (*doxa*) was originally, not a matter of method or even of consciousness, but an attribute of the Divinity.

3. THE PROBLEM OF CHURCH DEFINITIONS

So far in this chapter nothing has been said about error; not because it was out of place in this context, but because it has been assumed throughout as a self-evident possibility. For it must have been obvious to everyone throughout everything we have said about these human propositions that always fall short of reality, are always liable to be misunderstood, are not always translatable, are constantly on the move, shifting and changing their meaning, are so susceptible to ideology and never absolutely clarifiable – it must have been obvious, in short, that they are subject to ambiguity, distortion, mis-understanding and error. There are so many sources of error that it is hardly worth trying to classify them. Those we are told about include tacit identification and false analogy, incomplete disjunction and the tendency to fabrication, con-fusing the modes of being, and interference with pure appre-hension by emotional factors. It seems to be only too obvious that propositions can be true or false.

Error seems really to become a special problem only in regard to those propositions from which it is sought to exclude it *a priori* and in principle. This seems to be especially the case, not when we are concerned, for instance, with the self-evident first principles of philosophy (those of identity, contradiction, causality – though their self-evidence is now a matter of con-troversy too), but with propositions that are not regarded as self-evident in the philosophical sense, though theologically infallibility is attributed to them. Does not such a claim call for the deepest scepticism? All that we have said in the two previous sections makes it seem unlikely that the doctrines of the Church – which it admits are human propositions – can be inherently free from the human inadequacy and dubiety inherent in them and can thus be free from the capacity to err. Moreover, it can be shown that in propositions of faith in the form of negative definitions the problems inherent in propositions in general are especially evident. A previous study of mine on the problem of Church definitions went beyond the statement made above that propositions can be true or false and concluded that they can be true and false.[4] We must pursue this matter a little way here too.

If every human statement of truth, with its human limitations, borders on and easily turns into error, this holds good for polemical Church definitions in a special way. A definition has a target; it is aimed at a specific error. But since there is no error without a kernel of truth, there is always a danger that a polemically aligned proposition will strike, not only the error, but also the truth contained in it. If a Protestant, for instance, states quite unpolemically that the just man lives by faith, the shadow of error that accompanies the proposition does not appear. But if he polemically makes the same statement in reply to the error of a legalistic Catholic who exaggerates the importance of good works, there is a danger that the shadow of error may obscure the truth of his statement by the un-expressed implication that the just man lives by faith (without doing good works). The converse also holds good. If a Catholic states unpolemically that the just man does works of charity, the shadow of error accompanying the proposition does not appear. But if he states polemically, in reply to the error of a quietist Protestant who attaches too much importance to faith, that the just man does works of charity, there is a danger that the shadow of error will obscure the truth of his statement by the unexpressed implication that the just man does works of charity (and does not live by faith).

This classic example of Catholic-Protestant argument shows that a polemical statement of truth, never mind from which side it comes, runs the risk of being understood merely as a denial of an error. It thus necessarily ignores the kernel of truth contained in the error. This statement of truth thus becomes a half-truth; what it says is correct; but what it does not say is also correct. From the point of view of the person who makes it, it refutes the error at which it is directed; from the point of view of the person to whom it is addressed, it fails to refute the truth. To the former it seems – rightly – to be true; to the latter it seems – not wrongly – to be false. In short, because a half-truth is also a half-error, the two parties fail to understand each other. Each clings to his truth and sees the other's error. Though the truth of each includes the truth of the other, each excludes the other because of its lack of truth.

This sort of thing has constantly recurred throughout Church history. Definitions condemned errors without excluding from the condemnation the truth contained in them. Thus to the other party a true condemnation of error seemed a false condemnation of truth. Thus the Council of Trent condemned the doctrine of justification 'by faith alone' in so far as the latter was empty, presumptuous and dogmatical. It did not define the real meaning that can be given to 'by faith alone' and what the Reformers meant by it, namely faith that put its whole trust in the Lord alone. Thus to the Protestant the true condemnation of the false doctrine of *sola fide* was false condemnation of the true doctrine of *sola fide*.

Thus consideration of Church definitions was bound to lead to the conclusion that every proposition can be both true and false, depending on its aim, circumstances, meaning. It is easier to establish what it says than what it means. In every instance it should be the task of theology to detect the truth in the other party's error and the possible error in one's own truth. Thus the abandoning of unintended error would lead to a meeting of minds in intended truth.

If a theology, a Church, fails to take seriously this dialectic of truth and error, it is inevitably on the way from dogma to dogmatism; the functionalism of a definition, its connection with the circumstances surrounding it, come to be overlooked; the idea of dogma is strained and exaggerated, and dogmas themselves are undialectically and uncritically isolated and absolutized; the outcome is dogmatism, which consists of the exaggeration, isolation and absolutization of dogma. The valuable teaching contained in dogma is transformed into doctrinalism and its binding nature degenerates into juridicism. The partial becomes the particularist, the authoritative the authoritarian, the intellectual the rationalist, and the trend to formulation and objectification finally leads to a formalism, objectivism and positivism that crush the truth with truths. Such is the dogmatism recently subjected to a penetrating study by Josef Nolte. His many-levelled criticism was a bitter necessity, though it may be painful to many. As against dogmatism, he rightly pleads that theology and the Church should adopt a 'metadogmatic' approach that would deal seriously with the problem of 'dogma in history'.[5]

If a theology, a Church, takes the dialectic of truth and error seriously, it is protected from dogmatism in its handling of dogmas. It conducts itself with modesty and therein with wisdom. It allows itself to be sustained by a faith that regards every definition as a hazardous undertaking, a necessary one in extreme emergencies, but one never embarked on without risk, the delimitation of a frontier that can only too easily bring one close to that frontier oneself – not a bad thing so long as one does not stop still in the process. That is the faith of *Homo viator*, who knows that he has no permanent lien on knowledge and understanding, but must constantly wrestle afresh and pray for them, and knows too that he will not be spared the darkness either of sin or of error on his way; the faith of the *Ecclesia peregrinans*, which knows that in all its wanderings error is not the most shameful but only the most human of its human weaknesses.

The question nevertheless arises whether this argument has not rendered meaningless the promises given to the Church.

4. THE DILEMMA AND THE WAY OUT

Where do we stand now? Having got so far, a brief glance is sufficient to show that we have landed ourselves in a situation from which it is difficult to see a way out.

a. *The Dilemma*

On the one hand, it is clear that the promises given to the Church must be acknowledged. No believing Christian who bases himself on the New Testament can dispute this. We need only recall the scriptural texts constantly quoted in this connection: Matthew 16:18, 'The gates of the underworld can never hold out against it'; Matthew 28:20, 'And know that I am with you always; yes, to the end of time'; John 14:16, 'And he [the Father] will give you another Advocate to be with you for ever, the Spirit of truth'; John 16:13, 'The Spirit . . . will lead you to the complete truth'; 1 Timothy 3:15, 'The Church of the living God, which upholds the truth and keeps it safe'.

On the other hand, the Church's errors must be acknowledged. No thinking person can fail to recognize this. There is no need to expatiate on the matter; it will be sufficient briefly to make the following points:

1. The possibility of error must be taken into account in the Church's doctrines (in the broadest sense of the word, in so far as these are human propositions); Catholic theology admits, at any rate in regard to certain office-holders and communities, certain propositions and formulas of faith, that errors (fallible teaching) cannot be excluded.

2. In particular, we must take into account the possibility of error in negative definitions (in the broadest sense of the word), in so far as these are polemical propositions aimed at the condemnation of error that can easily condemn the truth also; Catholic theology does not deny the possibility of error in negative definitions, which can be pronounced by very diverse office-holders and organs in the Church.

3. The only question at issue is whether there are not exceptional propositions of the Church that are inherently free from error and cannot be erroneous. We can summarize our reply as follows:

(1) As we saw at the outset of our discussion, at least one doctrine that, according to the ordinary teaching office, counts as an infallible doctrine of the Church (the immorality of 'artificial' methods of birth control) is regarded by a large part of the Church and many theologians as false and erroneous.

(2) The vital point that no one, neither Vatican I nor Vatican II nor the textbook theologians, has shown is that the Church, its leadership or its theology, is able to put forward propositions that inherently cannot be erroneous. The burden of proof lies with the makers of the claim.

(3) It is impossible honestly to deny objective errors committed by the Church's 'teaching office', both ordinary and extraordinary. All apologetics in the matter, as we have seen, lead only to greater difficulties, whether by bending or even denying historical facts, or by being forced back on making anachronistic distinctions (denying the *ex cathedra* character of past statements, etc.).

Is there a way out of this dilemma? With the disappearance of infallible propositions, the promises given to the Church seem to have disappeared too, and the infallibility of the Church itself seems to have gone by the board as well. But does the infallibility of the Church really stand or fall with the existence of infallible propositions? As we saw, Vatican I failed to raise that question. It nevertheless urgently requires an answer.

b. *The Way Out*

1. There is no escaping from the dilemma by coming down, unbelievingly or superstitiously as the case may be, in favour of either of the following alternatives: that the promise has failed, which is the view of an unbelieving world and is unacceptable to the believer; or that there are at any rate some errors that must never be admitted, which is the line taken by a triumphalist Church and is likewise unacceptable to the believer.

2. Nor does blunting and rendering innocuous one of the horns of the dilemma at the expense of the other offer a way of escape. In fact infallibility in principle used to be granted to the teaching office, and errors were regarded as exceptions. In spite of all the efforts of the extreme ultramontanists, that position could not be maintained and came to an end with Vatican II. Later the position was adopted that the teaching office was fallible in principle, except in the case of certain infallible propositions. This position, which was adopted by some long before Vatican I, turned out to be untenable too.

3. The dilemma can be resolved only by raising the alternatives to a higher level and asserting that the Church will remain in truth in spite of all the errors that are always possible.

In regard to this assertion let us begin by briefly stating:

(1) It can be supported from Scripture, which bears witness to the maintenance of the Church in truth, but makes no mention whatever of infallible Church propositions.

(2) It is consistent with the facts of Church history: the many errors of the teaching office on the one hand, and on the other the maintenance and survival of the Church and its proclamation through 2,000 years.

(3) The problem was not stated or tackled either at Vatican I or at Vatican II, nor is it dealt with in neo-scholastic textbook theology.

(4) Finally, such an answer to the difficulties was not considered in all the discussions that preceded the encyclical *Humanae Vitae* which we took as our starting-point.

On this last there is a point that arises immediately. Nowhere has the Achilles' heel of the Roman doctrine of infallibility been more revealed than in connection with this encyclical. In Chapter I we granted much – to many, perhaps unexpectedly much – to the conservative minority on the papal commission on birth control. But on one point we must energetically protest. The minority report on which the Pope based his decision culminates in the following passage: 'What weighs more heavily, however, is that this change [in the Church's teaching on the subject of birth control] would involve a heavy blow to the doctrine of the assistance of the Holy Spirit promised the Church to lead the faithful on the right way toward their salvation . . . For the Church to have erred so gravely in its grave responsibility of leading souls would be tantamount to seriously suggesting that the assistance of the Holy Spirit was lacking to her.'[6]

And here we believe it incumbent upon us to say that – contrary to the intention of its defenders, who talk so much about faith – the Achilles' heel of the Roman theory of infallibility is in the last resort lack of faith. Surely it is clear that just at the point where faith is especially called for, when faced with error, error on the part of the Church, it failed and was dismayed. Identification of the 'Church' (it would be better to say the 'hierarchy') with the Holy Spirit had become so habitual that it was assumed that admitting certain errors, aberrations, deviations and mistakes by the Church would be attributing them to the Holy Spirit. As if the undeniable errors and mistakes of the hierarchy (and of theology) were errors and mistakes of the Holy Spirit, and the errors, deviations and digressions of the Church were those of God. True, God acts on the Church through the Holy Spirit, is testified to by the Church, he founds, maintains and rules it, it is he who is *Deus qui nec fallere nec falli potest*, God who can neither deceive nor be deceived. But the human beings who constitute the Church can err, miscalulate and blunder, mishear, misunderstand and go astray; they are *homines qui fallere et falli possunt*. He who has faith in God will act with sobriety and confidence. He will distinguish between the Spirit of God and the Church, and not identify them. Thus liberated, he will be able to see without illusions that the development of the Church has always included misdevelopment and that her advance has always included retrogression. Faith in God's guidance and providence in the history of man and of the world does not falter in the face of disaster, great or small. It persists in the face of ineptitude and adversity, personal blows and world catastrophes. Faith in the special presence and assistance of the Divine Spirit in the community of the faithful does not fail or lose heart, even though mistakes can be and often are made by everyone in all circumstances in every field. Rather does it prove itself in the face of mistaken conclusions, assessments and attitudes of the Church and false steps by its leaders and teachers.

When the ship of the Church is in rough water there are always nervous and doubting disciples who believe they must awaken the Lord because they are perishing. The answer has already been given: 'Why are you so frightened, you men of little faith?' (Matthew 8:26).

5. THE CHURCH ON THE ROAD TO TRUTH

The Church, consisting as it does of human beings – and that includes the whole body of believers, including its leaders and teachers – would always like to be left in peace, accepted and assimilated by society, satisfied with the conditions prevailing in society and in the Church itself, and also with the truth that it received and 'possesses' as 'the deposit of faith'. As if this truth – like the Spirit which the Church has received – were not merely an 'instalment', the truth of the gospel of Jesus Christ that calls her out on to the road into the future that alone will bring the whole truth, the full revelation, the Kingdom of God.

It is the truth of the promise that summons the Church, which can never be an end or aim in itself, continually to make a fresh start and set out on the march again. In the words of J. Moltmann, the Church is an 'exodus community', whose path leads through the desert with only a few oases, living, indeed, not only under the mysterious sign of the cloud, but also under the cross expressly set up as a sign: 'Let us go to him, then, outside the camp, and share his degradation. For there is no eternal city for us in this life but we look for one in the life to come.' That is the culmination of the Epistle to the Hebrews (13:13–14), which so vividly describes the Church as the wandering people of God.[7]

Possessing the truth of the promises which she herself proclaims and announces, the Church must ever again venture on a new exodus. The people of Israel wandering in the desert is the prototype and counterpart of the people of the new covenant (cf. especially Hebrews 3:3–4:13). The word of revelation went out to the new people of God as it did to the old (4:12–13), not so that it should settle down in peace in 'possession' of the truth, but so that, summoned by the word of truth, it should set out on the road in obedience and faith. The new people of God enjoys no more security than did the old; it must continue on its way through temptation, trial and sin, menaced by weariness, despondency and weakness of faith; and, also like the old, the new people of God has been given a promise that, after the toil and trouble of a long journey, a long probation in faith, endurance and persistence, borne with firm trust and unshakable faith through struggle, suffering and death, it will enter into peace.

There is, however, a vital difference: the 'word' of revelation that has gone out to the new people of God is final and definitive. Danger and threats can therefore never finally overwhelm them; for all their weaknesses, they are assured of salvation. The promise given to the new people of God is the eschatological promise that cannot be annulled, for it is assured by a better covenant of God with his people, and thus gives them ultimate confidence in their wandering. But it remains a wandering, with all the risks and perils – from which Christ alone as the new Moses and leader of God's people is exempted (cf. 3:7–4:11; 4:15) – in which the individual can be isolated, go astray and be left behind in the desert of this world, in which the people of God have no abiding home. Ultimately they are only guests and strangers in the world, a great cloud of believing witnesses, all on the road to the homeland that can never be lost (11). Only there does faith, '[guaranteeing] the blessings that we hope for, [proving] the existence of the realities that at present remain unseen' (11:1), pass over into the vision and the festival of 'the city of the living God' (12:22). Until then all 'created things' remain perishable, fallible, shakable (12:27). Only in the peace of the final consummation will the faithful receive the infallible, 'unshakable kingdom' (12:28).

Thus in the Epistle to the Hebrews the Church is seen as a pilgrim community of the faithful, exposed in all its members to temptation, error and upheaval, its only truth being the great promise revealed in Christ. The lesson is plain, and no one in the Church is exempted, not even the leaders, whose faith is held up as an example (13:7): 'So hold up your limp arms and steady your trembling knees and smooth out the path you tread; then the injured limb will not be wrenched, it will grow strong again. Always be wanting peace with all people, and the holiness without which no one can ever see the Lord. Be careful that no one is deprived of the grace of God and that no root of bitterness should begin to grow and make trouble; this can poison a whole community. And be careful that there is no immorality, or that any of you does not degrade religion like Esau, who sold his birthright for one single meal' (12:12–16).

The magnificent picture of the wandering people of God in the Epistle to the Hebrews is not by the apostle Paul, but in many respects it is in the Pauline tradition. Paul himself stated even more plainly than the author of the Epistle the provisional character of all our knowledge by faith. And what he says holds good for every human word spoken in the Church, including the most solemn: 'Our knowledge is imperfect and our prophesying is imperfect; but once perfection comes, all imperfect things will disappear . . . Now we are seeing a dim reflection in a mirror; but then we shall be seeing face to face. The knowledge that I have now is imperfect; but then I shall know as fully as I am known' (1 Corinthians 13:9–10, 12).

If that is the situation in regard to the imperfection, the incompleteness, the obscurities, the fragmentariness, of all our formulations of faith, and if the completion, the real sight of unsullied truth, is still to come, is it wise to speak of Church 'infallibility'?

6. INFALLIBILITY OR INDEFECTIBILITY?

There is a sense in which one can speak of Church 'infallibility'. We stand completely by the now much more completely assured view of the 'infallibility' or 'inerrancy' of the Church that we put forward on an earlier occasion.[8] To the extent that the Church is humbly obedient to God's word and will, it shares in the truth of God (*Deus revelans*), who can neither deceive (*fallere*) nor be deceived (*falli*), for lying and fraud (*omnis fallacia*) and all deceit (*omne fallax*) are remote from her. Infallibility, undeceivability, in this radical sense, therefore means that basically the Church remains in the truth that is unaffected by errors in detail.

By this is meant that, however dangerously the Church may deviate in detail, though like Israel it may ever again succumb to doubt and hesitation and sometimes err and go astray, he will 'be with you for ever, that Spirit of truth' (John 14: 16–17). The Church will not succumb to the power of lies. Because of God's promise, we know that she is undeceivable: infallibility, undeceivability, is bestowed on her by God's promise. In spite of all errors and misunderstanding, it is kept in the truth by God.

But we cannot evade the question whether it is essential to speak of the 'infallibility' of the Church, whether there may perhaps not be a better word for what is meant here. As we mentioned above, the liability to misunderstanding of the word 'infallibility' is largely admitted today, and was indeed admitted at Vatican I by the spokesman for the deputation on faith. Should we not draw conclusions from that? In view of the possibility of misunderstanding, would it not be better to sacrifice the word to save the thing instead of sacrificing it to the word?

There are two reasons in particular that at any rate at the present day make the term 'infallibility' open to misunderstanding and frequently actually misleading. In the first place, particularly in certain translations, it has moral overtones, suggesting faultlessness, of which it is impossible to rid it; when used of a person today, it generally has a pejorative meaning ('he thinks he's infallible'). Secondly, it has become far too much associated with certain infallible propositions. The object, as we have seen, must be to prevent the naïve misunderstanding that the infallibility of the Church is tied to infallible propositions.

We should therefore like to substitute for 'infallibility' the term 'indefectibility' or 'perpetuity' in truth. The concept of 'indefectibility' (indestructibility, permanence) and the positive concept of 'perpetuity' (imperishability, endurance) are ecclesiological concepts just as traditional as that of infallibility, and in practice it is often hardly possible to distinguish between them. And though in textbook theology perpetuity or indefectibility tend to be more closely linked with the existence than with the truth of the Church, it should be borne in mind that the Church's being and the Church's truth are inseparable. If the Church ceases to be in the truth, it ceases to be the Church. But the truth of the Church is not dependent on any fixed, infallible propositions, but on her remaining in the truth throughout all propositions, including erroneous ones. Meanwhile, to emphasize the truth of the Church in relation to the being of the Church, let us for the sake of clarity talk, not of the indefectibility or perpetuity of the Church, but of its indefectibility or perpetuity in the truth. What is meant by this is that the Church remains in the truth, and that it is not affected by any errors in detail. This makes it plain that we hold fast to the fact of infallibility, though for the reasons given we prefer the terms 'indefectibility' or 'perpetuity'.

Thus the word 'infallibility' would be restricted to him to whom it was restricted originally, God, his word and his truth, *Deus qui nec fallere nec falli potest*, who in the strict sense of the word is the *solus infallibilis*.

There is historical backing for this. Yves Congar recently made an exhaustive study of the concept of infallibility in the Middle Ages: 'The universally shared basic belief', he writes, 'was that the *Ecclesia* herself could err (Albert the Great, St Thomas Aquinas, Bonaventure, the Decretists). By *Ecclesia* is understood the Church in her totality, as *congregatio* or *universitas fidelium*. One part or another of the Church could err, and even the bishops or the Pope could; the Church could be storm-tossed, but in the end she remained faithful. In particular Matthew 28:20 was quoted in this respect, as well as Matthew 16:18, Luke 22:32, and John 16:13. Other conclusions regarding various hierarchical authorities are based on this basic belief in relation to the *Ecclesia*.'[9]

On the basis of Gratian's *Decretum* in particular it was assumed that the 'Roman Church' had never erred in faith. But what was meant in this context was not the local Church of Rome, which could err and had certainly done so, but the universal Church; it was this that was to be regarded as *inerrabilis*, or at least *indefectibilis*. As for the Pope, 'it was generally assumed that the Pope could err and fall into heresy, even though some have scruples about saying so at the present day. Sometimes a distinction was made between the *sedes*, the unerring see, and the *sedens*, its occupant; sometimes a distinction was made between the Pope as an individual and the Pope as head of the Church, but no use was made of that distinction. Instead it was stated that a pope who fell into heresy *ipso facto* ceased to be head of the Church, because he had ceased to be a member of it.'[10] Subsequently, though not so much with the canonists as with the theologians, a certain link came to be established between infallibility and the ecumenical council on the one hand and with the Pope on the other, though the latter's infallibility was always connected with the Church, in so far as he was its head. Side by side with the papal teaching office was another, similar one, that of the *doctores*, or theologians.

Congar's conclusion in regard to the High Middle Ages is: 'It cannot be said that the dogma of 1870 was accepted other than in embryo in the period under consideration. Basically, emphasis was laid on the infallibility, or rather indefectibility, of the Church. It had not yet been fully decided which personality in the hierarchy was assured of this infallibility, but this step was about to be taken. Meanwhile the problem of the Pope's supremacy over the council would have to be raised and settled. In the thirteenth century the two authorities were not regarded as competing.'[11]

Is it not astonishing that throughout the whole of the Middle Ages, which were so deeply marked by papal absolutism, the

only agreed and explicit teaching was on the infallibility, or
rather indefectibility, of the Church as such? In relation to the
modern age, Congar writes: 'Evidence of the uncertainty of
many minds at the beginning of the sixteenth century about
the Pope's primacy by divine right and his infallibility in particular is abundant. The Church was infallible, but what was
the precise nature of this infallibility? Uncertainty and controversy on this unsettled point continued until the middle of
the nineteenth century. One certain tradition existed, that of
the infallibility of the Church, and this continued to be maintained.'[12] The emphasis laid on papal infallibility in the
thirteenth century by St Thomas Aquinas in particular was
taken up again in the fifteenth century, after the conciliar
period, by Torquemada and others, and in the Counter-
Reformation period it was continued in particular by Bellarmine and Suarez and, of course, above all by the popes
themselves (notably by Innocent XI and definitively by
Pius IX). 'In the climate of excessive insistence on authority
and obedience in combating the Reformation, the infallibility
of the Church tended to become predominantly and almost
exclusively the infallibility of the bishops and particularly of
the Pope.'[13]

Our own conclusion is that if, as against the infallibility of
the bishops or the Pope in particular, we lay emphasis on the
infallibility or rather indefectibility or perpetuity of the Church
in the truth, all that we are really doing is returning to a good
and ancient and fortunately never extinguished tradition.

7. THE CHURCH'S REMAINING IN THE TRUTH

The basic question of infallibility in the Church may now be
regarded as answered. In the strict sense of the word, God alone
is infallible. He alone is *a priori* free from error (*immunis ab
errore*) in each and every instance; thus *a priori* he can neither
deceive nor be deceived. But the Church, which is composed
of human beings, who are not and can never become God, can
very humanly continually deceive itself and others at all levels
and in all fields. For the avoidance of misunderstanding, it is
better to ascribe to the Church, not 'infallibility', but, on the
basis of faith in the promises, 'indefectibility' or perpetuity, in-

destructibility and imperishability; in short, a fundamental remaining in the truth in spite of all possible errors.

All the assumptions and conclusions that follow from an answer such as we have given cannot be examined within the scope of the present study. But we shall briefly answer at any rate some of the more obvious questions that arise.

a. *Does a Church so liable to err differ from other human organizations?* The answer is that the Church of Christ – and we include under that heading all Churches that wish to be Churches of Chrlst – is not distinguished from other human organizations by the absence of error, or the presence of fewer or lesser errors, or by freedom from error on the part of certain individuals or in certain instances. It is only necessary to glance through the short list of exemplary errors we quoted at the beginning of Chapter I, or the Index of forbidden books . . . To err is human. It is also ecclesiastical. It has recently been pointed out that it is also papal – simply because Church and Pope are human, and human they remain. This has often been forgotten in the Church, and we have been sharply reminded of it.

The Church is distinguished from other human organizations – and this distinction is vital – only by the promise given to it as the community of believers in Christ: the promise that it will survive all errors and sins, that its truth will remain imperishable and indestructible through all storms, that the message of Jesus Christ will endure in it, that Jesus Christ will remain with it in spirit and thus keep it in the truth through all errors and confusion. This promise makes it superfluous for the believer to ponder on what would happen if there were no longer any community of the faithful. The promise means that God assures the continuance of the faith and the Church, and sees that in spite of all straying and wandering it ultimately keeps direction and carries onward the truth of Christ. Its faith is often weak, its love lukewarm, its hope wavering. But that on which its faith is based, its love rooted, its hope built, endures. And thus it too endures, not by its own strength, but by that of God, the imperishable and indestructible 'pillar and bulwark of truth' (1 Timothy 3:15). It did not give itself its indefectibility, but no one can take it away. The Church may forsake her God; he will not forsake her. On her path through

time she may go astray, may stumble and often even fall, she
may fall among thieves and be left lying for dead. Yet God will
not abandon her, but will pour oil on her wounds, raise her up,
and pay also what could not be foreseen for her healing. So the
Church will continue on her way, living on the forgiveness, the
healing and the strengthening of her Lord.[14]

This, then, is the promise, with all that it involves by way of
truth, life and strength for the present day, that distinguishes
the Church, the community of believers in Christ, from other
human organizations. The only question that remains is
whether all this is not too beautiful to be true.

b. *Is not this indefectibility merely an unreal, verbal theory?* The
answer is that it is a truth of faith. It is based, not on evidence
observable by me as a detached observer, but on a promise that
is a challenge to my confident commitment. He who accepts this
is rewarded with knowledge. Only the believer can know the
real meaning of love. The Church, though certainly not invisible, is only relatively visible. In spite of her often only too
massive visibility, that on which and by which and for which
she lives is hidden. Thus the promise that it will remain in the
truth is a challenge to faith; and he who responds to the
challenge with faith shares in the truth.

This does not mean that the Church's indefectibility is
unverifiable. That the Church of Christ has behind it a history
of twenty centuries is a fact that cannot be ignored. It is a
history with many, all too many, shadows; the mistakes, the
sins, the crimes in that long history are innumerable. If we look
at certain centuries in the Church's history – say the tenth, that
saeculum obscurum, or the fifteenth, the century of the Renaissance
popes – we may have the impression that practically everything
was done at that time to corrupt the Church and its truth. Yet
it ultimately turned out to be incorruptible. The Roman
Empire also had a long, impressive history, and much truth was
invested in it (the ideas of justice, law, order and peace). But
men – from the highest to the lowest – corrupted the Roman
Empire and it decayed, more from within than from without.
The old ideas no longer inspired and sustained it, it lost its
truth and perished. Shaken inwardly and finally destroyed, it
was never restored.

What guarantee have we that the same will not happen to

the Church of Christ? The answer is that no institution and no constitution can give any such guarantee. But so far, at all events, it has not happened, and 2,000 years of Christendom provide an illustration that is not to be despised (not proof) that in spite of all error and sin the Church in the last resort has not been corrupted, but has remained in the truth. All the numerous prophets of the Church's decline have so far turned out to be false prophets. It survived the tenth and fifteenth centuries, retrogression was followed by revival, and decadence by renewed knowledge of the truth.

History, of course, cannot be extrapolated to show the future. As in the past, the Church's being and truth will continue in the future to be dependent on the promise, and this cannot be demonstrated, but only apprehended by faith. As in the past it will continue in the future to depend on the living faith and love of Christians. Who is it, then, who ensures that the indefectibility of the Church is not merely an unreal theory or an empty divine promise, but a genuine reality in this community? Where was the Church's indefectibility manifested in its darkest ages?

Was it manifested through the 'hierarchy', which relied on its apostolic succession and its rights? Considering the behaviour of popes and bishops in those times, the final break-up of the Church seemed more likely than its imperishability, and – succession or no succession – popes like Alexander VI were not exactly witnesses to the truth of Christ. Was it manifested through theology, which relied on its cleverness and knowledge? At such times theology often failed as completely as the 'hierarchy'; only too often, while the bishops chased power, money and pleasure, the theologians remained silent or asleep, or by their apologies excused or defended the hierarchs in whatever they did or did not do. For all their scholarship, they were hardly witnesses to Christ's truth.

Where, then, in these dark times, was the indefectibility of the Church really manifested? Not in the hierarchy and not in theology, but among those countless, mostly unknown Christians, though there were always a few bishops and theologians among them, who, even in the Church's worst periods, heard the Christian message and tried to live according to it, in faith, love and hope. Mostly they were not the great and the powerful, the clever and the wise, but the 'simple people', those 'of no account' of the New Testament, who are those of great account in the Kingdom of Heaven. They were the true witnesses to the truth of Christ, and by their Christian life and Christian conduct they manifested the indefectibility of the Church in the truth.

If we think of the people of God discriminatingly and not mechanically, we can say with Vatican II that it 'shares also in Christ's prophetic office. It spreads abroad a living witness to him, especially by means of a life of faith and charity and by offering to God a sacrifice of praise, the tribute of lips which give honour to his name (cf. Hebrews 13:15). The body of the faithful as a whole, anointed as they are by the Holy One (cf. 1 John 2:20, 27), cannot err in matters of belief' (Constitution on the Church, Article XII). True, this assertion is again linked with certain propositions; if the 'sense of faith of the whole people . . . from the bishops down to the last member of the laity' is accepted uncritically and indiscriminately as revelation of 'the Spirit of truth', then in the course of centuries we should often have had to regard some very strange things as revelations of the Spirit. It must be pointed out that the 'sense of faith of the people of God under the lead of the sacred teaching authority' can never become the source and norm for the revelation of the Spirit that is and remains the source and norm for the Church's sense of faith. This means that anyone who wishes to find out what the Christian revelation is cannot establish it statistically by a public opinion poll of the people's 'sense of faith' – for we know by experience that the faith of the people (and perhaps sometimes also of the teaching office) is mingled with superstition and even unbelief – but has critically to examine this 'sense of faith' in the light of the original Christian message. The gospel remains invariably the source, norm and driving force of the faith and the perpetuity and indefectibility of the Church in the truth.

c. *Is certainty compatible with this indefectibility?* Certainty is essential to faith, and faith should provide it. Can the 'hierarchy' or theology provide the certainty of faith? Both would be overestimating their capacities if they claimed they were able to do so. Only the Christian message, no matter by whom it is proclaimed, confers the certainty of faith. It is

Jesus Christ, speaking in the Christian proclamation, who bestows faith. He is the invitation, the challenge, the encouragement to faith, so that through him the individual is placed before God, to answer to God for his life and death. The 'hierarchy' and theology – each in its own way, as we shall indicate later – are there to serve the proclamation of the Christian message that is incumbent upon all. By serving they can indirectly prepare the way for the faith that is awakened and bestowed by the Christian message, by Jesus Christ himself.

Thus it is the Christian message, and he who speaks through it, that provides the certainty of faith. To that extent the certainty of faith depends on the truth of the Christian message. But this truth is not to be confused either with self-evidence or with infallibility. The truth of the Christian message is not a system of self-evident propositions that produce certainty on Cartesian lines. The reality of God is not obvious in the Cartesian sense. Neither is the truth of the Christian message a system of infallible definitions that might provide certainty on neo-scholastic lines. The reality of God cannot be grasped in this way. The certainty of faith existed for at least a thousand years before infallible propositions were heard of; it existed nearly two thousand years before infallibility was defined. But inherently infallible propositions are, as we have seen, granted neither to any individual believer nor to any group of believers. Both the individual and the community of believers should certainly aspire to *true* propositions in proclamation, even though an ultimate ambivalence can never be eliminated even from the propositions of faith, and all language even in matters of faith remains dependent on dialogue. Certainty – of a kind different from that of mathematics, but no less assured – is not, however, established by these true propositions. It arises only when the individual opens himself to him who is proclaimed in that message, whether the truth of any single proposition is greater or less, or is more adequate or less adequate to that message.

This kind of faith does not mean accepting true or infallible propositions, believing this or that. Nor does it mean taking anything on trust from anyone, believing this person or that. It means committing the whole of oneself to the message, to him whom it proclaims, believing in Jesus Christ, in spite of all possibly ambiguous or perhaps false propositions. Only such faith can provide certainty, the peace that passes all understanding. How do I assure myself of another person's love? By expecting declarations of love? These are necessary, but are there infallible signs of love, and do they create unequivocal certainty? In the last resort I can be certain of love only by opening myself to it and thus experiencing it – possibly in spite of inept declarations or clumsy signs of it. I become certain of the love of God only when I myself love.

At the same time the individual believer has no need to be isolated. The individual is called on to believe, but without the community that believes and professes and proclaims the faith he does not come to believe. His faith comes neither from himself nor directly from God, but through the community that invites, encourages, challenges him to believe and then – if it is really a community of faith and love – constantly encircles and helps to sustain his faith. Thus the individual's faith can share in the faith of the community and in the common truth. And modern man, who even in his faith has become only too well aware of his historical relativity, isolation and loneliness, will feel it to be, not a burden, but a liberation that, for all his own personal responsibility, his faith is sheltered in the wider and more manifold faith of the religious community which is the Church. As we have said, the faith of the religious community can express itself in creeds, definitions of faith, symbols and dogmas, all of them having deep meaning and an important function without any claim to infallibility being made for any propositions.

8. ECUMENICAL PROSPECTS

The question of infallibility divides Christendom. A considered answer to this question on the part of Catholic theology has been outstanding since the Reformation. The earlier appeal to tradition, which is dubious on this point, was obviously no more convincing to other Christians and Churches than were the later statements of the two Vatican councils. But if we are to avoid fighting false battles on false issues, we must examine more closely, though with due brevity, what the Protestant position really was.

A. It was undoubtedly simpler to tie down Luther to the formal question of the capacity of Pope and council to err than to deal with the vital theological problems (particularly the doctrine of justification). In his reply to Prierias in 1518 Luther frankly admitted that both Pope and council could err.[15] And at the famous Disputation of Leipzig in 1519 John Eck skilfully pinned him down to the statement that councils had erred in practice (specifically the Council of Constance, which had condemned Huss a hundred years earlier and had him burnt at the stake in spite of promises of a safe-conduct).[16] And finally, at the Diet of Worms in the decisive year of 1521, Luther's insistence on the ability of councils to err was the chief reason why he was dropped by the Emperor Charles V and subjected to the imperial ban.[17] When he was called on by the imperial orator to concede the inerrancy of councils and to reject the propositions condemned at Constance, Luther unequivocally replied: 'Unless I am convinced by the testimony of Scripture or manifest reason – for I do not believe either Pope or councils alone, since it is certain that they have both erred and contradicted themselves frequently, I am bound by the scriptural testimony I have quoted and, since my conscience is caught in the words of God, I neither can nor will revoke anything, since to act against conscience is neither safe nor honest.'[18] It was on this occasion that Luther is said to have made his famous statement: 'I can do no other. Here I stand. God help me. Amen.'[19]

He adhered to this position throughout his life,[20] and the view that councils, and of course popes in particular, could and had erred was shared by all the Reformed Churches. Calvin in his *Institutio* displays a very lively sense of history in showing that there were true councils, subsequently acknowledged by the Church, and false councils, not acknowledged by the Church, that council had often contradicted council, that councils had been wrong, and that blind obedience to councils was irresponsible.[21] He also specifically rejects the view 'that councils cannot err; or if they err, it is not lawful for us to discern the truth, or not to assent to their errors.'[22] In his thorough study of Reformation confessions of faith, Benno Gassmann writes that in these the Church is regarded as free from error only so long and in so far as it bases itself on Christ and the 'foundation of the prophets and apostles', in other words, on Scripture. Inerrancy is not an incontestable possession of the Church; any Church can fall away from the truth, just as it can depart from Scripture. To the congregation Scripture is the standard and the norm. Inerrancy is a factor that lies between these two poles.[23]

Finally, the Thirty-Nine Articles of the Church of England soberly state: 'As the Churches of Jerusalem, Alexandria, and Antioch have erred; so also the Church of Rome hath erred, not only in their living and manner of ceremonies, but also in matters of faith.'[24] In regard to the authority of general councils, they state: 'And when they be gathered together (forasmuch as they be an assembly of men, whereof all be not governed with the Spirit and Word of God) they may err, and sometimes have erred, even in things pertaining unto God.'[25]

B. For all their rejection of the infallibility of Pope and councils, the Reformed Churches accept the infallibility or indefectibility and perpetuity of the Church. To Luther the councils have authority, not an inherent authority as representative of the Church, but an authority based on the truth of their decisions, that is, when they have the truth of the gospel behind them. The legitimacy of the Church is based on spiritual legitimacy. Luther also believed in the guidance of the Church by the Holy Spirit, which enabled him specifically to ascribe infallibility to it. After the apostles it could be said of no one except the universal Church 'that he cannot err in faith'.[26] That Church, however, is not to be simply equated with the official Church, with the Pope and bishops. It is rather the hidden but very real Church of those who truly believe that it cannot err, because Christ in accordance with his promise remains with it to the end of the world; it is 'the pillar and bulwark of the truth' (1 Timothy 3:15).[27] In this respect the Church had survived even under an erring papacy. Luther 'in spite of everything saw in the real history of the Church a continuity of truth, in as much as the promise that the Holy Spirit would lead the Church was always fulfilled anew. Thus in this sense the true Church was the object, not only of a faith that believed in spite of what it saw, but also of actual historical experience, of a manifest continuity that Luther constantly acknowledged. But this continuity of guidance by the Spirit, the maintenance of the true Church, was not identical with the official tradition and the alleged apostolic succession of the Church, and was not guaranteed by the latter. God always chose his witnesses to the truth how and where he willed . . . Guidance through the Holy Spirit must therefore not be understood in any hierarchical or supranatural evolutionary sense. God permitted the official Church to err in order to break down the trust in men to which she was constantly inclined instead of trusting in his word alone. But then he again sent her witnesses to his truth.'[28]

The famous Article VII of the Augsburg Confession must be seen against this theological background: 'They teach that the one Holy Church will remain for ever (*perpetua mansura sit*). Now this Church is the congregation of all the faithful, in which the Gospel is rightly taught and the sacraments rightly administered.'[29] The perpetuity and indefectibility of the Church are emphatically accepted here. In his apologia for the Augsburg Confession, Melanchthon says of this article: 'In order that we may be certain, not doubt, but firmly and entirely believe that a Christian Church will really be and remain on earth until the end of the world; that we may also not doubt that a Christian Church lives and is on earth, which is the Bride of Christ, although the troop of the impious is more and greater; that also the Lord Christ here on earth in the troop which is called Church is active daily, forgives sins, daily answers prayer, daily animates his followers with abundant and powerful consolation in their temptations and constantly raises them up: for all this we have the consoling article of our faith, "I believe in one Catholic, universal Christian Church". Hence no one may think that the Church, like an external state organization, is tied to this or that country, kingdom or class, as the Pope wants to say of Rome; but this certainly remains true that the troop and men are the right Church who continually in the world, from the rise of the sun to its setting, truly believe in Christ; who then have one gospel, one Christ, one sort of baptism and sacrament, are ruled by one Holy Spirit, although they have different ceremonies.'[30]

Calvin too accepts the infallibility or indefectibility of the Church though, unlike his Catholic opponents, he regards it as inseparably connected with the word: 'Their statement that the

Church cannot err bears on this point, and this is how they interpret it – in as much as the Church is governed by the Spirit of God, it can proceed safely without the word; no matter where it may go, it can think and speak only what is true; accordingly, if it should ordain anything beyond or apart from God's word, this must be taken as a sure oracle of God. If we grant the first point, that the Church cannot err in matters necessary to salvation, here is what we mean by it: The statement is true in so far as the Church, having forsaken all its own wisdom, allows itself to be taught by the Holy Spirit through God's word. This, then, is the difference. Our opponents locate the authority of the Church outside God's word; but we insist that it be attached to the word, and do not allow it to be separated from it.'[31] The Church's remaining in the truth is not annulled by the errors of councils. 'I am quite convinced that truth does not die in the Church, even though it be oppressed by one council, but is wonderfully preserved by the Lord, so that it may rise up and triumph again in its own time. But I deny it to be always the case that an interpretation of Scripture adopted by vote of a council is true and certain.'[32]

The Thirty-Nine Articles of the Church of England do not go more closely into this question, but take the same position in regard to the Church as the community of believers, in which the pure word of God is preached and the sacraments are administered in accordance with Christ's mandate,[33] as they do in regard to the authority of councils, the decisions of which have authority only when they are 'taken out of Holy Scripture'.[34]

C. What are we to conclude from all this? That ecumenical agreement on this, perhaps the most difficult point of Catholic-Protestant controversy, is perfectly possible, and that, if the critical new approach of Catholic doctrine proposed in this book turned out to be acceptable, ecumenical agreement could be attained. For there is no need of lengthy expatiation to make it evident that the Reformers, on the basis of their own assumptions, could accept the idea we have put forward here of an indefectibility or perpetuity of the Church that depends on the presence of the Spirit, the proclamation of the word, the community of believers, but not on infallible propositions.

That this idea will come to prevail in the Catholic Church

is wholly within the bounds of possibility. In recent Catholic publications on the question, though they do not come to grips with the problem of infallible propositions and the infallibility of the Church, a trend towards clarification is noticeable in two respects:

1. Papal infallibility is given a more limited interpretation than that of Vatican I and is connected with the infallibility of the Church;[35] and

2. the infallibility of the community of the faithful is emphasized as against the infallibility of the teaching office.[36]

The infallibility of the teaching office has been denied by Bishop Francis Simons, the Catholic missionary bishop of Indore.[37] The views of this admirably courageous Dutchman on faith, evidence and miracles seem to us to be excessively influenced by a neo-scholastic fundamental theology, and we share neither them nor his attitude to modern exegesis, particularly form-criticism. We agree, however, with his main thesis, which is: (1) that the infallibility of the teaching office requires to be substantiated from Scripture, but that (2) such substantiation cannot be provided. But he assumes an identity between the infallibility of the Church and infallible propositions, which he tests by an oversimplified concept of 'self-evidence'.

The author of the present book associates himself completely with the conclusion of W. Kasper's article on the road from Vatican I to Vatican II. 'The supersession of Church triumphalism by Vatican II also affects the Church's attitude to truth and calls for a new and deeper interpretation of the so easily misunderstood concept of infallibility', he writes. 'This concept belongs more essentially than any other to the still undealt-with heritage of Vatican I. Properly understood, it means the confidence of faith that, in spite of many errors in detail, intrinsically the Church is maintained in the truth of the gospel by the Spirit of God. Infallibility would then be regarded dynamically instead of statically. The eschatological conflict with the powers of untruth, error and falsehood would be regarded as continually taking place in and through the Church and, in accordance with our faith, truth would always ultimately prevail and never finally be lost. Thus, by reason of its faith, the Church in its struggle for the right perception of the truth would be a token of hope for human society. It must show by its own example that it is never senseless but always necessary to search and travel further, in the certainty that the truth will prevail. The road the Church travelled from Vatican I to Vatican II testifies to this hope.'[38]

The encyclical *Humanae Vitae* was a misfortune to the Catholic Church in many respects. But should it turn out to have been a catalyst, to have accelerated reflection on Church infallibility, it would not have been in vain, particularly for the *oikumene*.

9. THE TRUTH OF COUNCILS

No question with ecumenical implications addressed to the Catholic Church fails to have repercussions on those outside it. Our critical survey of Catholic as against Protestant doctrine should not create the impression that the question of infallibility presents a challenge to Catholic theology alone. This will become immediately evident when we raise some questions, not only in regard to Protestant theology, but also in regard to that of the Orthodox Eastern Churches, with which we shall begin.

It is doubtful whether there is a uniform doctrine of Church infallibility shared by all the Orthodox Christian Churches of the East. The question has evidently not been considered so urgent in the East and has not been discussed with the same intensity as in the West, which is not necessarily a bad sign. But Orthodox theology should be able to associate itself with the ecumenical consensus noted above, in as much as it regards 'infallibility' – in so far as it finds it necessary to mention it at all – as based on the Church as the whole of the people of God. While Rome concentrated on the Pope's infallibility, Orthodoxy concentrated on that of the universal Church; on the infallible Church, in other words, not on infallible individuals. The Orthodox patriarchs replied as follows to Pius IX in 1848 without, however, deterring him from promulgating either the definition of the Immaculate Conception or that of his own infallibility: 'Among us, neither patriarchs nor councils could ever introduce new teaching, for the guardian of religion is the very body of the Church, that is, the people (*laos*) itself.'[39] The important Russian theologian Alexei Khomiakov, commenting on these exchanges at the time, wrote: 'The Pope is greatly mistaken in supposing that we consider the ecclesiastical hierarchy to be the guardian of dogma. The case is quite different. The unvarying constancy and the unerring truth of Christian dogma does not depend on any hierarchical order; it is guarded by the totality, by the whole people of the Church, which is the Body of Christ.'[40]

The Orthodox Churches do not seem always to have been clear on the question of on what score the infallibility of the Church requires infallible propositions. This is shown by a recent study by John Karmiris who, however, as we shall see, cannot be regarded as representative of Orthodoxy as a whole: 'In regard to the infallibility of the Church referred to here,' he writes, 'it seems necessary to declare at the outset that the Church is infallible as a whole, as a *pleroma*, consisting of all Orthodox believers, clergy and laity. As organ of her infallibility she needs only the ecumenical synod, which alone has the right to formulate dogmas infallibly and to whose supreme leadership and authority all are subject. This includes both patriarchs and popes, as well as all the other hierarchs, just as all the apostles, together with Peter, were subject to the apostolic synod. The totality therefore, the *pleroma*, or the body of the Church, is regarded in Orthodoxy as the bearer of infallibility, while the ecumenical synod serves as organ and, as it were, as mouthpiece of the Church. At the ecumenical synod the ecclesiastical *pleroma* is represented by its bishops, who establish dogmas under the inspiration of the Holy Spirit. "The Church consequently is infallible, not only when assembled at ecumenical synods, but also as a totality independently of the synods, so that the infallibility of ecumenical synods follows from the infallibility of the Church as a whole, and not conversely, the infallibility of the Church from the infallibility of ecumenical synods" (K. Dyovouniotis). It must be observed that neither the ecclesiastical *pleroma* nor its two big divisions – the clergy and the laity – each for itself alone, nor – which would be still worse – one person, a bishop, a patriarch or pope, could authoritatively lay down dogma, since this, as we have said, is the sole and exclusive prerogative and duty of ecumenical synods and of the bishops taking part in them.'[41]

If the infallibility of the Church is thus identified with the infallibility of propositions – laid down, not by the Pope, but by ecumenical councils – Orthodoxy, for all its opposition to Rome, exposes itself to the same difficulties from which the Roman doctrine suffers, arising from the artificial restriction of the apostolic succession to the bishops, the questionable legitimacy of deducing the infallibility of ecumenical councils from the infallibility of the Church, and, finally, the question whether it is possible to make infallible propositions at all. Here again it is insufficient for theologians to assert; they must establish their claims theologically. The argument for the infallibility of ecumenical councils seems, however, to over-shoot the mark, for if a hundred ecclesiastical office-holders can represent the Church infallibly, why should a single one theoretically be unable to do so? In fact, however, all the considerations that cause one to question the infallibility of papal propositions apply equally to the infallibility of propositions enunciated by any assembly of bishops. As we have seen, no assurance of infallibility to such an assembly is to be found anywhere in Scripture.

It is, however, more than doubtful whether this concentration of the infallibility of the Church in the propositions of an ecumenical council is really the Orthodox position. The emphasis of certain Eastern theologians on conciliar infallibility seems sometimes to be dictated, not so much by their own ancient tradition, as by opposition to the Roman Pontiff and a desire not to fall short of him in the matter of infallibility.[42] This results in their adoption of their opponents' superficial position in the matter and their taking too much for granted their identity with the Church of the New Testament and the early Church in general. Among recent Orthodox theologians, Timothy Ware is much more discriminating and at least states the difficulty clearly. 'But councils of bishops can err and be deceived',[43] he writes. Thus he raises the problem, cursorily dismissed by Karmiris, of how we can be certain whether a particular assembly of bishops is an ecumenical council or not.

We shall now refer to two groups of problems belonging to the early Orthodox and common Christian tradition that suggest there is no such thing as the inherent, automatic infallibility of an ecumenical council.

1. The ecumenicity of a council is not *a priori* certain. After the First Ecumenical Council of Nicea in 325 its acknowledgment by the Church as a whole was regarded as of fundamental importance. Athanasius, the champion of the Council of Nicea, often enumerated all the Churches taking part.[44] The more modern *sobornost* theory, which dates back to Khomiakov and is supported by many Slavonic theologians (in the present century by Sergii Bulgakov in particular), sees recognition by the Church as a whole as a necessary qualification for the ecumenicity of a council. Recognition of an ecumenical council by the particular Churches must not, of course, be understood as a kind of retrospective referendum that might deny such a council the right of making binding decisions on questions of faith.[45] But the necessity of recognition or acceptance of a council by the Church as a whole that is documented by history implies at least that it does not necessarily follow from the fact that a council has been convoked and conducted as an ecumenical council that is has the truth on its side. This last becomes evident only when its propositions come to prevail in the Church, that is, when the Church recognizes in these propositions its own experience of faith.

Actually there were councils that were not convoked or conducted as ecumenical but have nevertheless come to be accepted as ecumenical; such were the Second Ecumenical Council at Constantinople in 381 and the Fifth at Constantinople in 553. Also the canons of smaller Eastern synods, such as those of Ancyra in 314, Neocaesaria (Pontus) in 320, Antioch in 329 (?), Gangra (Asia Minor) in 342, and Laodicea (Phrygia) in 350, by gaining acceptance acquired importance in the West too. But the converse is also true. Councils that were convoked as ecumenical failed to establish themselves; such were the Council of Sardica, the Second Council of Ephesus in 449, the Second Trullan Synod, and also the general synods of the West at Arles in 314 and Rome in 341.

The historian H. Jedin rightly observes that 'for the first thousand years and beyond, the intention and will of the convokers of a council were not sufficient to establish its ecumenicity; nor did the acknowledgment of its decisions by the Pope during this period serve as formal confirmation of its ecumenicity as it clearly did in the case of later councils.

The recognition of these twenty councils as ecumenical is not attributable to any comprehensive legislative act by the papacy covering them all, but established itself in the theory and practice of the Church.'[46]

If the ecumenicity of a council is not *a priori* certain, its infallibility is still less so. The determining factor is not the will to make infallible definitions, but the intrinsic truth of the council's decisions that inevitably imposes itself on the Church's sense of faith.

2. Councils have corrected one another. When ecumenical councils began, there was not the feeling that came into existence later that their words were, as it were, inspired. At the early christological councils in particular there were a very large number of terminological and conceptual changes. The councils of Nicea and Sardica assumed, with many of the Fathers, that there was only one hypostasis of the Godhead; the First Council of Constantinople and the Council of Chalcedon assumed, with many others, that there were three. Also there were instances in which an earlier council was specifically rejected. The Council of Chalcedon in 451 rejected the decisions of the Second Council of Ephesus of 449, the ecumenicity of which was therefore not accepted, though it had been convoked as ecumenical; and the Council of Constantinople in 754 rejected the veneration of images, which the Second Council of Nicea in 787 approved.

Finally, there are instances of decisions by ecumenical councils being amended by a later council. Thus the Council of Chalcedon in 451 specifically amended the decision of the First Council of Ephesus in 431, which was recognized as ecumenical and under the leadership of Cyril of Alexandria had condemned and excommunicated Nestorius of Antioch. Though Chalcedon commended Cyril and the condemnation of Nestorius, by its new formulation of faith it nevertheless recognized the claims of Antioch theology and specifically rejected the central doctrine of Alexandrine christology which had dominated the two councils of Ephesus, the idea of the *one* nature in Christ. Thus the Patriarch Nestorius, who was condemned at Ephesus in 431 and 449, would have been able to subscribe completely to the formulation of faith laid down at Chalcedon in 451, to which Cyril, the leading spirit at Ephesus I, could have subscribed only with open or secret reservations, and to which Dioscorus, the leading spirit at Ephesus II (who was excommunicated by Chalcedon), could not have subscribed at all (Ephesus II came to be known in history as the 'robber synod').

There is a *locus classicus* in St Augustine that says: 'Who would not know that the holy canonical Scriptures both of the Old and New Testament have a priority over all subsequent writings of bishops such that there cannot be any doubt or dispute at all as to whether whatever is written there is true or right; but that the writings of bishops after the settlement of the canon may be refuted both by the perhaps wiser words of anyone more experienced in the matter and by the weightier authority and more scholarly prudence of other bishops, and also by councils, if something in them perhaps has deviated from the truth; and that even councils held in particular regions or provinces must without quibbling give way (*sine ullis ambagibus cedere*) to the authority of plenary councils of the whole Christian world; and that even the earlier plenary councils are often (*saepe*) corrected (*emendari*) by later ones, if as a result of practical experience (*cum aliquo experimento rerum*) something that was closed is opened, something that was hidden becomes known?'[47]

Now, if ecumenical councils differ with one another, disavow one another, specifically reject or actually correct one another in this way, it is impossible, not only in the light of the gospel message, as we have shown, but also in the light of council history to accept the *a priori* infallibility of ecumenical councils, meaning by that their ability to formulate infallible propositions. The Second Vatican Council, consciously under the influence of John XXIII, though without thorough theological consideration of the matter, therefore did well to renounce the making of infallible definitions.

To sum up, then, ecumenical councils *can* be the means of expression of the infallibility or indefectibility of the Church. But they are not so *a priori*, by virtue of the will of the convokers or participants, as if the latter were granted inherent infallibility by the Spirit of God in response to their wishes and prayers; it is precisely that that it is impossible to demonstrate by any means whatever. But they may be seen retrospectively to have been the vehicle of the infallibility or indefectibility of the Church if and in so far as they bear authentic witness to the truth of the gospel of Jesus Christ. Thus there is no such thing as conciliar pronouncements that are infallible in advance. But there are conciliar pronouncements that in fact are true, i.e. those that are in agreement with the original Christian message and are recognized as such by the Church. Councils do not have authority over the truth of Christ. They can strive to attain it. It is for this that the Spirit of Christ is promised to the bishops and all participants, as it is also to every Christian.

'Is it not astonishing to see how many Orthodox theologians question the infallibility of councils?' the Catholic theologian M.-J. Le Guillou exclaims almost indignantly. He mentions the names of S. Zankov, B. Zenkovsky, N. Arseniev and N. Milash, and goes on to say that 'this influence is discernible even in Bratsiotis . . . and, even more surprisingly, in V. Lossky.'[48] Is such a broad consensus really so surprising? Only to a Catholic theologian who does not take seriously the questions posed by Orthodox theology and believes himself able to dismiss the problem by a reference to the wicked Luther and the Disputation of Leipzig and the noxious influence of Protestantism on Orthodox theology.

If we look at Orthodox theology, and also the Orthodox tradition, without preconceptions or prejudices, we can discern the outlines of a thoroughly gratifying ecumenical consensus in regard to the true infallibility, or rather indefectibility, of the Church. We therefore fully agree with J. Meyendorff – of whom Le Guillou says that 'the following passage is perhaps still more representative of present-day Orthodox ecclesiology'[49] – when he says: 'It is not "ecumenicity" but the truthfulness of councils that makes their decisions binding on us. Here we touch on the basic secret of Orthodox doctrine on the Church. The Church is the miracle of God's presence among mankind beyond any formal "criterion" or any formal "infallibility". It is not sufficient to convoke an ecumenical council to proclaim the truth, whatever the historical reality may be that is attached to the idea of the council; what matters is that among those assembled there should be present he who said: "I am the way, the truth and the life." Without this presence the assembly, however numerous and representative it may be, is not in the truth. Protestants and Catholics usually have difficulty in grasping this basic truth of Orthodoxy. Both materialize God's presence in the Church: the former in the letter of Scripture, the latter in the person of the Pope. They do not thereby evade the miracle, but give it concrete form. To the Orthodox the sole "criterion of truth" is God himself, who lives mysteriously in the Church, guides it on the way of truth, and makes known his will in the wholeness ("catholicity") of her life. In the course of history councils – particularly "ecumenical" councils – have been merely means of proclaiming the truth; for it is quite obvious that the Orthodox faith is not exhaustively contained in the decisions of the seven councils, which merely established some basic truths about God and about Christ. The totality of the Orthodox faith remains continually in the Church; it finds its expression in local councils (the councils of Constantinople in the fourteenth century, for instance, that defined the Orthodox doctrine of grace) and in the works of various theologians; it is likewise always and everywhere professed in Orthodox liturgy, in the sacraments, and in the lives of the saints. This life did not come to a standstill with the last ecumenical council (in 787): the truth lives and works always and everywhere in the Church. It might also declare itself in a new "ecumenical" council that gathered together not only the Orthodox Churches but also the Christians of the West.'[50]

We have arrived at the question, raised by Orthodox theologians, which we shall now put to the Protestants in the form of a Catholic counter-question to Protestantism: the question of the infallibility of the Bible.

10. THE TRUTH OF SCRIPTURE

The question we put to Protestants must be stated as follows: Is it sufficient to replace the infallibility of the teaching office with the infallibility of the Bible, to substitute for the infallibility of the Roman pontiffs or of ecumenical councils the infallibility of a 'paper Pope'?

Catholic insistence on tradition and the infallibility of certain doctrinal propositions was met at an early date by the Protestant principle of dependence on Scripture (*sola scriptura*) and the attribution of infallibility to biblical propositions.

Here too polemics between the two sides led to distortion of the problem. The Reformers themselves countered the accepted traditions in Church, theology and piety, not by the infallibility of Scripture, but by the testimony of the content of Scripture; Calvin engaged in philological and historical criticism of the Bible, and Luther occasionally engaged in it (on the Epistle of James or the Book of Revelation). But Lutheran and Reformed Orthodoxy, on the defensive against the claims of the Church reinforced after the Council of Trent, systematically developed the theory of inspiration that was shared by the Reformers and the Council of Trent into a theory of literal inspiration, which was extended to the most minute details, both subjective (how inspiration took place in the sacred writer) and objective (how inspiration took objective form in the book).

Thus revelation came to be identified with the production of the words of Scripture as it took place through the unique and once-and-for-all working of the Holy Spirit in the biblical author. The authors of the books of the Bible consequently came to be seen as unhistorical, phantom-like beings through whom the Holy Spirit did everything directly. Every single word of Scripture shared uniformly in the perfection and inerrancy of God himself. The human authors of the Bible had therefore to be exempted from human imperfection and liability to err; the slightest imperfection or error would in fact have to be charged to the Spirit of God himself, who can neither deceive nor be deceived. Thus 'inspiration' and the inerrancy deduced from that hypothesis were extended with systematic rigour to every single word of the Bible (literal inspiration and literal inerrancy), with the result that the vocalization of the original Hebrew (but not of the translations) was regarded by some as inspired. The Bible was declared in every respect – linguistic, stylistic, logical and historical – to be the perfect and infallible sacred book. Complete infallibility and inerrancy were attributed to every word it contained.

The theory of literal inspiration and literal inerrancy was profoundly shaken by the Enlightenment. Historical and critical exegesis subsequently unexpectedly brought to light the humanity and historicity of the biblical authors. Their liability to error became more than evident. But biblicism remained a constant danger to Protestant theology. The idea of the literal inspiration of the Bible has survived, not only in many sects, but also in some Protestant Churches, particularly in modern American fundamentalism and certain trends of European pietism. The real basis of faith is not the Christian message, Christ himself as preached, but the infallible words of the Bible. Just as some Catholics believe not so much in God and Christ as in the Church (confusing *credere Ecclesiam* with *credere in Deum*), so do many Protestants believe in the Bible. In the case of the former the living Christian message has been swallowed up in the infallible propositions of the teaching office, just as in the case of the latter it has vanished into the infallible propositions of the Bible. The apotheosis of the Church in one case corresponds to the apotheosis of Scripture in the other; and both are arguments in a circle; 'I believe it because the priest says so' corresponds to 'I believe it because the Bible says so'. Even scholarly Protestant theologians up to the present century put forward some strange and unverifiable ideas about the 'personal inspiration' of the apostles or authors of the Bible, the 'spirit of authorship' active in them, the 'strength of their memory' that was reinforced by the Spirit, their ecstatic 'emotion' and charismatic 'fervour'.

Now, it cannot be overlooked that in the early Church a theory of inspiration developed that was subject to manifold extra-Christian influences and gave rise to misunderstandings. While Palestinian Judaism saw God himself at work in the authors of the Bible, but took seriously their human and historical peculiarities, wholly in the spirit of the Old Testament, in Hellenized Judaism (Philo in particular) an attempt was made to eliminate these peculiarities, as human individuality was dissolved in ecstasy under the influence of the divine frenzy. Early Christian theologians regarded the authors of the Bible as tools who wrote under the 'impulse' or 'dictation' of the Spirit (like a secretary, or a flute in the hands of a flute-player). Finally, it was above all St Augustine who, under the influence of Hellenist theories of inspiration, regarded man as merely the instrument of the Holy Spirit; the Spirit alone decided the content and form of the biblical writings, with the result that the whole Bible was free of contradictions, mistakes and errors, or had to be kept free by harmonizing, allegorizing, or mysticizing.[51] St Augustine's influence in regard to inspiration and inerrancy prevailed throughout the Middle Ages and right into the modern age. The Council of Trent declared that the books of the Bible and the unwritten traditions were received 'orally from Christ or dictated by the Holy Spirit' (D 783).

It is significant, however, that the Tridentine decree makes no mention of the inerrancy of the Bible as a result of inspiration. It was only in Protestantism that the theory of literal inspiration was rigorously maintained and systematically developed. It was only towards the end of the nineteenth century that the popes, under the pressure of destructive critical exegesis, took over the theory of literal inspiration worked out by Protestant Orthodoxy, at a time when it was strangely out of phase. But Vatican I, which made an explicit statement on the inspiration of the Scriptures ('under the inspiration of the Holy Spirit, they have God for their author'), restricted itself to the indirect and reserved comment that they 'contain revelation [!] without error' (D 1787). But from the time of Leo XIII, and particularly during the modernist crisis, the complete and absolute inerrancy of Scripture was explicitly and systematically maintained in papal encyclicals (D 1951 f., 2011, 2102, 2186–8, 2315). It was thought that the only way of meeting the threat of rationalism was to adopt the rationalist (Cartesian) attitude to truth (as in the case of infallibility) and assert an inerrancy of propositions in Scripture too, even in regard to scientific and historical matters. The Curial preparatory commission even tried to impose a theory of this kind on the Second Vatican Council in the schema on revelation.[52] Completely in the style of nineteenth-century apologetics, an attempt was made to deduce 'directly and necessarily' from the universal extension of divine inspiration an 'absolute immunity from error of the whole of Scripture', which was to apply specifically to the whole religious and profane sphere, this being described as the ancient and constant belief of the Church. The whole schema, however, was rejected by the Council by an overwhelming majority at the first session in 1962, and John XXIII personally intervened to remove it from the order of the day to counter a Curial voting trick.

To the general surprise, Paul VI put discussion of revelation back on the order of the day for the third session.

But the debates at the third session of the Council were to mark a turning-point on the question of inerrancy. In the new schema the lengthy six articles were condensed into a single brief one (under the heading, not of inerrancy, but of inspiration).[53] The sacred writer was no longer described as an 'instrument' of God, but as a 'true author', and God, not as 'principal author', but simply as 'author'. 'Inspiration does not mean the elimination, inhibition, or displacement of the human activity of the sacred writers. All memory of old theories of verbal inspiration was to be eliminated, and with it all forms of an impersonal, mechanistic, interpretation of the origin of Scripture.'[54]

The vital address on the issue – the negative term 'inerrancy' had in the meantime been displaced by the positive term 'truth' – was made by Cardinal König of Vienna, whom later speakers supported. Oriental studies, he said, showed 'that the Scriptures in matters of history and natural science are sometimes lacking in truth (*a veritate quandoque deficere*)'. According to Mark 2:26, for instance, David entered the house of God and ate the loaves of offering under the high priest Abiathar. According to 1 Samuel 21:1 ff., however, this took place, not under Abiathar, but under his father Ahimelech. Matthew 27:9 relates the fulfilment of a prophecy of Jeremiah's which was in fact a prophecy of Zechariah's (11:12 ff.), and so on and so forth. Thus on the question of inerrancy, according to the Cardinal, speech should be 'honest, unambiguous, unequivocal and fearless'. An unhistorical attitude in these matters did not save the authority of the Bible, but merely rendered its exegesis incredible. Deviation from the truth on historical or scientific matters in no way endangered the authority of the Scripture at the present time. Theologically, it rather provided evidence of the divine condescension (*condescensio Dei*). God took the human author with all his weaknesses and fallibility and still achieved his aim of teaching man the 'truth' of revelation. 'Thus the Cardinal implicitly abandoned the assumption derived from the aprioristic and unhistorical thinking that has dominated teaching on inerrancy since the age of the Fathers; the assumption that the admission that a sacred writer has erred is equivalent to an admission that God has erred.'[55]

As in a number of other important matters, however, the outcome was a compromise. Apart from the constant Curial pressure on the Council and the theological commission, 'this new view of and approach to the doctrine of inspiration and inerrancy . . . had unfortunately been insufficiently prepared for in theological literature, and was therefore unfamiliar to most of the Fathers.'[56] The clear way out would have been to omit the phrase 'without any error' (*sine ullo errore*) and state positively that the books of the Bible teach the truth integrally and unshakably (*integre et inconcusse*). This was precisely what Cardinal König had suggested (a fact that should not be overlooked in commentaries). But what happened? The commission adopted two positive terms (*firmiter* and *fideliter*), but left in 'without error', omitting only the word 'any'. This compromise had a great deal to do with politics and very little to do with theology. The ambiguous text (author's italics) now runs: 'Therefore, since everything asserted by the inspired authors or sacred writers must be held to be asserted by the Holy Spirit, it follows that the books of Scripture must be acknowledged as teaching *firmly, faithfully and without error* that truth which God wanted put into the sacred writings for the sake of our salvation' (Article XI). Thus, after a whole series of Curial manoeuvres and massive interventions by Paul VI in the work of the theological commission, the problem of inerrancy, together with those of inspiration and the relationship between Scripture and tradition, was left to post-conciliar theology. 'The development of the text has shown us that "monophysitism" in the interpretation of inspiration and inerrancy as represented in the teaching on verbal inspiration and also in the 1962 version of the teaching on inerrancy (and in the scriptural encyclicals), is to be given up. So much can be said on the basis of Article XI. It remains for theology to examine inerrancy even more thoroughly on the basis of the new approach.'[57]

It is not our intention here to deal with all the questions that arise in connection with the theory of inspiration. At all events, to use Grillmeier's terms, a 'demythologization' and 'depsychologization' of the doctrine of inspiration seem to be urgently required.[58] There are two points that seem to be of special importance in relation to the problem of infallibility; there should really be agreement on them among Catholic, Orthodox and Protestant Christians:

1. God himself acts with us and on us through the human word of Scripture in so far as he thereby moves us to faith and causes the words of man in proclamation to be the instrument of his Spirit; behind all the mythological ideas and often misleading concepts associated with it, that is the real truth in the theory of inspiration.

2. At the same time the Scriptures are completely human documents, written by human authors with their human gifts and limitations, their human potentialities both for knowledge and for error, with the consequence that errors of the most varied kind cannot *a priori* be excluded; this should be the real limitation of the theory of inspiration in all positive statements about the workings of the Spirit.

But how are these two points to be reconciled? Just as in the Church, which is composed of men, so too in the Bible, which was composed by men, God gains his end, without doing any violence to man, through human weakness and historicity. Through all the human frailty and the historical conditioning and limitations of the authors of the books of the Bible, who are often able to speak only stammeringly and with inadequate conceptual means, it comes about that God's call, as it was finally sounded aloud in Jesus, is truthfully heard, believed and realized.

Just as it is wrong in the case of the Church to link the work of the Spirit of God (in the sense of *assistentia*) with any particular definitions by a Pope or council, so is it wrong in the case of Scripture to restrict the working of the Spirit of God (in the sense of *inspiratio*) to any particular statement by an apostle or biblical author. The truth is rather that the whole process, the origin, collection and transmission of the word, the acceptance in faith and further proclamation of the message, is under the guidance and control of the Spirit. In this sense not only the history of the writing of the Scriptures, but the whole of their prehistory and subsequent history is 'inspired' by the Spirit; not dictated by it, but soaked and filled with it. Thus the Bible is not a miraculous book like the Koran, a sacred, error-free book, containing innumerable in-

fallible propositions, directly revealed by Heaven to the
Prophet (through angels), that therefore has to be accepted
literally and consequently may not be interpreted or commented on. Before touching the Bible one does not have to
wash one's hands. Nowhere do the books of the New Testament
claim to have fallen directly from heaven; on the contrary,
often enough they quite candidly emphasize their human origin
(Luke 1–2 is especially revealing on the origin of the Gospels).
And though the witnesses know they are moved by the Holy
Spirit, the listener or reader is not called on to recognize the
presence of any act of inspiration, but it is simply assumed that
proclamation and acceptance of the gospel takes place 'through
the Holy Spirit' (1 Peter 1:12; cf. 1 Corinthians 7:40).

Thus the revelation of the Old and New Testaments cannot
be simply identified with Scripture. Scripture is not revelation;
it attests it. Here God is only indirectly and covertly at work.
Only in faith is the proclaimed gospel known and felt to be in
truth God's own word to men (cf. 1 Thessalonians 2:13). Thus
the humanity, individuality and historicity of the authors of the
Bible is fully preserved. Never at any time are they turned into
unerring, almost superhuman but fundamentally inhuman
tools, inhuman because without choice or responsibility. The
working of the Holy Spirit excludes neither defects nor errors,
neither concealment nor dilution of the truth, neither human
limitations nor human fallibility. The witness of the New
Testament, though all of it proclaims the God who acts on us
through Jesus Christ, is not of equal and uniform value throughout; there is brighter and darker, clearer and less clear,
stronger and weaker, first-hand and second-hand witness. All
in all, it is very diverse and multiform, liable to divergency,
contrast, and even sometimes to contradicting itself.

Thus in Scripture we are confronted with the work of the
Spirit within unqualified human historicity. This not only
makes biblical criticism possible, but actually calls for textual
and literary, historical and theological criticism. Serious
biblical criticism can only help to prevent the glad tidings
from remaining enclosed in a book and to ensure that it will
always be vividly proclaimed anew. This message can and
should of course never be simply handed down in the form
linked with a particular age. The first witnesses remain

fundamental. But the gospel was not dictated to them in fixed forms of words or rigid doctrine, nor did they slavishly transmit it in that way. Rather, they accepted it in their particular place with their special peculiarities and proclaimed it in the light of their own interpretation and theology. In the same way the present-day proclaimers of the gospel should pass it on in new form in their place, in their time, in their way. Scripture certainly is and remains the record, acknowledged by the Church, of the original testimony. As such it has a permanent normative authority and significance that cannot be displaced by any later testimony; it remains the standard by which all later Church proclamation and theology must constantly be measured. But the freedom, multiplicity and diversity of the testimony at that time justify the freedom, multiplicity and diversity of the testimony of the present day, the unifying simplicity of which lies in the message of man's salvation through Jesus Christ.

What do we really believe in? What is the real basis of Christian faith? Is it the Church or the Bible? It is neither, for that is a false alternative. The ground of faith is God himself in Jesus Christ; it is thus Jesus Christ himself who is attested in the Bible and is constantly proclaimed anew by the Church. The Christian does not believe in the Church, or in the Bible; he believes in God, in Jesus Christ. He believes, not in the Gospels, but in the gospel and in him who speaks through it. Thus Jesus Christ remains the Lord also of Scripture; as the source and yardstick of its authority, he is the ultimate authority in matters of faith and theology. It is he who is the spiritual power of Scripture, with the result that the latter, notwithstanding all biblical criticism, as the history of exegesis shows, constantly asserts and gains recognition of its truth anew. Thus I do not, for instance, first believe in Scripture or in the inspiration of the book, and then in the truth of the gospel, in Jesus Christ. I believe in the Jesus Christ who was originally attested in Scripture and, by thus experiencing Scripture as gospel in faith, I see how filled and permeated with the Spirit Scripture is. My faith in Jesus Christ originates in Scripture, because Scripture testifies to Jesus, but it is not based on Scripture; Jesus Christ, not an inspired book, is the ground of faith.

Is infallibility, then, to be attributed to the Church or to the Bible? It is to be attributed to neither, but to God alone and to his Word, which became flesh in Jesus Christ; and to the gospel message as such, which is the unerringly true testimony to the plan of salvation. Scripture – to Christians primarily the New Testament, but also the Old Testament as its prehistory – is the written record of that originally unerring testimony; in itself it is not infallible, but in spite of all its human and only-too-human weaknesses, imperfections and errors it announces 'the truth' of the gospel, which is Jesus Christ himself. Just as scientific and historical errors in a Shakespearean historical play can sometimes help rather than hinder understanding of the play's import and purpose, so may the scientific and historical errors in the Bible help us in the same way; though God, quite unlike Shakespeare, writes straight even on crooked lines. Taking the account of creation in Genesis 1 as a literal and infallible statement of truth caused the great message of the first page of Scripture to be frequently overlooked. Now that we have given up surrounding every sentence of that chapter with an apologetic gloss, seeking to establish a false harmony with scientific facts and juggling with unscientific ideas, we can see with new eyes what the passage is really about. The same applies to the reference to original sin in Genesis 3, the conflicting traditions about the Resurrection, and the mythical descriptions of the end of man's history.

Just as there is no inherently infallible teaching office, so is there no inherently infallible teaching book in Christendom. The Church as the community of the faithful cannot make infallible propositions, but possesses a fundamental indefectibility in the truth. Scripture, as the record of the original faith in Christ, possesses no inherent freedom from error in framing propositions, which in no way detracts from its unique pre-eminence in the faith of Christians. On the contrary, the impact it makes comes from him whom it announces. Because it speaks of him, it exercises a living authority (its power of truth) by virtue of its content, and this authority continually overwhelms faith anew. To him who proclaims its message and to him who hears it at vital moments it is always freshly clear and accessible (its perspicuity). It provokes assent and renunciation and thus, in a completely unmagical and intangible way, it works (its efficacy). And God's work of salvation through Jesus enables us to see its unity. Looked at in this way, this basic testimony to the original Christian faith for the whole of Christendom at all times seems, not to diminish, but to grow in significance.

It is in this comprehensive but qualified sense that we can speak of the truth of Scripture, not attributing any inherent inerrancy to its propositions, but regarding it, in spite of all minor defects, as broadly true and faithful testimony to Jesus Christ. Even though there are no inherently inerrant propositions in the Bible, it nevertheless contains true propositions attesting the gospel. Thus the truth of Scripture means more than mere truth as *adaequatio intellectus et rei*, the philosophical definition of truth, made in the light of Greek philosophy, that has been accepted since the Middle Ages. The more modern doctrine of inerrancy, like the orthodox Protestant doctrine of inspiration, is a product of the rationalism that sought to make the divinity of Scripture clear, distinct, obvious and manifest in its propositions, which was bound sooner or later to turn into a domination of reason over Scripture.

In the last resort the truth of Scripture, over and above all true propositions, means truth as the term is used in the Old and New Testament. In this sense truth (*emet, alétheia*) means, over and above the truth of words and sentences, loyalty, constancy, reliability; that is the loyalty to his word and to his promise of the God of the Covenant. There is not a passage in Scripture that speaks of its inerrancy. But every passage in Scripture bears witness in its immediate or wider context to the truth of God, who never deceives, remains true to himself and his word, and thus also to men, and finally fulfilled his word in him who is 'the Word' and 'the truth' (John 1:1 ff.; 14:6). In this sense Scripture, which is not inerrant, testifies to the everlasting truth of God, who cannot deceive or be deceived. It thus testifies to the infallibility of God himself.

II. A TEACHING OFFICE?

As we have seen, there is no basis in theology for infallible propositions in Scripture, or by councils, bishops or the Pope. What, then, is a teaching office for? We shall put forward only a few points for discussion on this broad and complex question. As we approach the end of our survey it is perhaps as well to repeat that the whole of it is meant to be open to discussion, to dialogue. As the subtitle clearly indicates, it is to be regarded as an enquiry. An enquiry takes place when a question has arisen that calls urgently for an answer. Anyone who has a better answer than he who raised the question will not keep it back. He who has no, or no better, answer will not dispute the validity of the question.

A. The expression 'teaching office' is much used in the Catholic Church today, and it is referred to on all sorts of occasions. But the 'teaching office' is a relatively recently introduced and unclarified concept.

1. Its modernity.[59] 'The teaching office' in the modern sense – the college of prelates who possess public teaching authority – assumes the distinction between the Church teaching (*Ecclesia docens*) and the Church taught (*Ecclesia discens*). For all the frequency with which it is used today, this distinction was introduced only in the modern age, at the end of the seventeenth and the beginning of the eighteenth century, significantly enough in connection with the distinction of which we are already aware between active infallibility (of the Pope or the bishops as the case may be) and passive infallibility (of the Church, or of the faithful). But it was only after the beginning of the nineteenth century that the distinction between the Church teaching and the Church taught began to occur more frequently. Soon, however, it became current in theological discussion; and one who played a big part in this was G. Perrone, the Roman Jesuit who was one of the theological 'fathers' of the definitions of the Immaculate Conception and of papal infallibility. The term *magisterium* in its modern ecclesiastical technical sense appears frequently in the debates and documents of Vatican I: 'It has the meaning sometimes of teaching, sometimes of the teaching function and competence to teach, and finally sometimes – and this is new – of the body of prelates who possess public teaching authority: the teaching office.'[60]

Thus it is clear that the term has no basis either in Scripture or in older tradition, but was a modern introduction in connection with the doctrine of infallibility of Vatican I and the distinction between the Church teaching and the Church taught which we have already criticized because in this exclusive sense it is completely unscriptural.

2. Its obscurity. The Latin *magisterium* corresponds to the Greek *hegemonia* (leadership) and *didaskalia* (teaching). The Latin *magisterium* also frequently has associations with *magistratus*. This is completely echoed in the modern ecclesiastical sense of *magisterium*: the bishops, who are the leaders of the Church, are consequently also regarded as its teachers. At the same time it is also apparently taken for granted that teaching should take place through an office or authority ('teaching office' as a kind of parallel to 'Foreign Office').

But this also raises the question whether it is really obvious that there should be a teaching office in the Church in the form of an authority, that the bishops and the Roman Pontiff in particular should combine in their persons the functions of both leading the Church and teaching it. It will not be disputed that the bishops – though in this respect they are not dogmatically distinguished from the presbyters – are leaders of the Church. But it is not equally certain that they are also its teachers, and still less, as textbook theology claims, that they are the sole authentic teachers in their dioceses and, together with the Pope, in the universal Church. Our previous observations[61] about the apostolic succession of the bishops, and the Bishop of Rome in particular, suggest doubts about this. But let us take a closer look.

B. At this point we must consider the basic question of who can and should teach the Church. It depends on what is meant by 'teach'. If by 'teaching' is meant the proclaiming of the message that is always fundamental for the Church in small things as in great, the answer must be that every member of the Church, every Christian, may and should proclaim it.[62] In this respect there is no distinction between the Church teaching and the Church taught.

Testifying to the word is the duty of the universal priesthood (cf. Hebrews 13:15). Its proclamation of the word is entrusted not only to a few but to all: 'But you are . . . a royal priesthood . . . to sing the praises of God who called you out of the darkness into his wonderful light' (1 Peter 2:9; cf. 3:15). The reference to darkness and light recalls the saying of Jesus in

Matthew 5:14, which is likewise addressed to all believers: 'You are the light of the world.' Therefore 'what I say to you in the dark, tell in the daylight; what you hear in whispers, proclaim from the housetops' (Matthew 10:27). The proclamation of the message is the primary task entrusted by Jesus to all his disciples (Mark 1:35–8; 16:15; Matthew 28:18–20; Acts 1:8; 1 Corinthians 1:17). Hence the abundance of terms in the New Testament – about thirty altogether – referring to preaching and proclamation: proclaim, call, preach, teach, declare, expound, speak, say, testify, persuade, confess, charge, exhort, reprove . . . The variety of forms of proclamation permits each and every one to make his particular contribution.

It is the word that creates and constantly assembles the Church anew by rousing faith and obedience; the word must constantly go out afresh (cf. Romans 10:14–17). Believers, being those 'called' by the word (Romans 1:6; 1 Corinthians 1:24; Hebrews 9:15), should concern themselves with it. All must not only hear the word of the apostles, bear witness in deed before the world and pray for the success of the proclamation of the word (cf. 2 Thessalonians 3:1), but proclaim the message themselves, even take up the word at divine worship, according to the charism granted to each individual: 'At all your meetings, let everyone be ready with a psalm or a sermon or a revelation, or ready to use his gift of tongues or to give an interpretation; but it must always be for the common good' (1 Corinthians 14:26). By the very fact that all believers have the right and privilege of the word in any form, together they bear powerful witness to the faith that is also capable of conquering unbelievers (cf. 1 Corinthians 14:24–5).

The Christian message spread so rapidly from the outset only because it was proclaimed, not just by a few missionaries with a special mandate, but by all, each according to his gifts and opportunities; not only by apostles and evangelists, but also by traders, soldiers and seamen . . . The Acts of the Apostles lays emphasis on the fact that 'they were all filled with the Holy Spirit and began to proclaim the word of God boldly' (4:31; cf. 8:4; 11:19). St Paul several times corroborates this (cf. 1 Thessalonians 1:18; Philippians 1:12–18). When he bade women keep silent in the congregation (1 Corinthians 14:33–5; cf. 1 Timothy 2:12), this must be understood in the context of its time and not as a principle for all eternity. According to Hebrews 5:12, Christians should be given, not just milk, but solid food if they are not to remain in the initial stages of Christian faith, but are themselves to be teachers.

In 1 Thessalonians 4:9 St Paul says that the faithful 'have learnt from God', and this idea is stated much more strongly in the First Epistle of John. 'Anointing' by the Holy Spirit gives true Christians complete knowledge of everything vital to salvation: 'You have all received the knowledge' (1 John 2:20; cf. John 14:26; an alternative reading is 'you have received all knowledge'). And, since the Spirit remains in the faithful, they are told: 'You do not need anyone to teach you' (1 John 2:27; cf. 2:21). This does not mean that the faithful have no need of the witness handed down by men (cf. John 1:15; 2:17, 24; 3:11). But the Spirit is the force that works within them, independently of men, that gives them truly convincing teaching and ultimate certainty.

Thus it is plain that only someone who, over and above human testimony, is instructed by God, by the Holy Spirit, can authoritatively transmit the message. But the New Testament testifies that that is every Christian. Every believer, having been taught by God, can and should teach others; as recipient of the word of God, he can and should also be its proclaimer in one way or another.

Every Christian is thus called on to proclaim the word in the widest sense, even though, because of the diversity of gifts, by no means everyone can or should do everything. Here we must make at least a brief reference to lay preaching, which – as we have just seen – was perfectly normal in the very charismatic congregations of the first phase of Christendom, but in the second and particularly in the third century was pushed into the background by the preaching of office-holders.[63] But, in spite of all prohibitions, lay preaching continued to be practised and tolerated, and from the twelfth century onwards was actually again approved in the case of certain renewal movements. But the Council of Trent reserved preaching in the strict sense to the bishops and their assistants, and finally lay preaching was subjected to a general prohibition in the Code of Canon Law of 1918.

At the present time a suitably adapted and orderly renewal

of lay preaching is a pastoral necessity. Not only is it justified and desirable in principle in the light of the New Testament, but it is urgently called for by the present state of society (its declericalization, or alternatively, the maturation of a secular world) and of the Church (its lack of preachers on the one hand, the maturity of the laity on the other). Vatican II met this situation to the extent that the revised services that it introduced can be conducted by the laity. In this connection the sociological and psychological barriers that reserve preaching to the male sex must be overcome. There are no dogmatic objections to services conducted by women (radio and television should not be overlooked in this connection). There must be an end of the denigration of women in the Church, its law and its worship.

This certainly does not mean that any man or woman who feels like it should climb into the pulpit on Sunday. Though every Christian is called on to proclaim the word and bear Christian witness, and is thus entitled in principle to preach, that does not mean that he is called on to preach in that particular congregation; according to Paul, there is a diversity of gifts. And those who like 'preaching' at home and elsewhere are not always adapted to preaching in the pulpit. For preaching in the strict sense, the proclamation of the gospel to the assembled congregation, someone in the congregation must be *called*. Bishops and priests can and should gratefully acknowledge the charism for preaching granted to members of the laity and allow it to be used to good effect. If this were done, public lay preaching would take place with specific Church endorsement, and possibly also after some training had been given. It only remains to be pointed out that in the Protestant world (with the exception of the Methodists and the Free Church) lay preaching, like the universal priesthood, has remained largely theoretical. The Orthodox Churches also theoretically permit laymen to preach.

C. Even though every Christian is called to proclaim the word, and at any rate in principle is authorized to preach, is he thus also called on to teach in the proper, technical sense of being a teacher in the Church? Is the leader of the Church automatically also its teacher?

It is essential that any Church order inspired by the New

Testament should present us, not with a uniform ecclesiastical 'hierarchy' (the term, meaning 'sacred rule', was first introduced by the Pseudo-Dionysius in the fifth or sixth century), but with a multiform, diversified ecclesiastical *diakonia* ('service' in the ordinary, everyday, sense of the term); that there should be 'Church diversity in the diversity of its disciples, witnesses and servants (ministers)'.[64] The position of the 'pastors' or leaders of the Church – in the Church today these are normally bishops and presbyters – so far from being impaired by such biblical pluralism, would be strengthened by it.

As we have previously pointed out, it cannot be shown either exegetically or historically or theologically that the bishops are in the direct and exclusive sense that is often claimed for them the successors of the apostles (and still less of the college of the twelve); the modern order of three offices – bishops, presbyters and deacons – is a later historical development,[65] and in itself a perfectly reasonable one. The apostolic succession applies primarily to the universal *Ecclesia apostolica*, in as much as every Christian should strive for agreement with the fundamental apostolic testimony (Scripture, succession in apostolic faith and confession) and for connection with the apostolic service (missionary progress in the world and the building up of the Christian community, succession in apostolic service and life). But within the apostolic succession of the universal Church there is a special apostolic succession of Church leaders or pastors, in as much as without being apostles themselves they continue the special apostolic function of founding or leading Churches. As such they do not form a ruling group enjoying a unilateral power to command and entitled to blind obedience. Nevertheless, by reason of their special service, their ministry, they enjoy a special authority and, when they fulfil their service in the spirit of the gospel, they are entitled to count on co-operation and recognition of their authority.

It would certainly imply an unbiblical clericalization of the Church if we concluded that the service of leadership involved authority over the community, the universal priesthood. On the other hand, an equally unbiblical secularization of the Church would be implied by deducing the authority of the service of leadership from the authority of the community, the universal priesthood. According to the New Testam, entall authority in the Church comes from the Lord of the Church by virtue of the Spirit. Leaders and community therefore must be seen both in their inseparability and in their separateness. The general entitlement of each and every Christian to proclaim the word and take part in the sacraments is one thing; the special authority of individuals who are called – normally by the laying on of hands or ordination – to public service to the congregation by proclamation of the word, administration of the sacraments, many kinds of pastoral care for the members of the congregation, is another. For all the necessary criticism of the present leadership of the Catholic Church that we have frankly expressed, nothing we have said implies that Church leadership is not essential. It is not no Church leadership that we need, but Church leadership in accordance with the gospel. We do not need less authority, but more qualified authority: authority based on service, and capable of subordinating itself to the subordinate if the latter has the gospel and reason on its side. For its office-holders, the bishops and presbyters, are there for the Church; the Church is not there for them. Bishops and priests should not be appointed without the backing of their communities, and the whole of their conduct in office should have their backing and should also be subject to constant scrutiny. For all their relative independence, the leaders of the community should respect its right to a say in its affairs and should promote the active co-operation of all in every way.

A Church leadership is truly in accordance with the gospel only when it does not 'rule' with the aid of spiritual power and veiled force, the imposition of laws and the use of authoritarian methods, but leads the Church and the congregation with the helping, encouraging, exhorting and comforting word of the gospel. This holds good at all levels of Church leadership, and it applies in particular to the bishops. A bishop's primary duty (and the first call on his time) should not be travelling round conducting confirmation services, blessing church bells, attending ecclesiastical-secular functions of all kinds; all these things could either be done by others or are totally superfluous. A bishop's first task should be the proclamation of the gospel (which cannot be done by pastoral letters and confirmation sermons), and the practical consequence of this is the need to visit parishes and their priests to help and fortify them.

But an episcopal (or papal) teaching office? If by this is meant the proclamation of the gospel (which is possible in such diverse forms), there is nothing to be said against it and everything to be said for it. If that was what the teaching office did, the Church would have the spiritual guidance, the real leadership, that it sorely needs. But it would certainly be better to call it, not a teaching office, but an office of guidance or, better, a guidance service, or simply the Church leadership, for short.

But if what is meant by the episcopal (or papal) teaching office is not the proclamation of the gospel, but the official regulation of all teaching, with the result that the leaders of the Church are the sole authority for its teaching, thus becoming the teachers of the Church as well as its leaders, it must be pointed out that such restriction and monopolization of charisms, such channelling of them into a hierocracy of pastors, is in clear contradiction to the New Testament message and the New Testament Church. No one has the right to imagine himself the sole possessor of the Spirit and to curb or muffle the spiritual possession of others. 'Are all of them teachers?' (1 Corinthians 12:29). When a leader of the Church regards himself simultaneously as apostle, prophet and teacher, and so tries to be all things in one, he is absolutizing his ministry in completely unbiblical fashion, even if he should quote in his favour the triple role of Christ (royal, prophetic and priestly). Such a one-man system is foreign to the New Testament. Everyone has his own charism. One man has one gift, and another has another (cf. 1 Corinthians 7:7,17). No one, not even a bishop or a pope, can be everything, according to St Paul. 'Are all of them apostles, or all of them prophets, or all of them teachers?' (1 Corinthians 12: 29).

D. After the apostles and the prophets, the third group of those who continually and regularly exercise public charismatic functions in the congregation, according to St Paul, are the teachers (*didáskoloi, doctores*). While the apostles are the original witnesses and messengers of the living God, the prophets – who in Ephesians 2:20 together with the prophets are called the foundation of the Church – are those in whom the Spirit directly speaks and who, in a particular situation in the Church, aware of their vocation and responsibility, light the way in the present and future. The teachers are those who take endless pains about

the handing on, demonstration and correct interpretation of the
original Christian message. Both, prophets and teachers alike,
speak in the light of the original apostolic witness for the
present and future of the community. The prophet speaks more
intuitively, while the teacher develops his thoughts more
systematically and theologically.

In the present context it is not so important to analyse the
original function of the teacher – particularly in regard to the
interpretation of the Old Testament, the beliefs and injunctions
of the early Church. It is more important to note that, if we
rightly speak of succession to the apostles in the various pastoral
ministries, we have just as much right to speak of a succession to
the prophets and the teachers. In post-apostolic times teachers
turned out to be indispensable, though their position and status
– like those of the pastors – changed greatly. Only when there
were not enough prophets and teachers in the congregation,
according to the Didache, was it to choose bishops and deacons
to 'minister unto you the ministry (*leitourgia*, or the Eucharist)
of the prophets and teachers' (15:1). 'So there would seem to be
justification for enquiring in the light of Scripture whether an
unbiblical structural displacement did not take place in a
Church that seems to attach supreme value to a succession of
bishops, but does not mention any successors to or a permanent
class of charismatic teachers.'[66]

Here the author can reiterate a point that he systematically
developed elsewhere.[67] What becomes of a Church in which the
teachers are silent? The question will be better understood if, in
accordance with present-day terminology, we speak of theologians instead of teachers. What becomes of a Church in which
scholarly reflection on and interpretation of the original
Christian message, the true transmission, the true translation of
that message into the terms of the present day, have ceased? A
Church in which theologians had to be silent would become an
untruthful Church. Its teaching might be very correct and
unchanged and conscientiously handed on. Its faith might seem
secure from doubt, and its teaching might seem to present no
serious problems. Yet it would often be evading men's real
problems, and would fail to notice that it was bogged down in
an outdated theological system, that it was handing on superannuated ideas and the empty husks of traditional concepts as

truth, and that both in teaching and in life it had departed from the original message. Meanwhile the leaders who did not want to listen to the theologians in the Church, having little interest or time for well based theology because, perhaps through fear, they did not want to be disturbed in their faith, or naïvely believed that they already knew everything that mattered – those leaders would in their ignorance the more confidently seek to impose their personal teaching as the teaching of the Church, confuse their antiquated ideas with the genuine tradition, close their minds to learning anything and, though unqualified themselves, claim the privilege of judging the qualified. Then, though gifts are diverse, they would claim to be successors, not only of the apostles, but also of the teachers. There can be pastors who are also teachers but, according to St Paul, they are the exceptions rather than the rule.

But how fruitful it can be for them and for the Church if they listen – as the best of them have always done – to the theologians who try to help the Church by critical examination of current teaching and by reference to the original message; who exercise their theological skill, not for their own sake, but for humanity, the Church and the world; who by critical examination of the Church's proclamation in the light of the gospel are out, not to destroy, but to build, to stimulate and to lead the way to better proclamation and action. By raising the question of truth in the light of the original message, theology performs an immense service to those responsible for preaching, instruction and pastoral care. It helps them and the Church to distinguish, in the light of its own origins, the great, the genuine, the abiding, the true tradition from all that has been handed down with it, the traditional falsities and pettinesses in teaching and life, so that the message may again be seen in all its purity and so passed on. In the light of that message, continually thought out anew with the aid of all the resources of scholarship and research, theology is able to lay its hands again on the Church's mislaid keys and reopen locks grown rusty in the course of centuries, thus paving the way to renewal, to truer teaching in accordance with the gospel. What would the Church be without Origen, St Augustine, St Thomas Aquinas, or Luther and Calvin, or the many great and small teachers of the Church? The Church has never been without its teachers. St Paul believed that every congregation had its teacher. And when there is willingness in the Church to listen to its teachers, the teachers will speak. Here too the spirit must not be quenched, but allowed to express itself.

We have been talking about true prophets and good teachers. There are also false prophets and bad teachers, false prophecy and sterile theology. Prophets and teachers, like leaders, must be scrutinized by the whole congregation to make sure they are what they are supposed to be: providers of an unpretentious but courageous, modest but resolute, dedicated but free service that can constantly help the Church to new alertness, new preparedness, new vitality. In their grave and responsible pastoral duties, which neither prophets nor teachers can take from them because of the service that they provide, the leaders of the Church are not alone. They have the support of reciprocal service.

E. Pastors and teachers in the Church, leaders and theologians, each have their own charism, their own vocation, their own function. The service of leadership and the service of teaching must be regarded functionally; not as hypostatized and also in fact largely bureaucratically anonymous 'offices' primarily interested in maintaining their own power and authority, but as different though interdependent services working in the same field and with the same purpose, and manned by believers endowed with different gifts.

In recent times a number of popes – not including John XXIII – have repeatedly tried to reserve to themselves (and, when it suited them, also to the bishops) the exclusive absolutist privilege of 'authentically' explaining the 'deposit of faith'.[68] Here there is no need to repeat the instances we quoted that show sufficiently that the teaching authority that declared itself to be juridically authentic only too often turned out in practice to be inauthentic. After all that we have said in the course of this book, it is clear that it is not only to the Pope and bishops that the Holy Spirit is authentically granted for the salvation of the Church, that the Church is not identical with its leaders, that the truth of the Christian faith is not 'deposited' in Roman offices and episcopal chanceries, and that the 'authentic' proclamation and explanation of the Christian message is not 'reserved' to anyone. The Spirit of God bloweth where it listeth, it is greater than the Church, and the Church is greater than its leadership.

In the light of the original Christian message, and also in the light of the oldest and best tradition of the Catholic Church, which in the Middle Ages still left the 'teaching office' to the theologians (in practice, though not always fortunately, the Sorbonne), there can be no question of the Church leadership (in the guise of the 'teaching office') taking the place of the gospel as the standard of truth for theology and theologians. There can be no question of the leaders of the Church instead of the Lord of the Church exercising authority over them (and doing so, moreover, in the form of an Inquisition exercising juridical supervision and scorning human rights). There can be no question of theologians being able to practise theology only as delegates of the Church leaders, which – as experience has shown – necessarily leads to a juridicization of doctrine at the cost of freedom and its codification at the expense of scholarship. And thus there can be no question of theology in the Church contenting itself with a privacy convenient to the Church leadership and leaving to the latter the field of publicity and official action. Still less can there be any question of its doing what Pius IX, for instance, wanted, that is, seeing its 'most noble task' in seeking out documentation for the definitions of the 'teaching office'.

After so many unhappy experiences right down to the most recent past, there can be no more evasion on this point if things are to improve. We can only applaud Max Seckler's clear exposition of the dilemma involved in the Roman conception of theological scholarship and the 'teaching office', which he subjected to careful analysis. 'On the one hand,' he writes, 'there is a Church office enjoying absolute autonomy, sovereignty and self-sufficiency, that by virtue of these characteristics regards itself as the "office for teaching" and claims direct access to God, to the Spirit, to truth. On the other, we have the picture of a theology that is a creature of the hierarchy, bound in conscience, regulated in its thinking, supervised in the lecture-room, regulated in its speech, exposed to disciplinary measures of every kind, and able to earn love and respect only by subjecting itself to the will of the sovereign "in whom it lives, moves and has its being". Are these structures willed by God? It may be objected that things are not as bad as that, that the theologians are not so nervous and the dangers not so great. That is certainly true. The reality is largely different. But is not the real dilemma that the redeeming features of all this, the *clementia Caesaris* on the one hand and the scholarly conscience of the theologians on the other, present themselves, so to speak, in the wan light of the abnormal? For the sake of the service that it has to perform in the Church and for the Church, theology will have to come to grips with this pattern of things. In the first place the degree of theological binding force possessed by this imposing structure will have to be clarified by historical, canonical and systematic studies. Since the events connected with *Humanae Vitae*, but not only for that reason, these tasks have acquired a special urgency.'[69]

We hope that in this book we have made a critical and constructive contribution to the clarification of this question. But a theoretical clarification is only one aspect of the problem, as is shown by the now celebrated declaration on the freedom of theology addressed to the Roman authorities, first by 40 and then by 1,360 professors of theology all over the world, who introduced their concrete proposals for the reform of the Roman supervision of doctrine and supervisory practices in general in the following words: 'In complete, genuine and unambiguous loyalty to the Catholic Church, the undersigned theologians feel compelled in real and sober earnest to point out publicly: the freedom of theologians and theology in the service of the Church, regained by Vatican II, must not now be jeopardized again. This freedom is one of the fruits and exigencies of the liberating and redeeming message of Jesus himself, and remains a fundamental and essential aspect of the freedom of the sons of God in the Church, as preached and defended by Paul. All the teachers in the Church must therefore preach and proclaim the word, pressing it home on all occasions, convenient, welcome or unwelcome.'[70]

There is no need to dwell on the fact that all that we have said here about theology and theologians in the Catholic Church at the present day applies to lay as well as to clerical theologians. The Church leadership nowadays recognizes the theology of members of the laity, both men and women, though still with many reservations (particularly in regard to the theological colleges). Here we need only point out that most of the great early Christian theologians were laymen: Justin, Tertullian, Clement of Alexandria, Origen, and many more in later years. Many theologians began their theological work as laymen (and a number had ordination pressed upon them against their will): Cyprian, Basil, Gregory of Nazianzus, Jerome, Augustine, Paulinus of Nola, Diodore of Tarsus. Lay theology never wholly died out in the Church, but it was only in the present century, particularly in connection with the Second Vatican Council, that it again became a widespread phenomenon, with the result that the medieval clerical monopoly of education in this field can now be regarded as outdated. The obvious consequence of this development should be open access in principle to all teaching positions in theological faculties for lay theologians – men and women – equipped with appropriate academic qualifications. But in theology as elsewhere everyone should not assume that the field is open to him to do what he likes in the Church. Theologians are not born, but made by hard work. But here too charisms are granted that must be acknowledged and made use of; one of the most gratifying effects of the Church's renewal is the lay theology of our time.

F. Our criticism of the unhappy relations between leadership and teaching in the Church has been so outspoken only in order to clear the way for positive co-operation. In the Catholic Church today everything depends on the trusting co-operation to which we referred earlier. Should that really be so difficult to attain?

Leaders and teachers in the Church certainly each have their specific task; that of the bishops and priests is leadership, that of the theologians scholarship. But the two are not on different fronts; a class-war ideology would be totally inappropriate. Both take their stand on the same gospel of Jesus Christ, and their common purpose is to bring it home to men. The task of the former is leadership by proclamation of the word; that of the latter scholarly investigation of it. Leaders should not try to act as theologians by involving themselves in the complex problems of theology, and theologians should not try to play the bishop by deciding the difficult problems of Church leadership. Both sides have every reason to listen to, inform, criticize, inspire each other. Not only do both take their stand on one and the same gospel and serve the same Lord, but the efforts of both are directed to the same humanity with its cares and hopes, the countless 'poor devils' of all kinds in the world (who are the 'poor' of the New Testament). The leaders and teachers of the Church exist for them; the former to do their work by spiritual guidance, the latter by spiritual learning, both in the same Spirit. It helps the theorist to be told the cares and wishes of the practical man, and it helps the practical man if he can make fruitful the insights and visions of the theorist. Nowhere is dialogue more necessary in the Church than it is here.

It is for man that the Sabbath exists, as well as all prohibitions and commandments, institutions and constitutions, all power of leadership and scholarship, and it is also for the sake of man if in case of need the one takes over the functions of the other; if the Church leaders have to speak and act for the theologians, or the theologians for the Church leaders.

A theological emergency exists if the theologians can no longer cope with their problems, if as a result of hopeless theological confusion and hopeless theological muddle-headedness the proclamation of the gospel practically ceases, heresy shakes the Church to its foundations and perhaps combines with a political system, and the very life of the Church of the gospel is at stake. In such circumstances a *status confessionis* exists, and the leaders of the Church cannot be content to look on. They will then meet and – certainly in co-operation with all theologians of good will – say clearly, trusting in God's Spirit, what is the Christian faith and what is not. That happened repeatedly in the past, and it may happen again in the future. In such a crisis, *in extremis* and only *in extremis*, resort is had, not to endless discussion, but to resolute but unpretentious definition in the service of faith and the faithful. Such definition, as we have explained at length, is both binding on the Church and provisional, being related to a specific situation, and is made in full awareness that *nemo infallibilis nisi Deus ipse*, no one is infallible but God himself.

An emergency of the Church leadership exists if the leaders of the Church can no longer cope with their problems, if their eyes are closed, whether through nervousness or indolence, ignorance or arrogance, to crushing human problems, if they will not or cannot see, if by passivity or aggressivity they endanger the unity of the Church, block the way to renewal and try to restore the past, if the gospel and humanity are betrayed or forgotten, if the life of the Church of the gospel is therefore at stake. In such circumstances a *status confessionis* exists for the theologian, and he cannot be silent or withdraw into his esoteric science. He must speak out loud and clear, whether what he has to say is welcome or unwelcome, without respect for persons, however highly placed. He must bear witness for the sake of the gospel and humanity, must state the truth and not shrink from practical intervention, in a spirit of modesty and objectivity and full awareness that no one is infallible but God himself.

We have now closed the circle of our reflections and can return with deeper understanding to what was said in the Foreword.

Document I

THE NEW STATE OF THE DEBATE
ON INFALLIBILITY (1979)

Can a great public question be laid to rest before it has been answered? The old infallibility of the kings, emperors and czars ruling by the grace of God has long ceased to be an issue. And the more recent infallibility of the autocrats and dictators ruling by their own power, the Duces, Führers, Caudillos, General Secretaries, etc., has crumbled after a Second World War, Auschwitz, the Gulag Archipelago, democratization in Spain and the beginnings of a dethronement of Chairman Mao in China. However, the question of the infallibility of *parties*, which 'are always right', and their present representatives is still being suppressed – from Moscow to Havana – with every means of oppression and repression. And – many people then go on to ask – what about the infallibility of *churches*, which 'are always right'? What about their former or present representatives who appeal to the Holy Spirit? No, at least one thing, quite apart from all the other differences, has become clear: since the Second Vatican Council the question of this infallibility can no longer be simply suppressed, even in the Catholic Church.

At the centenary celebrations of the definition of papal infallibility by the First Vatican Council in 1870 the widespread, vague question of infallibility had taken the form of a precisely formulated 'enquiry': *Infallible? An Enquiry* (1970) was something like a parliamentary question put by His Majesty's Loyal Opposition in a free commonwealth. The Roman Congregation of Faith attempted with the help of the conferences of bishops to silence it by a decretal, since it had become such a live issue, and end the discussion once and for all. But this question, though condemned to death, would not lie down, and discussion in the community of faith has not ceased.

Even the unprejudiced among Roman observers surely did not expect that the question of *'Infallible?'* could still be given a definite answer in our generation by the repetition of conciliar decisions, the infallibility of which was questionable from the

start and which was now again being put in question. The kings
and generals, the fathers, teachers and often also professors had
earlier made similar attempts to rescue their own infallibility
once it had been put in question: we are infallible, because we
have said that we are infallible!

But there was always the unavoidable retort: with what right
did you, did your forebears, say that you are infallible? And
even more in the Church: what right do you have to claim the
infallibility of the holy Spirit of God which blows where and
how it wills, you who are human beings and not God? Is it not
also human for you to err? Or has God somewhere promised
you his own infallibility? That needs to be proved beyond all
ambiguity! The men of the Bible and of the New Testament
Church – beginning with Peter, the 'rock' – do not give us the
impression of being infallible. The cock did not crow only for
Peter – who once called the Lord 'Satan' and three times denied
him; who also proved himself fallible after Easter and even
more so in Antioch in his dispute with Paul. Moreover for long
decades there was no talk of any infallibility of the Bishop of
Rome (or at first even of ecumenical councils), so that on close
inspection it must seem to historians that infallibility is an
innovation of the second millennium, indeed basically of the
last century. What, then, is the foundation for the infallibility of
Pope and councils in scripture and early Catholic tradition?

Or are we not allowed to ask that at all? Is merely to ask the
question a sin, and to make an enquiry a mortal sin? No, after
the understandable first shock, people in Rome cannot seriously mean that. That would be a sign of anxiety – even more, it
would provoke the child's question about the emperor's new
clothes. No, in a Church which has nothing to fear from the
truth, which has no more to fear than the untruth which claims
to be the 'pillar and foundation of the truth'; in such a Church
there must be a vital interest in not 'keeping down' the truth but
constantly making it 'manifest' once again. Too much is at
stake here for silence to be permissible in the long term. For is it
not the problem of infallibility which is still, as before, blocking
renewal over wide areas of Catholicism? Does not the doctrine
of infallibility represent the most serious obstacle to ecumenical
understanding? Is it not the claim to infallibility which makes
the Catholic Church, despite all its indisputably positive

contributions and its far greater possibilities in present-day society, look increasingly inefficient and lack credibility? Poverty and underdevelopment in the Third World – the population explosion – birth control – the encyclical *Humanae vitae* – the infallibility of traditional church teaching: all this is now so closely connected that those who shout so loudly at the outside world should shout even more loudly inside the Church, instead of remaining silent on this question.

Certainly, anyone who has said and repeated unmistakably what needs to be said on such a question need not constantly keep on talking. Particularly in a heated atmosphere, that could be more a hindrance than a help to self-criticism and practical reflection – on both sides! A constant readiness for discussion is as necessary as careful consideration of those involved – all without compromises over the substance of the matter. Criticism and self-criticism are always to be expected. But no 'cease-fire agreement' can be struck on such a fundamental question, nor has it ever been. Not only because the Roman Congregation of Faith has so far never acceded to such action in 'partnership', but also because in the long run the enquirers would be committing themselves to a silence which went against their consciences, against the freedom of scientific research and against the true interests of the Church and its leaders.

Indeed the Catholic Church and its leaders should not regard an investigation and examination of this question as an attack from outside, but as help from within. After all, the Catholic Church and its leaders have the greatest interest in seeing:

that the deideologizing of the absolutist and authoritarian magisterium which began with John XXIII and Vatican II is brought to a conclusion in favour of an authentically spiritual authority, so that the Church is finally rid of all the arrogance, compulsion and indeed dishonesty of curialist theology and administration;

that the consequences of the new beginnings of Vatican II are consciously drawn: under John XXIII this council deliberately avoided infallible definitions, and in the face of traditional dogmatism called for a constructive form of Christian pro-clamation today, which to some degree is also put into practice;

that the historicity of the truth and its formulation should be recognized in the Church, thus making possible a better foundation for Christian faith, taking further the contemporary renewal of the Catholic Church, and in all this helping the cause of Jesus Christ once more to break through in a 'church' system which often contradicts the message of the one to whom it appeals.

Happily, as was shown as early as 1973 in a survey which has yet to be refuted (H. Küng, *Fehlbar? Ein Bilanz*, Zürich, Einsiedeln and Cologne), the most recent phase of the debate on infallibility has already made a number of things clear:

1. *The justification of the enquiry.* Both those engaged in this critical enquiry and the Roman authorities are agreed that the inconvenient texts of Vatican I and II are to be taken literally. The original sense of these texts must not be toned down and trivialized, as for obvious reasons Catholic theologians have constantly attempted to do, up until most recent times. Opportunistic reinterpretation to the point of contradiction instead of precise interpretation – as is usual in all authoritarian systems – simply conceals the problem, offends against intellectual honesty and delays a comprehensive solution. If the texts on infallibility are taken on the basis of modern scholarship as they were originally meant, they pose an even greater challenge to all Catholics than they did a century ago. A theological ostrich policy leads nowhere, and theological enlightenment is as unavoidable here as it once was in the Galileo question. Catholic faith must not degenerate into the faith of the charcoal burner who believes only because this is what the priest has told him. Here there is a need to examine more than the infallibility (the 'extraordinary' infallibility) of the Pope who is making the definition ('how the Pope became infallible'). There is another question which was already too much neglected by the anti-infallibilist minority at Vatican I, namely the infallibility (also 'extraordinary') of the whole episcopate dispersed through the world, which even after Vatican II is said to be infallible if bishops and the Pope are unanimous in teaching that a particular doctrine of faith or morals (for example the immorality of 'artificial' means of birth control) is definitively binding. So the question of the unanimity of the teaching of Pope and bishops, crucial for *Humanae*

vitae, which is guaranteed even without an explicit definition of infallibility (Vatican II: 'in this way they infallibly proclaim the teaching of Christ'!) proved and constantly proves to be a catalyst which does not allow the question of infallibility to rest. Traditionally inclined theologians often see these connections more clearly than the so-called 'progressives'. However, as a result, perplexity over the infallibility of this everyday, 'ordinary' magisterium emerges even more clearly.

2. *The present Catholic consensus.* A fundamental agreement is emerging on three important points:

(*a*) That the magisterium can err is a fact: in Catholic theology today it is being conceded with an openness which was previously unaccustomed that even the organs of 'infallible' doctrinal decisions can err at least in principle (though perhaps not in certain well-defined situations) and often have erred. 'No one who looks objectively at the history of the Church can deny that the Church as a whole and also those authorities in it which in accordance with their self-understanding are regarded as organs of infallible doctrinal decisions, namely the Pope and the ecumenical councils, and the whole episcopate in the everyday practice of the proclamation of faith as this is done in unison, have often enough in the course of history proclaimed errors' (O. Semmelroth).

(*b*) Scepticism is appropriate in the face of the concept and praxis of infallibility: even conservative theologians think that the term is open to misunderstanding and indeed is largely incomprehensible today. There is no mistaking the fact that since the most recent debate, the term 'infallible' has largely disappeared from theological terminology and even from the official language of the Church. No one today wants infallible definitions any longer, either to cultivate piety or to clarify the complex problems of today. Certainly infallibility of the Pope would not be defined today had it not already been defined earlier. The structures of plausibility for the definitions of Vatican I, the political, social, cultural and theological presuppositions which already existed in the nineteenth century, no longer exist today, so that the Catholic people is left only with the definition itself, and in practice neither ordinary believers nor theologians nor the Popes themselves know what to make of it. There are often complaints about the 'exaggerations' and 'misuses' of the papal magisterium in the past centuries. However, people are less ready to concede that the negative developments in the Vatican definitions have themselves contributed towards this. But the line from Pius XI and Vatican I through the anti-Modernist campaign under Pius X to the *Humani generis* purge under Pius XII can no longer be overlooked. This 'Pian' era of more recent church history ended with John XXIII.

(*c*) The Church continues to be maintained in truth despite all errors: even for the conservative defenders of infallible statements, the indefectibility of the Church in the truth is more fundamental than the infallibility of particular statements. And since there is no disputing errors by the Church's magisterium generally, at least there is fundamental and general agreement with the positive statement that the Church is maintained in the truth of the gospel – despite all errors. But we must go on to examine how this is to be understood in concrete terms.

3. *The decisive question.* Are there not perhaps – over and above this fundamental indefectibility – verdicts, statements, definitions, dogmas, *propositions of faith* which are not only *de facto* true (which is undisputed) but *infallibly true*: namely because particular subjects (those in office or the authorities) *a priori* cannot err in a particular situation because of special support from the Holy Spirit (!)? That is in fact the clear and precise question to be put to Vatican I, for which the authorities (Pope and bishops) are infallible not constantly, but only in very specific verdicts, statements, sentences, definitions, 'propositions'. So far the debate has focussed on these infallible propositions of faith which are not only not false *de facto* but because of the support of the Holy Spirit cannot be false (for example the Marian dogmas). And what has been the result? In brief, no single theologian and no single official authority has so far been able to put forward a proof for the possibility of such infallible statements of faith (and the authorities standing behind them) which are guaranteed by the Holy Spirit. According to the exhaustive discussion which has been carried on so far there are no solid foundations in scripture and in the great Catholic tradition for the assumption of such

infallibly true propositions or authorities. Assertions to the contrary are not in themselves arguments to the contrary. And it is obviously begging the question to cite as proof the magisterial texts from Vatican I and II, since these are the very propositions which are in question. Moreover, what was still not seen as a problem in either Vatican I or Vatican II has not been answered by either Vatican I or Vatican II.

4. *The unexpected confirmations.* By contrast, the more recent (in fact earlier) Catholic position has been unexpectedly confirmed – and indeed from the Catholic side:

(*a*) With respect to *Peter*: in the most recent exegetical investigations, Catholics, too, have worked out afresh the authentic but fallible authority of Peter and the problems of a succession in a 'Petrine service'. Important though the symbolic figure of Peter remained for the Church of the subsequent period, there is little support in the New Testament and in the first three centuries for an infallibility of Peter (the biblical witnesses characteristically always combine both positive *and* negative features), far less for an infallibility of the Roman bishops. Vatican I's main evidence for papal infallibility, Luke 22.32 ('I have prayed for you, that your faith shall not waver'), was never used by mediaeval canonists as support for papal infallibility: what is promised to Peter here is not freedom from error but grace to keep faith to the end. And even this is not applied by the mediaeval canonists to the Roman bishops, but to the faith of the whole Church. To apply Luke 22.32 to an infallibility of the Bishop of Rome proves to be an innovation with no support in the text.

(*b*) With respect to the *ecumenical councils*: the first ecumenical council, that of Nicaea (325), managed without any claim to infallibility. Most recent historical research has shown how the leading man at this council, Athanasius, and with him many Greek church fathers and also Augustine, provide the foundation for the true but in no way infallible authority of the council: the council does not speak the truth because it was convened with no legal objections, because the majority of the bishops of the world were assembled, because it was confirmed by some human authorities, because it had some extraordinary support of the Holy Spirit and therefore could not *a priori* be deceived.

Rather, it speaks the truth because despite its use of new words it was not saying anything new, because it was handing down the old tradition in new language, because it had the gospel behind it. This classical Catholic view of the council is to be distinguished from the later mystical or legal *Byzantine* 'council evaluations' in the East and from the *specifically Roman* developments in the West – especially with reference to the authority of the papacy – which clearly emerged in the time of the fifth-century Popes, became established with the Gregorian Reform and in a *Roman Catholic* form were made a dogma at Vatican I.

(c) In respect of the origin of the Roman doctrine of infallibility. Perhaps the greatest surprise in the debate has been that the most recent historical investigations have un-earthed the unorthodox origins of the Roman doctrine of infallibility at the end of the thirteenth century. Scholarship owes this discovery to the American historian Brian Tierney: there is no slow 'development' and 'unfolding' of the doctrine of papal infallibility, but a more sudden creation at the end of the thirteenth century. So papal infallibility and irreformability – both of which belonged together from the beginning – were not, as previously supposed, 'invented' by the orthodox papal theologians and canonist Popes of the high Middle Ages, but by an eccentric Franciscan often accused of heresy, Petrus Olivi (died 1298). At first Olivi's view was not taken at all seriously, and in 1324 it was condemned by John XXII as a work of the devil, the father of lies. The Popes of the Reformation period could not yet appeal to a generally recognized infallibility, since remarkably enough the Council of Trent did not define the infallibility of the Pope in any way. In terms of the history of ideas it was the ideologists of the counter-revolution and restoration, de Lamennais and above all de Maistre, who were primarily responsible for Vatican I's definition of infallibility: essentially, infallibility is 'a new nineteenth-century idea' (C. Langlois). The mediaeval canonists – and at that time the Church's teaching was a matter for canonists – had not claimed that an infallible head was necessary to preserve the faith of the Church. Rather, they asserted that divine providence would see to it that the whole Church would not err, however much its head might err.

On the basis of exegetical, historical and systematic research so far, it can hardly be disputed that to a greater degree than might have been expected the fundamental criticism of the more recent Roman doctrine of infallibility coincides with scripture and the great Catholic tradition. In many respects this is now also confirmed by the new book of an insider, a Catholic theologian, historian and long-term collaborator with the Vatican Secretariat for Unity, August Bernhard Hasler: *How the Pope Became Infallible*, New York 1981. I could not refuse my fellow-countryman when he asked me to write a preface to his book. What new contribution does it make to the discussion of infallibility?

1. *Hasler's book tells the story of how the definition of infallibility came about.* Anyone who has read Butler-Lang's history of the First Vatican Council or the works by the Catholic historian Roger Aubert of Louvain about Pius IX and Vatican I knows essentially what to expect. However, on the question of infallibility, Hasler's report is more systematic, more detailed, more vivid and less sparing. The important thing here is not the historian who is producing the narrative but the story that he tells; it is largely a scandalous affair which Hasler relates unsparingly and without toning anything down, a story of the manipulation of the debate on infallibility; of the preparation, passing and implementation of the definition of infallibility; and constantly about Pius IX. Here at last is a Catholic historian who also takes very seriously the arguments of those who were defeated at the time, arguments which have often been endorsed in the meantime, and who goes right through all the lists not only of the bishops opposed to infallibility (which are still available) but also of the most hard-line supporters of infallibility – often just as inconvenient for interpreters intent on harmonization – and presents the evidence without toning it down, trivializing it or reinterpreting it. As a result, through an understandable one-sidedness he corrects and balances the previous one-sided historical accounts, also using new sources.

Where the *Enquiry* violated a tabu, Hasler seems to probe the open wound, which may explain some isolated Catholic reactions which tend to defame him rather than argue against his previous academic publications: all possible psychological defence mechanisms, inhibitions, repressions, anxieties and ideological interests make a rational examination of rational arguments difficult in this question. But it is natural that for all the examination of previous historical tendencies, developments and structures, in particular the figure of Pius IX should be illuminated both historically and psychologically, like other figures of world history. For this history was shaped by no one more than by this man: without him Vatican I would never have defined the dogma of infallibility. However, that what Hasler has to say about Pius IX and Vatican I can be demonstrated from the sources is shown better by his earlier academic historical study which underlies this new book: *Pius IX (1846–1878), Papal Infallibility and Vatican I. The Dogmatization and Implementation of an Ideology*. Given the overabundance of converging testimony from participants and observers of the council, we can ask whether all that is questionable, all that is reported there of the genesis and implementation of the definition of infallibility, does not bear on the question of the *truth* of this definition.

2. *Hasler's book sharpens the enquiry into the foundation of the definition of infallibility.* To see this book simply as the narration of the story of how this late, special Roman development came about – now told for a wider public – would be to trivialize it. No, it works through in detail fundamental questions which are raised by the history itself, most of which were already being discussed during or immediately after Vatican I. Subsequently, however, they faded into the background and are now taking on a new explosiveness in the light of the most recent debate on infallibility. Historians may discuss verdicts on individual sources, the ordering of certain details and the like. But one would have to have ploughed through the story with dogmatic blinkers if, in view of the quantity and quality of the material that has been accumulated, one did not want to ask questions like the four which follow:

(*a*) Was Vatican I a *really free council?* Of course freedom is historically a very relative term. But what if it can be demonstrated that already at that time a highly significant part of the Council itself did not feel free? Anyone who wants to parry the question of the freedom of Vatican I by referring to the lack of freedom which was also a characteristic of other councils (like Ephesus in 431) is only making the question sharper. Non-Catholic church historiography is unanimous in disputing the freedom of Vatican I in the debate on infallibility (and that is all that we are concerned with here). And more recent Catholic church history also concedes that freedom was considerably restricted. However, it usually plays this re-cognition down by a claim which is grounded more in apologetics and dogmatics than in history, that there was sufficient freedom at least for the decrees to be valid.

Now already at that time numerous prominent council participants and observers were denied the necessary freedom in the debate on infallibility, so that today this question needs to be looked at again. Indeed, how free was a council whose discussion was *a priori* prejudiced, whose agenda allowed only limited freedom of speech or real influence, and whose course from beginning to end was subject to the excessively powerful influence of the Pope, whose very own claim to rule and power was what the whole discussion was about? On top of a repressive agenda and procedure, on top of a one-sided and partisan selection of leading theological experts and com-position of council commissions and the council praesidium, the bishops of both the anti-infallibilist minority *and* the infallibilist majority were exposed to numerous pressures (moral, psychological, church-political, financial, from the press and from the police). And the definition of infallibility was carried through by various manipulations practised by the Pope himself, before the council, in the council and after the council. Consequently one cannot be surprised that the old, but suppressed, question of the freedom of the council should have returned today, prompted by the most recent debate on infallibility. Painful and grievous though it may be to say so, in many respects this council was more like a well-organized and manipulated totalitarian party congress than a free assembly of free Christians.

(*b*) Was Vatican I a *really ecumenical council?* Ecumenicity, too, is a historically relative term. But it is also clear from church history that not every council which claimed to be ecumenical has been accepted, 'received' by the whole Church as ecumen-ical. And the fact that the questionable freedom of Vatican I also jeopardizes its ecumenicity is something that a new objective investigation should consider.

What the French bishop François Lecourtier wrote at the time is confirmed by numerous similar testimonies from bishops and observers at the council: 'Our weakness at this time comes neither from the scriptures nor from the tradition of the fathers, nor from the testimonies of general councils and history. It comes from our lack of freedom, which is radical. An imposing minority, representing the faith of more than 100 million Catholics, i.e. almost half the whole Church, is oppressed by the yoke of restrictive agendas which go against the conciliar traditions; it is oppressed by deputations which have not really been elected and which dare to insert undiscussed paragraphs into the text that is being discussed; it is oppressed by a commission for the postulates which are enforced on it by the authorities; it is oppressed by the absolute lack of discussion, replies, objections, the impossibility of making statements; by newspapers which are invited to hound the bishops and stir up the clergy against them; by the nunciatures which add their contribution when the newspapers are no longer enough, and which attempt to raise up the priests against the bishops as witnesses to the faith, but leave the really godly witnesses only the role of delegates from the lowly clergy, indeed blame them if they do not act in this way. The minority is oppressed above all by the whole weight of the supreme authority which burdens it with the praise and encouragement that it extends in the form of letters to the priests. It is oppressed by the demonstrations in favour of Dom Guéranger and against M. de Montalembert and others.'

The questions posed by this situation cannot be avoided. Did the other 'half' of the Catholic Church have a sufficient say? Were the representatives of this half not *a priori* in a hopeless situation in the face of the preponderance of Italian city bishops and the supremacy of the Pope and the curial apparatus? Was this council in its quantitative majority really representative of the whole Catholic Church – not to mention the whole Christian ecumene? And was this council's definition of infallibility subsequently accepted, 'received', in freedom by the whole Catholic Church?

The drama of Bishop Lecourtier, mentioned above, who finally in despair hurled the council documents into the Tiber, left early and as a result was deposed from his see of Montpellier after the council, is representative of the drama of conscience of so many of the most significant and best educated bishops, who went off before the decisive vote and subsequently assented to the dogma only under indescribable pressure from above and below – often simply for the sake of the unity of the Church, watering it down in their interpretation and without inner conviction. All the use of the Index and all the dismissals, sanctions and excommunications, all the means of manipulation and oppression, threats, supervision and denunciation, applied by Curia and nuncios, and finally the Old Catholic schism and the inner emigration of so many Catholics, especially of theologians and educated people – all this makes it seem quite justified to ask whether this council's dogma of infallibility was freely accepted, 'received' by the whole Church.

(*c*) *Were the sacrifices worth while?* The definition of infallibility is the crown of the Roman system which developed in particular after the Gregorian reform in the eleventh century. The dogma of infallibility had the function of a meta-dogma which covers and guarantees all other dogmas (and countless doctrines and practices associated with them). The dogma of infallibility – and the aura of infallibility attaching to the 'ordinary', everyday magisterium is sometimes more important than the relatively rare infallible definitions – seemed to give the faithful a superhuman security and protection which made them forget all anxiety about human insecurity, freedom and the venture of faith. To this degree the dogma of infallibility doubtless helped towards integration, towards removing psychological burdens, and in a highly effective way furthered the unity, coherence and power of Roman Catholicism, which increasingly saw itself as a bulwark (Cardinal Ottaviani used the term 'il baluardo') in the world. Could there be anything that better legitimized, stabilized and protected this system against criticism than the dogma of the infallibility of its (supreme) representative(s)? There remained only the question whether the dogma of infallibility itself had really been legitimated, stabilized and immunized; whether its *truth* had been safeguarded.

Up to Pius XII the system seemed intact; only in John XXIII did what had long been accumulated and suppressed break out, leading in a relatively short time – to the surprise of most people – to a new attitude of the Catholic Church to itself, to the other Christian Churches, to the Jews and the world religions, and to modern society. What under Pius IX had been tabu and condemned – for example religious freedom and toleration, ecumenism and human rights – was now loudly proclaimed as Catholic doctrine. Already during the council the infallibility with which the traditional positions had for a whole century been defended against modern tendencies seemed to many people in Rome and elsewhere already to have been shattered.

But think of the sacrifices with which the old authority, continuity and infallibility had been bought! This has been considered once again since John XXIII and Vatican II. John XXIII had named as official experts at the council theologians who had formerly been condemned, which caused problems for many council fathers. And even more traditional theologians, like Hans Urs von Balthasar, had gone on to ask whether Vatican I's definition of infallibility had not been 'an enormous accident'. Were that Old Catholic schism and the inward emigration of many educated Catholics, who no longer felt themselves at home in this authoritarian and now often totalitarian Church, really necessary? Had the demotion of the bishops to being mere recipients of orders from Rome, had the purges of theologians under Pius IX, Piux X (the encyclical *Pascendi* and anti-Modernism) and Pius XII (the encyclical *Humani generis* and worker priests), and still even under Paul VI (the encyclical *Humanae vitae*) really been worth it? And what about all the prohibitions on speaking and writing, the prior censorship and self-censorship, the condemnations and bans on books, the excommunications and suspensions, the restrictive policy on the archives and the personal politics along party lines (Curia, episcopate), and on top of this finally the self-imposed isolation of one who in many respects was a 'prisoner in the Vatican'? Was Ignaz von Döllinger quite wrong when in 1887 he wrote to the Archbishop of Munich that the papal dogmas had been achieved with force and violence and would have to be paid for time and again with force and violence?

Indeed we cannot avoid noting what a great price Catholic church history, exegesis, dogmatics, moral theology and preaching generally did have to pay after Vatican I for this infallibility and irreformability, which did not allow any real corrections and reforms but at best 'interpretations' and adaptations! The price was a constant conflict with history and the modern world, which deeply shook the credibility of the Catholic Church. It was constant apologetics against new information and experiences, against all scientific criticism, against all possible enemies, real or supposed. There was a gulf between the Church and modern science, between theology and historical research, and also increasingly within theology between the history of dogmatics and dogmatics, between exegesis and dogmatics. Tremendous sacrifices were also required indirectly of the 'little people', in the interests of the authority, continuity and infallibility of doctrine: the ban on contraception is only a particularly explosive example of all the burdens imposed on human consciences in catechisms and penitential rules, religious instructions and preachings, as *de facto* infallible teaching. The result was the exodus of countless intellectuals, the unexpressed dissent of many believers, the lack of creative individuals and initiatives in the Church, repressive processes, and symptoms of hardening and fossilization, disturbances of consciousness, loss of reality, very often a spiritual apparatus which functioned only externally, without an inner life. I shall not continue my lament, but the question comes home to us: was all this necessary? Was it all worth while?

(*d*) Should *Pius IX be beatified*? Markedly conservative forces in Rome are now again pressing hard for the canonization of the 'infallible teacher of faith' – for reasons which are obvious in terms of ideology and power politics (with Pius IX and Vatican I against John XXIII and Vatican II and thus against all openness of the Catholic Church to Christianity and the modern world). But the negative statements of so many contemporary bishops and other contemporaries about Paul IX are so important and so numerous that they are hardly compatible with the 'heroic degree' which is required, not only of the theological virtues (faith, hope and love), but also of the four cardinal virtues (wisdom, justice, boldness, moderation):

an exaggerated consciousness of mission, a double tongue, a
disturbed psyche and a misuse of his office. All negative factors
which probably cannot be made positive with an appeal to an
allegedly providential mission of this Pope for the Church. In
addition to his notoriously weak theological education there is
also his anti-Jewish, anti-ecumenical and indeed anti-demo-
cratic attitude. A saint of the twentieth century? The discussion
here should concentrate less on hypothetical and speculative
questions (the after-effects of epilepsy, Cardinal Guidi the
illegitimate son of the Pope) and the like than on the
indisputable facts which tell against a beatification of this Pope
and which suggest that it would be advisable to bring a halt to
this process as soon as possible – if the problems of such
beatifications (and particularly the beatification of papal
predecessors by their papal successors) are not to become even
more manifest.

The desire of church historians that the Vatican archives
should be opened up comprehensively thus becomes particularly urgent. What is the use of the great announcement that
the Vatican secret archive will be opened for the whole
pontificate of Pius IX (and most recently of all also for his
successor Leo XIII) if in particular the archive material of the
First Vatican Council and other important documents are still
to be kept from researchers? *A priori* one can speak only with
qualifications of a real opening of the Vatican secret archive as
long as the most important archives – those of the Congregation
for the Extraordinary Affairs of the Church and the Congregation of Faith (formerly the Holy Office and before that the Holy
Inquisition, and the earlier Index Congregation) remain
closed. If the Church after Leo XIII, who opened the Vatican
secret archive for the first time, does not need to fear the truth,
why then do we also have the continuation of a repressive policy
here?

The questions which arise from Hasler's historical work are
extremely inconvenient ones – who could fail to see that? But
even someone who would want to give different answers to
them must concede that they are all without exception
questions which may and indeed must be put – for the sake of
the truth and the credibility of the Church. Anyone who is to
take offence here should see the offence where it really is and not

attack those who report it and who have the right to an unprejudiced, free and critical discussion of their findings.

However, critical destruction and historical reconstruction are only half of the theological business. No less important than the question 'How the Pope became Infallible' is another question: 'How can the Pope (again) be the Pope without infallibility?' Here are some thoughts on that which I already formulated in connection with the 1973 infallibility debate.

How could the Pope 'function' without infallible definitions of doctrine? In our day we have got to know both possibilities. There was Pope Pius XII, who not quite a century after Vatican I thought that he finally had to claim the authority attributed to the Pope by the Vatican but never hitherto actually exercised, in order to proclaim *Urbi et orbi* an infallible doctrinal definition, a new Marian dogma. But none of his doctrinal statements remained so disputed in Christianity and even in the Catholic Church as this 'infallible' definition! Even its pastoral effects on the piety of the Catholic people and the conversion of the world which were hoped for at the time were assessed in a more than sober way at a distance of thirty years. Vatican II distanced itself from extreme Marianism, which made the doubtful character of the definition even more evident.

The other example is the next Pope, John XXIII. From the start he never had the ambition to pronounce an infallible definition. On the contrary, he continually emphasized in a great variety of ways his own humanity, his limitations, and indeed now and then even his fallibility. The aura of infallibility departed from him. And yet no Pope in this century exercised such influence on the course of the history of the Catholic Church and indeed Christianity generally as this Pope who attached no importance to infallibility. With him and Vatican II a new era of church history began. Without any infallible statements he succeeded in many ways in finding a new hearing for the gospel of Jesus Christ in the church. So he had an authority inside and outside the Catholic Church which would have been inconceivable in the time of his predecessor. At all events, with all his weaknesses and mistakes – more spontaneous than planned, more symbolic than programmatic – he gave

a glimpse of how the Pope could be the Pope even without any
claim to infallibility: not ambitiously grasping for powers and
prerogatives and exercising authority along the lines of the
ancien régime, but with an authority of service in the spirit of the
New Testament in the face of today's needs: brotherly collaboration in partnership, dialogue, consultation and collaboration above all with the bishops and theologians of the
whole Church, including those concerned in the decision-
making process, and inviting them to share the responsibility.
That is how the Pope should exercise his function even in
questions of preaching and teaching – in the Church, with the
Church, for the Church, but not above or outside the Church.

Again, that does not exclude the possibility that a Pope can
also sometimes take a stand against something – indeed in some
circumstances he must do so. It did not need any infallible
definition: a clear, understandable word by the 'representative'
spoken at the level of the Christian message would have been
enough in the face of the attack on Poland or the mass murder of
the Jews. But remarkably, in recent times there was no
'infallible' pronouncement even when countless people would
have expected one. Conversely, for all his fallibility the Pope
(together with the other bishops) can serve the church
community and its unity, inspire the missionary work of the
Church in the world and intensify its efforts for peace and
justice, disarmament, human rights, the social liberation of
peoples and races, and work for those handicapped in all
manner of ways. Without any claim to infallibility, in his life
and work he can continually make the voice of the Good
Shepherd heard in the Christian ecumene and far beyond. He
would then be an inspiration in the spirit of Jesus Christ and a
leader in Christian renewal, and Rome would become a place of
encounter, dialogue and honest and friendly collaboration.

It follows from all this that the Pope can 'function' even
without infallible teaching definitions; indeed, under the
present conditions of church and society he can perform his
service *better* without infallible doctrinal definitions. So anyone
who puts the infallibility of papal statements in question is not
putting the papacy itself in question. This must be said quite
emphatically, in the face of constant confusions, distortions and
suspicions. Much in the service of Peter has become question-

able, above all the mediaeval and modern absolutist forms which have lasted down to our days. A Petrine service has a future only if it is understood in the light of the Peter symbol of the New Testament. The exegetical foundation for a *historical* succession of bishops of Rome has become questionable. But the substance of a Petrine service has continued to be meaningful if it is a service to the whole Church in a *functional-practical* succession: a *primacy of service* in the full biblical sense.

Such a primacy of service, the outlines of which at least began to emerge in the figure of John XXIII, is a real *chance* for the Catholic Church and all Christianity. A primacy of service would be more than a 'primacy of honour'. Such a primacy is not to be had in a serving Church and in its passivity it cannot help anyone. A primacy of service would also be more than a 'primacy of jurisdiction': understood as pure authority and power, such a primacy would be a fundamental misunderstanding, and understood literally it says nothing about the decisive factor, namely service. Petrine service, understood biblically, can only be a 'pastoral primacy': a pastoral service to the whole Church. As such it is *in substance* backed by the New Testament – despite all the questions of historical succession, which have not been and probably cannot be clarified. As such it could be of great use for the whole of Christianity today.

All this also applies to Hasler's questions about my own position: yes, Catholic church communion was and again is possible even 'without a strictly authoritarian leadership (a monopoly for the Church's magisterium in the interpretation of scripture and tradition!)'. Free, unprejudiced scientific research, which also of course includes historical-critical investigation of the New Testament evidence (see *On Being a Christian*), and critical reflection on the relationship between faith and understanding (cf. *Does God Exist?*) does not lead to the 'self-destruction' of the church but to its renewal. In this introduction I do not want once more to go into the basic theological question of the indefectibility of the Church in truth – which, to be sure, is a question of faith. That topic is covered in my theological meditation *The Church – Maintained in Truth?*.

There remains, finally, the question: can a Catholic theologian who adopts such a critical position *remain Catholic?* Excom-

munication, suspension, the withdrawal of the licence to teach
– superficial observers sometimes overlook this – are indeed
always possible, and will still be used where they are effective.
They themselves would not be an easy condemnation to bear
for Catholic theologians who have economic and legal support
from the Church. This is something which is only understood
by a person to whom belonging to a particular community of
faith means something.

But excommunication, suspension, withdrawal of licence
have not yet happened in the new debate on infallibility, nor
are they probable in the future: and not just because individual critical theologians allegedly have so much popularity,
influence and power that they could not be punished. Rather,
this is because throughout the Catholic Church and also in
Rome it has been noted that the substance of the question and
the situation in which it is asked are both complex and
difficult. There are too many doubters: opinion polls show
that in many countries only a minority in the Catholic Church
believes in papal infallibility. So it has so far proved impossible to brand the critics of infallibility un-Catholic before all
the world. They resemble the former critics of the papal
church state who were threatened with excommunication and
yet were proved right – though some of them only after their
death. Here a distinction must be made:

Those are not un-Catholic who oppose the *Roman system*
(Roman Catholicism) which in the eleventh century came to
dominate teaching, morals and church government and because of its centralism, absolutism, triumphalism and imperi-
alism was already constantly being criticized in Vatican II
and also in the post-conciliar period by numerous Catholic
bishops, theologians and laity. A special position for the
bishops of Rome, linking up with Peter and the great Roman
tradition, in the sense of a pastoral service to the whole
Church, is not to be repudiated in the light of the gospel. But
there must be repudiation of any absolutist curial system
which regards the free Catholic community of faith as Rome's
'spiritual' empire and bears the main responsibility for the
schism with the Eastern Churches, for the Protestant Reformation, and for the fossilization of the Catholic Church
itself.

Those are un-Catholic who want to depart from the *Catholic Church* (the whole, universal, all-embracing Church), or more precisely those who give up the continuity of faith and community of faith which persists over all breaks (catholicity in time) and the universality of faith and the community of faith for all groups (catholicity in space), and thus fall victim to a 'Protestant' radicalism and particularism which has nothing to do with authentic gospel radicalism and concern for the community. The question emerges even more clearly than ever whether the infallibility of propositions (like the former infallibility of the Church state) is not more part of the curialist system than of the Catholic Church as it has understood itself from the beginning.

But of one thing the author of this new book on infallibility can be certain: anyone who as a Catholic theologian goes this way of discerning criticism is treading a narrow and dangerous path which can easily incur him censure from two sides:

A theology which does not shrink from asking critical questions will doubtless be censured by unenlightened defenders of the faith: there, it may be said (for partly understandable reasons), the theologian may not plead his own cause in a new way. One might be departing from the teaching authority of the Church if one does not think and speak of God and the Church along the lines of official Church tradition.

A theology which constantly presses for positive answers through all the negative criticism will doubtless also be censured by those apparently enlightened despisers of the faith. There, they will say (again for partly understandable reasons), the theologian may not speak of God, far less of the Church in today's world and society; with their flat one-dimensional approach such people have not noted that the enlightened in particular can think and speak in a different, new, better way of transcendence, of God and also of the Church.

The former will readily brand anyone who attempts to take this critical course a heretic who is outside the Church, and the latter will claim that he is falling into line with the Church. What the former say out of pastoral concern, the latter say cynically: 'Be consistent, either come over to us or go over to the other side. You cannot be half and half.' Cannot be? As if one had consistently either to adapt completely or emigrate if one noticed serious defects and false developments in the democratic state! No: true consistency is not a matter of drawing all the conclusions; drawing all the conclusions is false consistency. Difficult though it may be to walk along, and exposed though it may be to misunderstanding from both sides, there is a consistent way between conformism and escapism, between uncritical adaptation and hypercritical sectarianism: loyalty to the Church to which one feels an obligation, but always a critical loyalty which manifests itself in loyal criticism. In this sense, obligation to the Church and its message harms a critical theologian as little as obligation to the state and its constitution harms a critical lawyer. Loyalty and criticism, obligation and freedom, sympathy and absence of prejudice, faith and understanding, are not mutually exclusive, but inclusive.

I certainly hope that the author of this book, too, may consistently continue along the way of critical loyalty, unswervingly but not unaffected by well-meant Church verdicts and less well-meant journalistic spite, in honest scholarship and unshaken belief in the cause to be advocated, in hope of a fair balance of opposites.

In hope of a fair balance of opposites. A *'re-reception of the papal dogmas of Vatican I'* has been called for by the French theologian Yves Congar, who did more than anyone else to prepare theologically for the new understanding of the Church at Vatican II: historical (Aubert, Torrell, Schatz) or theological-historical studies (Thils, Dejaifve, Pottmeyer), radical questions (Küng) and then the fact of Vatican II itself and the revival of local and particular churches, and finally the re-presentation of the principles of Eastern ecclesiology – according to Congar all this allows us better to recognize the historical conditioning of Vatican I and calls (in 'our Catholic loyalty') for a re-reception of the Vatican dogmas and especially of the dogma of papal infallibility. According to Congar, taking note of an authentic understanding of 'magisterium', of the best exegetical, historical and theological studies of these decades, of the ecumenical theological dialogue which has been opened up under such new conditions, and the reality of the local church, in conjunction with the other Christian churches we should reconsider and reformulate what was defined in Vatican I and then accepted by the totality of

Catholics under the conditions of the time. According to Congar such a 're-reception' should in fact issue in a *revision* of the resolutions of Vatican I. This would give not only the Catholic Church and theology but also the whole ecumene a way out of a situation which has become intolerable, into a new future.

I hope that I may be allowed to take up Congar's suggestion and make it more specific, not in order to provoke a new dispute over infallibility but definitively to do away with the old one:

Now, under the new pontificate, a new exegetical, historical and theological investigation could be made of the question of infallibility, in objectivity, scientific honesty, fairness and justice.

As formerly in the matter of birth control, an ecumenical commission could be appointed which would consist of recognized experts in the various disciplines (exegesis, the history of dogma, systematic theology, practical theology and the relevant non-theological disciplines).

With a shifting of accents, less weight might be placed than hitherto on the negative, critical aspects and more on the positive, constructive aspects, so that it could be asked whether the *abiding of the Church in the truth despite all errors* does not have a better foundation in the Christian message and the great Catholic tradition, and whether this would not be something that it would be better to live out in the Church today.

Here is an application: the rejection of any means of birth control by Pope Paul VI was grounded, according to the Roman view, in the authority, continuity, traditionality, universality and therefore *de facto* infallibility and irreformability of the traditional doctrine. Since then in this question – as in some others – Rome seems to have been blocked: *non possumus*, 'we cannot', it is said to the present day (as it was said about giving up the church state). Only a solution to the question of infallibility could also bring a solution to the question of birth control. The church authorities, who all too often content themselves with admonitions to the whole world, could here themselves provide powerful help in humility and self-criticism: by a bold revision of the doctrine of the alleged immorality of any (!) birth control which allegedly stands behind the encyclical *Humanae vitae*. What represents a severe burden on the conscience of countless people even in our developed countries with their falling birth rates does incalculable damage to people in many under-developed countries, especially in Latin America, for which the Church must bear part of the blame: poverty, illiteracy, unemployment, malnutrition and disease have a cause-and-effect relationship with high birth rates. During the past two decades in the Third World the rates of increase in food production (which are by no means small) have largely been swallowed up by the higher birth rates.

Pope John Paul II returned from Latin America in particular with new experiences. Is it too much to hope that the man who there spoke out so clearly against poverty, underdevelopment and the misery of children, and who also wants to work for ecumenical understanding, might take a decisive step towards an honest clarification of the oppressive question of infallibility – in an atmosphere of mutual trust, free research and fair discussion?

Tübingen, February 1979   Hans Küng

Director of the Institute
for Ecumenical Research
in the University of Tübingen

Document II

THE CHURCH – MAINTAINED IN TRUTH:
A THEOLOGICAL MEDITATION (1979)

NO EXTRAPOLATION

Futurologists 'extrapolate': from developments at the present time they draw conclusions about the still unknown future. Cannot the future of the Church also be extrapolated, projected in advance, in the light of the present? Can it not be predicted more or less exactly, from the history of the Church up to now, that there will be a Church also in the third millennium and even later?

Certainly the negative prophecies of Feuerbach, Marx, Nietzsche and Freud have not been fulfilled. There is as yet no sign of an end of Christianity, a fading away of religion, a death of God. And faith in progress and science, disseminated in both East and West, which claimed as a substitute religion to solve all the problems of man and society, has meanwhile run into a crisis of its own and frequently turned into hostility against science and technology.

At the same time sociologists of religion are pointing to the continually surprising, persistent vitality of the great religions, which are much older than any of the political systems: they cannot be expected to die out in the foreseeable future. Judaism and Islam, for instance, have displayed an amazing capacity for renewal in our time. Continually surprising also is the new vitality of Christianity as it finds expression in numerous initiatives to cope with world problems (racial equality, world peace, social justice) which, despite all failures, are repeatedly taken by the Christian churches and by individual Christians. Hence it is undoubtedly possible to extrapolate some trends from the history of the Church up to now, even though extrapolations by religious sociology are more in danger than others of failing to allow for the element of surprise in future happenings and of being no more than 'prognoses of the past'.

But, despite everything, looking at the situation as a whole, who would venture from the past two millennia of the Church

to extrapolate an entire third? And who would promise in
particular a steady, unrestricted continuity (perenniality),
indestructibility (indefectibility), or – if it is not misunderstood
as referring to individual propositions – inerrancy (infallibility)
of the Church? For who knows? Perhaps science, technology
and rational enlightenment may yet make possible and even
bring about a fulfilled, contented life without belief in God,
rendering superfluous both Christianity and churches. Who
would venture to prophesy about these things?

No, it is not possible to extrapolate indestructibility for the
Church. Nor should there be any attempt to do so. For the
indestructibility of the Church, its maintenance in truth, can be
meaningfully asserted only as a *truth of faith*. That is, Christians
are confident that there is a living God and that in the future
this God will also maintain their believing community in life
and in truth. Their confidence is based on the promise given
with Jesus of Nazareth: he himself is the promise in which
God's fidelity to his people can be read. How is this to be
understood?

A TRUTH OF FAITH

If we want to provide an adequate theological justification of
the indestructibility of the Church today, it cannot be done in
textbook fashion in biblicist-fundamentalist terms with the aid
of an odd text or two, as if at least in the Bible individual
propositions were a priori infallible. No, the Bible is not like the
Qu'ran, a compendium of infallible propositions dictated by
God or by an angel, to be understood literally and observed
strictly, including the prohibition of alcoholic drink, the veiling
of women, and cutting off the hand of a thief. The Bible is a
collection of human documents which are meant to bear
witness in human weakness, limitation, and frailty to God's
word and deed. The indestructibility of the Church can be
given adequate theological justification only if it is supported
not by individual biblical texts but by *the Christian message as a
whole*. As a believer I can rely on its call, even though one or
another line of Scripture is uneven, even though one or another
proposition reflects the message only obscurely, with some
distortion, or perhaps fails entirely to reflect it. God writes

straight, even on crooked lines. And because of the crooked,
very human lines, literary and factual criticism is unavoidable
for a modern understanding of the Bible.

But again, what is not contained in a single proposition, but
the basic conviction running through all the New Testament
writings, in fact the Christian message itself, is:

- that the historical Jesus of Nazareth is more than merely one
  of the prophets, is not simply different from other prophets;
- that in him God's ultimate, decisive call, God's definitive
  truth about himself and man, found expression;
- that Jesus was and is therefore rightly called the true Lord,
  God's word made flesh, the way, the truth, and the life;
- that for believers – allowing for all genuine progress and all
  development and involvement – he cannot be surpassed or
  replaced by any new Lord, any other word, any better truth.

This is the message of faith of those believers who with good
reasons first committed themselves to him – the one who was
crucified and raised to life by God – and who for their part want
to provoke faith and hitherto have repeatedly provoked faith.
Obviously I can reject this provocation; I can say no. Faith is a
free decision which presupposes open-mindedness, a readiness
to believe. And the less ordinary and banal, the higher and
more meaningful, the truth is, so much more open-mindedness,
so much more readiness, is required, even though faith itself is
by no means a blind and irrational, but a justified and
intelligent faith.

Since for believers Jesus is the decisive call of God, his final
word, his definitive revelation, from time immemorial the
conviction of the believing community has been:

- that God will always continue to find faith through this Jesus
  Christ;
- that consequently there will always continue to be human
  beings who come to believe in him;
- that there will always continue to be also a community of
  believers, that is, a Church of Jesus Christ in the broadest
  sense of the term.

Here then something fundamental has become clear. Faith
in the indestructibility of the Church – that is, in its being
maintained in truth – is related primarily to the whole Church
as believing community. It is not primarily related to certain

ecclesiastical institutions or authorities, which for the most part
did not exist at all or did not exist in this form from the
beginning and need not exist or need not exist in this form for
ever.

Thus not only has the plane of institutions and authorities
been penetrated but also that of propositional truths, in order –
if necessary through very varied statements – to point to one
and the same reality which lies behind the individual statements and alone gives them their truth. It is only in the light of
this reality, lying behind all talk of faith, which was laid open by
God through Jesus for a community of faith, that the invitation
to faith can actually be justified. To commit oneself to this
reality, to rely on the indestructibility of this faith and this
believing community, undoubtedly involves a risk, a venture.
Faith cannot be 'proved' in the same way as other things are
proved; it is a matter of trust, naturally of reasonable trust. If
someone has to cope with the reality of God, he cannot have the
assurance that is provided by ordinary reality. But this very
risk, the adventure of faith, involves a hope. Faith is related to a
future still to be realized, but already inaugurated. When
human beings have to cope with the reality of God, faith can
provide a certainty which infinitely surpasses all banal,
ordinary security.

DESPITE ALL ERRORS

This hope of the believing community in its future finds
expression in various texts of Scripture, which are repeatedly
cited in this connection by both Catholic and Protestant
theologians as 'classical' texts: 'The powers of death shall not
prevail against it' (Matt. 16.18); 'I am with you always, to the
close of the age' (Matt. 28.20); 'And he [the Father] will give
you another Counsellor, to be with you for ever, even the Spirit
of truth' (John 14. 16–17); 'The church of the living God, the
pillar and bulwark of the truth' (I Tim. 3.15).

It is notable, however, that these 'classical' statements about
the Church and truth do not a priori exclude errors either of
certain persons or in certain statements. On the contrary, the
many failures and errors of men are continually taken for
granted in the Bible from Genesis to Revelation. Only too often

– even with the patriarchs and Moses, with the judges, kings and prophets; and finally also with Peter and the apostles – these failures and errors are clearly demonstrated to us.

There are of course those who ask: If in faith we accept an indestructibility (indefectibility) of the Church, why not accept in the same faith an infallibility on the part of certain authorities or in certain statements of faith? But the difference is obvious. In the original Christian testimony, on which we are dependent for the definition of what is Christian, truth is promised to the Church, but inerrancy is not guaranteed to any ecclesiastical authorities either permanently or in certain cases. On the contrary, the very prototype of the disciple of Jesus, Simon Peter, whose faith in Jesus as the living Christ became fundamental, even a 'rock', to the Church, even he continually fails. On one occasion Jesus tells him, 'Get behind me, Satan' (Mark 8.33). In this very way Peter is the type, the symbol, of the Church: his faith 'may not fail' (Luke 22.32), although he too even in decisive situations does not act in accordance with the truth of the gospel and has to be severely corrected by Paul (cf. Gal. 2.11–15). That is, if truth is to be continually in the Church, this will not be because the members or at least certain members in certain situations do not make mistakes or because their liability to error is sometimes excluded by higher influence. The reason why truth remains in the Church is because, in the face of all human failings and mistakes, God's truth proves to be stronger and because the message of Jesus continually produces faith, so that Jesus remains in the community of believers and his Spirit constantly guides them afresh into the whole truth.

Yes, what is truth? 'Truth' (Hebrew *'emet,* Greek *alētheia*) in the Old and New Testament means essentially more than true, or correct, propositions or statements. 'Truth' in the biblical sense means fidelity, permanence, reliability: the absolutely reliable fidelity of the God of the Covenant to his word, to his promise, and so to us. This is the truth of God: the absolute fidelity and reliability of God in regard to humankind, of a God who does not deceive himself or us; who never becomes a liar, however often he is cheated; who never refuses fellowship, even though it is constantly broken; who does not allow those who lapse to fall away for ever. It is from this truth, fidelity and reliability of God that the believer and the believing community can, should, and may live.

Why then does the Church remain alive as a community of faith? Not because there is no threat to life, no fatal illness, within it. But because God keeps it alive, *despite* all infirmities and weaknesses, and constantly endows it with a new continuity (perenniality).

Why does the Church remain in grace? Not because it is itself steadfast and faithful. But because, *despite* all sin and guilt, God does not dismiss it from his favour and grace and constantly grants it a new indestructibility (indefectibility).

Why does the Church remain in truth? Not because there is in it no wavering or doubting, no deviation or going astray. But because God maintains it in truth, *despite* its doubts, misunderstandings and errors, and constantly gives it a new inerrancy (infallibility).

For the clarification of the traditional theological terminology it should be noted that in the New Testament the terms 'life', 'grace' and 'truth' mean the same reality in which knowing and loving, talk and action, and man's living assent in everything to God are combined. Thus the terms 'perenniality', 'indefectibility' and 'infallibility' overlap. They too mean one and the same reality, but in theological usage they can be more closely defined in one way or another and distinguished from each other. Since the terms 'indefectibility' and 'perenniality' have been traditionally connected more with the 'being' than with the 'truth' of the Church, but since also the being of the Church depends on its truth, in our context we have made use of the term 'indefectibility' (perenniality) while defining it more closely: *indefectibility*, indestructibility (not only in being but also) *in truth*. The term 'indefectibility' is oriented less than the term 'infallibility' to certain statements or authorities. Above all, it is not encumbered with the many misunderstandings attached to the term 'infallibility'. Consequently 'indefectibility' or 'indestructibility' is to be preferred for current usage. If then the term 'indefectibility' (of the Church) is used as opposed to 'infallibility' (of individual propositions or authorities), it means the fundamental permanence of the Church in truth, a permanence which is not suspended by individual errors. An indefectibility of the Church in truth is supported by the New Testament as a whole, but an infallibility of certain authorities or statements cannot be proved. Instead, we must speak of an indefectibility of the Church despite all fallibility on the part of its human authorities and statements.

Guided by the Spirit

JESUS CHRIST AS TRUTH, WAY AND LIFE

Talk of the Church being maintained, remaining, in truth sounds very theoretical. But everything depends on understanding its concrete meaning. *Two misunderstandings* must be rejected from the very outset. The concrete meaning may fail to appear, but it may also be overemphasized and then it will be self-destructive.

Against a defective concrete expression it must be said that what remains is not merely God. To say that God remains is more or less a tautology. What is meant here is that God's truth remains, not only in heaven but also on earth, that God's truth is therefore effective in the Church. In this sense it is the Church itself which is maintained and remains.

Against an excessively concrete expression it must be said, after all our reflections, that the Church's persistence in truth cannot be given expression in infallible propositions. A genuinely concrete form of persistence in truth must be conceived differently. It is not a question of the permanence of certain propositions, but again of the permanence of the Church itself in truth.

How can the fact of being maintained in truth be positively defined? From what has been said hitherto it should have become clear that, for the Church, it is not a question of abstract truth – 'What is truth?' – but of *Christian* truth, the *truth of the gospel of Jesus Christ*.

Hence the *first* answer to our question is that, in the concrete, the Church is maintained in truth whenever *Jesus himself* and not some other secular, political, or clerical figure *remains the truth* for the individual or the community. Jesus does not simply know or tell the truth. He personifies, he is the truth that leads to life. But he remains the truth for the individual and the community not simply because he is known, recognized and acknowledged as the truth but because we live by the truth that he is: so that this Jesus – his message, his behaviour, his lot – in the concrete existence of the individual and the believing community, is the orientation and the standard for relationships both to one's fellows and to human society, as also to God himself.

From this the *second* answer follows immediately, that the Church is maintained quite concretely in the truth of Jesus Christ not only where the right words are produced but wherever *discipleship is fully realized in practice*: wherever, that is, Jesus is not only proclaimed and believed but imitated and given living expression in a spirit of faith. For believing in him means committing oneself trustfully to him. And this again means participating quite practically in him and in his way, following my own way of life (and every person has his own way) in accordance with his guidance, in order in this way to reach true life through his living truth. He himself then is our way of salvation and way of life to God. He himself is the answer in regard to the right way, the permanently valid truth, the true life. And so too he is the answer to the question of meaning, the question of salvation, the question of life, for this age and beyond the limits of this age. In the language of John's Gospel: 'I am the way, and the truth, and the life' (John 14.6).

So then the Church is maintained in truth, in the truth of the gospel, in the truth of Jesus Christ. The Church does not keep itself in truth. It *is* maintained by God, through Jesus Christ, in the Spirit.

THE SPIRIT BREATHES WHERE AND WHEN HE WILLS

God, Jesus Christ are not remote from the believer or the believing community. It was always the conviction of the Christian community that God, Jesus Christ are close, are present to the believer and to the believing community. How? Not only through memory. But through the spiritual reality, presence, efficacy of God, of Jesus Christ himself. In brief, God, Jesus Christ are close to the believer, close to the believing community, *in the Spirit*, present in the Spirit, through the Spirit, in fact as Spirit.

'Spirit', the 'Holy Spirit', seems for many people a very

mysterious figure. What is the *Holy Spirit?* Palpable and yet not palpable, invisible and yet powerful, real as the energy-laden air, the wind, the storm, as important for life as the air we breathe: these are some of the varied ways in which men from the very ancient times have imagined the 'Spirit' and God's invisible operations. This Spirit is not the spirit of man, his knowing and willing living self. He is the *Spirit of God*, who is rigorously distinguished as *Holy* Spirit from the *unholy* spirit of man and his world. The Holy Spirit is no other than God himself in so far as he is the power and strength of grace gaining dominion over man's mind, man's heart and indeed the whole man, in so far as he is inwardly present and bears witness to himself in the believer and in the believing community.

As God's Spirit, however, he is also the Spirit of Jesus Christ raised up to God. Thus God's Spirit cannot be interpreted as an obscure, nameless divine force, but is quite unambiguously the *Spirit of Jesus Christ*: as the Lord raised from death to life, Jesus is possessed of God's power, strength and Spirit so fully that he himself exists and operates in the mode of existence and operation of the Spirit. The risen Jesus acts at the present time through the Spirit, in the Spirit, as Spirit. In the Spirit Jesus is the living Lord, the way, the truth and the life, the standard for the believer and also for the believing community, the Church. Neither a hierarchy nor a theology nor a fanaticism, seeking to go beyond Jesus – his word, his conduct, and lot – to appeal to the 'Spirit', can appeal to the Spirit of Jesus Christ, to the Holy Spirit. Consequently, the spirits – ecclesial and unecclesial, whatever they may be – are to be tested and discerned in the light of this Jesus Christ.

It is therefore clear now that, as Spirit of God and of Jesus Christ for men, he is never man's own potential, but the strength, power, gift and *grace* of God. He is not an unholy spirit of man, spirit of the age, spirit of the Church, spirit of office, spirit of fanaticism. He is and always remains the Holy Spirit of God who breathes where and when he wills and does not permit himself to be claimed as the justification of absolute teaching and ruling power, of unsubstantiated theology, pious fanaticism and false security of faith.

The Spirit works *where* he wills. The Spirit of God cannot be restricted in effectiveness by the Church. The Spirit works not only from above but very decisively from below. He works not only in church ministries but where he wills: in the whole people of God. He works not only in the 'Holy City' but where he wills: in all churches of the one Church. He works not only in the Catholic Church but where he wills: in the whole of Christendom. And, finally, he works not only in Christendom but again where he wills: in the whole world.

The Spirit works *when* he wills. Certainly, the free Spirit is not a spirit of arbitrariness, of pseudo-freedom, of enthusiastic fanaticism, but of true freedom; he is not a spirit of chaos but of order, not of contradiction but of peace: not only in the world but also in the Church. Paul in particular had to insist on this against the Corinthians who appealed to their gifts of the Spirit to justify their neglect of church order: 'God is not a God of confusion but of peace' (I Cor. 14.33). Arbitrariness, disorder, chaos in the Church, then, cannot be justified by an appeal to the Holy Spirit.

And yet this does not mean that God's Spirit breathes when he *must*. It is a question of when he wills. No church order in teaching and practice, no dogma and no rite compel him now to act and now not to act. God's Spirit is under no law other than that of his own freedom; under no justice other than that of his own grace; under no power other than that of his own fidelity. God's Spirit therefore is not in any way under the law of the Church, the justice of the Church, the power of the Church. God's Spirit is not governed by the law of the Church, the justice of the Church, the power of the Church. He himself governs and controls supremely the Church's law, the Church's justice, the Church's power. If then anyone in the Church thinks he can possess the Spirit by any means of law, justice and power, he is bound to fail. The Church does indeed try continually to take over the Spirit, but it cannot 'possess' him, cannot control, restrain, direct or master him.

The Church can do none of these things either by its word or by its sacrament, either by a dogma or by a rite. Certainly God commits himself in the Spirit to the Church's word and sacrament; he does so, however, not in virtue of a law of the Church but in virtue of his own freedom; not in virtue of the

Church's justice but in virtue of his free grace; not in virtue of the Church's power but in virtue of his fidelity. Which means that, if he commits himself to the Church's word and sacrament, it is an obligation not for him but for us. It is not we who make demands on him, but he makes demands on us: he requires our unconditional *faith*. Neither the word nor the sacrament operate automatically: if they are not received in faith, they are without effect. If someone thinks he can compel the presence of the Holy Spirit with word or sacrament, or even with law and justice, power and order, he must be lacking precisely in that faith which the Spirit requires of him: the faith, that is, which depends not on his or the Church's justice and law, on his or the Church's power and order, but on God's free grace and fidelity. It remains true then, even in the Church, that the Spirit breathes, not when he must but when he wills.

Could we – we who are the Church – ever forget that we, though justified, are sinners and are ever freshly aware that we are sinners, that we are consequently opposed to God's Spirit, 'grieve' him, and, for our part, may lose him? Could we forget that our faith too, although it gives us certainty, is continually freshly challenged and threatened, that we can only continue to trust in God's fidelity and grace? Is it not clear that we cannot by any means take for granted the *persistence* of the Spirit in us and in the Church? Have we any alternative but to pray continually in a spirit of penance not only, 'Come, Holy Spirit,' but also, 'Remain, Holy Spirit. Remain with us in your fidelity despite our infidelity?' Despite its continual failure in all its members, the Church has not lost the free Spirit of God. This is not something natural, but the miracle of God's fidelity, a fidelity which may not be assumed, but which must be continually believed and sought again in prayer.

BETWEEN TRADITIONALISM AND MODERNISM

But has not the Spirit hitherto always guided the Church into all truth? This saying about the Spirit who 'will guide into all truth' (John 16.13) has often been misused: misused by those who thought they could invoke the Holy Spirit and then be content to leave everything as it was; misused also by those who thought they could invoke the same Spirit and then be able to regard and accept every novelty in the Church as a truth of the Spirit. Both the former and the latter understand the saying in a way contrary to its true meaning.

The former, the slothful *traditionalists* who invoke the Spirit and then defend everything that has become established in the Church, overlook what is said *before* the statement about the Spirit who guides us into all truth: that is, that the Spirit continually comes to 'convince the world [and this means the evil, sinful world, hostile to God] concerning sin and righteousness and judgment' (16.8). He comes to judge the world indeed, but also the Church, which is in this world and which only too often appears as a worldly Church. And the Spirit must continually disclose afresh the guilt of this worldly Church. He must open its eyes to sin, justice and judgment: to sin which is fundamentally unbelief in regard to Jesus Christ, to justice which consists in overcoming through Jesus the world hostile to God, to judgment which has already been passed on this hostile world in Christ's death and resurrection.

The Church too – and this is what we all are – has every reason to ask continually whether it accords with faith in Jesus Christ, whether it lives by his justice, whether it takes account of the judgment that has been passed. The Church has continually every reason for penance and reflection and thus for its own part for conversion, reform and renewal. Unfortunately, the history of the Church is not a continual ascent, a continual improvement. The idea of perpetual progress even of the Church is an idea of the Enlightenment, not an idea of Christian revelation. In the history of the Church there is a certain progress, but repeatedly also a regress. In the history of the Church there is an ascent, but repeatedly also a descent. In the history of the Church there is a development, but repeatedly also entanglement and aberration.

The Church, believing in the Spirit of Christ who guides it continually into the truth, knows that the Spirit again and again confronts it also with its own sin, with the justice of Christ, and with judgment. It knows that in this very way the Spirit demands of it once more a new faith in Christ, a greater fidelity to the gospel, a life lived more seriously according to his message.

In this sense the Church under the Spirit may never simply leave things as they are, but must continually allow all things to become new in this Spirit who renews the face of the earth and also of the Church, who is the Spirit of him who says, 'Behold, I make all things new' (Rev. 21.5).

The saying about the Spirit who guides the Church into all truth, however, is wrongly understood, not only by those who think they can appeal to the Spirit to guide them into all truth and then leave everything as it was but also by those who think they can appeal to the same Spirit and then accept every novelty in the Church as a truth of the Spirit. The latter, the superficial *modernists*, overlook what *follows* the statement about the Spirit who guides into all truth: that is, the Spirit who 'will not speak on his own authority, but whatever he hears he will speak, and he will declare to you the things that are to come. He will glorify me, for he will take what is mine and declare it to you. All that the Father has is mine; therefore I said that he will take what is mine and declare it to you' (John 16.13–15).

What the Spirit then has to tell the Church are not any *new* revelations, *new* teachings, *new* promises, which might be added to supplement or surpass what Christ said. What is said of the Spirit is not that he will guide us into *new* truths, but that he will guide us into *all* the truth. This in fact is the basic conviction of the evangelists, that Jesus' word is the absolutely decisive word which decides life and death. The reason the officers give to the high priest for their failure to arrest Jesus is: 'No man ever spoke like this man' (John 7.46). The one who speaks here is not one of the Old Testament prophets, whose words are freshly inspired by the Holy Spirit *on each occasion*, but one who speaks and acts *continually* in virtue of his unity with God. No prophet has absolute significance: prophets succeed one another, one comes after the other. But after Jesus there is no new revealer: in him God's revelation is given once and for all to the world.

True, this revelation is inexhaustible. But what is bestowed by the Spirit on the Church as new knowledge does not supplement or surpass what Christ as revealer has said. It is merely the recollection of what Jesus said: the Spirit will only 'bring to remembrance' what Jesus said (14.26); he will not speak 'on his own authority', but will only say what he 'hears'

(16.13); he will 'take what is mine' (16.14); he will 'bear witness' to Jesus (15.26).

The Spirit then will teach *nothing new*. But all that Jesus taught and did he will manifest *in a new light*, in a new age, in the face of new situations and new experiences. Only in this way will the truth of Jesus Christ become freshly clear and intelligible in its meaning for today.

APPLICATIONS

These more precise definitions should help to make the maintenance of the Church in the truth of Jesus Christ by the Spirit more comprehensible.

1. If remaining in the truth is essentially a question of discipleship in the Spirit of Jesus Christ, this is *more a matter of orthopraxy than of orthodoxy*: it is realized more in the Christian life than in teaching, more in the deed than merely in the word.

For although what a person believes about Jesus Christ is by no means irrelevant, although this belief must determine his practical approach, it is nevertheless not the ultimate decisive factor. Merely saying 'Lord, Lord' is of no avail. The brother who says he will not obey and yet does so is preferred to the one who says he will obey and yet does not. In the passages on Jesus' calling of his disciples he never asks first for a profession of faith. The profoundly disturbing Sermon on the Mount is centred not on orthodox belief but on radical observance of God's will in service to one's neighbour. Why? Because Christian truth is concrete. According to Matthew, at the last judgment the verdict depends on what is done, on involvement on behalf of one's fellow human beings.

2. If remaining in the truth is essentially a question of discipleship in the Spirit of Jesus Christ, this is *a matter more of individuals and individual communities than of institutions*. Obviously Christian institutions also are bound by the gospel of Jesus Christ. But institutions as such cannot guarantee the persistence of the believing community in truth.

Because institutions are in the hands of men, they can be misused and corrupted. Often the individual and the individual community are maintained in the truth of Jesus Christ, despite the failure of certain institutions and their representatives to function evangelically (and therefore call for reform). However much institutions are necessary for a community and so too for a believing community, and particularly for a large believing community, in the last resort they are not essential for persistence in truth. They should foster this permanence, but may also prevent it. The Church is essentially a believing community, but decisions for faith occur in the heart of the individual. Institutions have no heart. There is an ultimate immediacy of the individual to God and to his truth over which no institution has power, not even by means of the stake or of excommunication. Discipleship of Christ therefore is continually possible even when it is more impeded than helped by institutions.

3. If remaining in the truth is essentially a question of discipleship in the Spirit of Jesus Christ, this is manifested *not only in the great, strictly orthodox churches but also among heretics*. This does not mean that heresy thus becomes truth. Whatever represents 'another gospel', thus rendering doubtful the foundation of the faith of the ecclesia and consequently opposed to the ecclesia, cannot be described as truth. But if we look at concrete individuals and communities, this distinction between truth and error is by no means easy to establish.

This is so because, on the one hand, there is truth in heresy: genuine heresies live not so much by error as by the truth invested in them and often exaggerated. On the other hand there is also error in the Church: errors, aberrations and deceptions, omissions, blockages and displacements, have often provided an occasion, a cause, an opening, for heresy. The latter often did not represent arbitrary action but understandable reaction: in good faith, in faith in the gospel, in the determination not to betray that gospel. Good faith, even good faith in Christ, must not be denied to the heretic. Errors may be condemned, but not erring individuals. Even the heretic can be influenced and can abide by the gospel and has been so influenced, often more than the self-important highly orthodox individual. It is because of this faith that discipleship of Christ is by no means impossible for him. Hence it must be said that, as the Church is preserved in the truth despite all errors, the heretic who strives for discipleship in virtue of his faith in the gospel is similarly preserved despite his heresy (which is not on that account justified).

4. If remaining in the truth is essentially a question of discipleship in the Spirit of Jesus Christ, this is manifested, *despite the failure of hierarchy and theology, in the living faith of the 'little people'*. There were times when little of the truth of the gospel could be observed in the lives and activities of hierarchs and theologians, when the Church came close to perishing and the promise of indestructibility seemed an empty phrase. But when popes and bishops pursued power, money and pleasure, and theologians kept silent, slept, produced apologias, or even collaborated, there still remained those innumerable, mostly unknown Christians (among them at all times even some bishops, theologians and particularly parish priests) who tried even at the worst times of the Church to live according to the gospel.

Thus it was not so much the high and mighty, the clever and wise, but the 'little people', the 'insignificant', who – and this is wholly in accordance with the New Testament – were 'witnesses of the truth' and manifested the indestructibility of the Church. That genuine renewal, which for the most part was not attained by any sort of dogmatic definition but by reflection on the gospel, by a change of awareness and genuine repentance, in prayer, suffering and action, came very often and at first unobtrusively from the circles of these 'little people'.

Under these circumstances what function is left to the various offices in the Church, especially those which provide a service, for the persistence of the Church in truth? Here we can only draw some provisional conclusions from what has been said. In any case offices do not establish truth in the Church. Officeholders too can err and frequently do err and, like institutions generally, can be corrupted. Officeholders therefore are not the cause of the Church's persistence in truth. It is despite the error even of many officeholders that the Church is maintained in the truth. The gospel itself is the source, norm and power for faith and for the continuity (perenniality) and indestructibility (indefectibility) of the believing community in the truth. Of course officeholders can and should have a positive, auxiliary function in this respect, in so far as they have to undertake in particular a service to the *truth* in the light of the special function of each office in the service of the gospel and of the believing community. As far as the Church's leaders are concerned, this is a service to the truth by the manifold proclamation of the gospel and the meaningful administration of the sacraments publicly before the congregation and consequently by active commitment in Church and society.

We shall have to return to this question. But before that we must discuss another aspect of maintaining the Church in truth: the concrete problem of errors in the Church.

Living with Errors

ERRORS ARE FACTS

In the course of discussions on infallibility people often ask with some anxiety what would happen if the Church, if a Pope or a council, were to err with reference to an important question of faith or morals in a solemn definition which would formerly have been regarded as infallible.

The question is understandable. What happens in the event of error? First of all the answer must be that there is no need at all for panic. Error on the part of the Church's magisterium in serious definitions of faith or morals is in any case a fact – and we are still alive. If anyone thinks that *Humanae vitae* is not sufficiently clear or serious, let him consider the definition of the Council of Trent on the transmission of original sin through procreation or the definition of the same council (which cannot be justified in the light of Christian origins) on the sacramental character of ordination as an indelible mark on the soul. Or, again, what about the solemn condemnation (understood in a dogmatic sense) of freedom of religion and conscience or the solemn proclamation in church documents from the time of the Galileo crisis up to our own century of the complete inerrancy of the Bible? We need not discuss here when an 'infallible' definition was involved and when it was not (this is a distinction introduced subsequently). According to Vatican I and II, the 'infallibility' not only of the 'extraordinary' but also of the 'ordinary' everyday teaching of Pope and bishops, extending to a variety of things, would have to be considered. In any case, even in the past century, quite a number of statements were presented as articles of faith (*de fide*) which are not admitted today (we need only recall the condemnations of the *Syllabus of Errors* of Pius IX which were regarded by some theologians after Vatican I as 'infallible', the theses against the scientific theory of man's origin, the antimodernist professions

of faith required of all the clergy under pressure of conscience
and compulsory oaths).

But whatever may be or may have been considered in
particular as 'infallible' teaching and what was not there is a
consensus on the fact of an erring magisterium even with regard
to the organs of 'infallible' dogmatic definitions (Pope, episcopate, ecumenical council). And the errors involved were
certainly sufficiently serious in themselves and in their consequences. For many this is now evident in the case of *Humanae
vitae*. Obvious also today more than ever are the negative
consequences of the Augustinian theory of original sin as
transmitted by procreation, consequences in regard to the
disparagement of sexual pleasure and in regard to the salvation
of unbaptized children; the consequences also of the doctrine of
the sacramental character (likewise going back to Augustine)
for dogmatically justified clericalism; of the doctrine of the
inerrancy of the Bible for the Church's attitude to the natural
sciences and history; of the condemnation of freedom of
conscience and religion for many persecuted Protestants and
for the position of Catholics in modern society.

Any minimizing of the errors of the ecclesiastical
magisterium is out of the question. Nevertheless . . .

THE CHURCH LIVES ON

In the believing community, as with conflicts, we must live or
learn to live with errors. The Church has 'survived' errors or
'survives' them up to a point in the immediate present with
some pain. But it continues to live and, despite all the serious
encumbrances, the truth can be perceived in the Church now as
before. For in the last resort the Church does not live by its
errors but by the truth of the gospel, which is able to prevail
even alongside numerous and serious errors.

To be more precise, there can be discipleship of Christ even if
a believer understands one or another point of doctrine in a way
that is contrary to the gospel. A truly evangelical basic attitude
can be no more nullified by individual erroneous propositions
than it is by individual sins. Correctly understood, 'simultaneously justified and sinner' (*simul justus et peccator*) has its
parallel in a rightly understood 'simultaneously believer and

unbeliever' (*simul fidelis et incredulus*). Every believer has reason to confess, 'Lord, I believe, help my unbelief!'

What is true of the individual can be said analogously of the ecclesial community. In the Church there will always be a sufficient number of people who so live according to the gospel that the message can be perceived and that to speak of the ecclesial community remaining in the truth makes sense, a permanence in the truth which cannot be nullified by individual erroneous propositions even if these have an official character. Like the *simul justus et peccator*, so too the *simul fidelis et incredulus* has an ecclesiological dimension. The Church is not a community of the perfect; it is on pilgrimage, *in statu viatoris*. More important than one or another false step, one or another wrong turn or detour, is the basic trend, determined by promise, of the believing community in the truth and toward the ultimate truth, which itself – as we have stressed – is a truth of faith. All detours and wrong turns in wandering through the desert did not in any way alter the fact that the ancient people of God were basically on the right road to the promised land. All the false steps, false conclusions, blunders and slips will not ultimately divert the people of God now wandering through many a desert from its destined course.

Even a possibly false dogma (and how many a dogma has been forgotten today or touches the Christian's sense of faith marginally at best) cannot destroy the Church's being and truth. The totality of faith consists in the integrity of commitment, not in completely correct propositions. And that commitment can be entire and unreserved even though something false is said at the same time. Errors of the Church's magisterium are a serious matter, but they are not a threat to the existence of the Church. This is precisely what is meant by the promise of indestructibility in truth. And this promise should really take away from Christians of little faith that fear of error which often appears to be greater than the fear of sin. Why does not the Holy Spirit prevent such errors from the outset? This was the kind of question raised by a number of people before and after *Humanae vitae*. The answer is that God's Spirit does not nullify man's humanity: to err is human. The more urgent question is why the Church in particular, which has written reorientation and repentance on its banner, has notable difficulty in correcting its errors. The answer is that the Church is inclined to identify itself with God's Spirit and thus ascribes to itself God's infallibility, from which it then deduces the irreformability, the incorrigibility, of its definitions. Should not the opposite be the case? Should not the Church under the gospel, as *ecclesia semper reformanda*, revise and correct its errors more easily and more rapidly than others and in this very way render credible precisely its indestructibility in truth.

If then we are to allow so concretely for errors on the part of the Church's magisterium, how can we know at all what is truth in the Church and what is not? The problem of *confirmation*, of *verification*, arises here.

Criteria of Christian Truth

THE GOSPEL OF JESUS CHRIST AS PRIMARY CRITERION

The first thing to be noticed is that recent teaching on infallibility is faced with quite serious difficulties when it comes to verification. Even if I accept infallible propositions as a fact, the question arises as to why these statements are true. Certainly their truth does not simply follow from their infallibility. Even according to the usual teaching, dogmas are not true because they have been defined; they are defined because they are true. Why then are they true? Why, for instance, is the dogma of Mary's immaculate conception supposed to be true, but not the dogma (desired at least by some people) of the immaculate conception of Saint Joseph? The more radical question might be: Why cannot both be true or both false?

What then is the *criterion* to be if we have to allow for errors on the part of the ecclesiastical magisterium and, under certain conditions, even in what were formerly regarded as infallible dogmatic definitions?

Certainly it cannot simply be practice: otherwise success would become the criterion of truth and what is there that is not successful in this world?

Neither can it simply be reason: otherwise Christian truth would be reduced to general truths of reason and thus become superfluous.

But it cannot be the faith, or the sense of faith, of the people: otherwise it would become only too often superstition.

Finally, the dogmas themselves cannot form the criterion: this would be to beg the question, an argument which turns out to be a vicious circle (dogmas are true because they have been made into dogmas).

The method of verification must be appropriate to the facts to be verified. There are various forms of verification. The criterion for what is supposed to be true in the *Christian* Church can be nothing but the *Christian message*, the gospel of Jesus Christ as originally recorded in the New Testament – in writing, making arbitrary changes and developments impossible – and thus *Jesus Christ* himself. The New Testament (as explained in concrete detail in *On Being a Christian*) may not be understood in a biblicist-fundamentalist sense as a collection of infallible statements, but must be given an historical-critical interpretation at the highest level of modern hermeneutics. At the same time it must be transmitted to the present, not only existentially with respect to the individual but also socially with respect to the community, a process in which practice in the second place has also a hermeneutical function: how far can this truth have its influence on life?

THE SIGNIFICANCE OF THE COMMUNITY AND TRADITION

Since Christian truth does not claim to be an eternal idea but is essentially historical truth, there are two factors which cannot be neglected in the process of verification.

The first is the factor of *community*. The truth reached me by way of the believing community and is still lived today in that community. Whether I want to do so or not, I cannot disregard this sociological context. But since I am part of that living, believing community itself, from which these testimonies have emerged and to which they continue to mean life, I could gain a deeper understanding of the meaning of these testimonies both originally and today.

The second factor is *tradition*. The Christian message was not devised by the present generation. It has been handed down through a history of twenty centuries. I am neither the author nor the first interpreter of Christian truth. History, like the community, can help me to break through the limits of my subjectivity and to perceive the truth more deeply and more comprehensively. The community and the tradition of the Church then form an essential part of the process of discovering Christian truth. This is precisely what is meant by catholicity in space and time.

The Christian and in particular the theologian is thus situated at a point between the original gospel and the present-day ecclesial sense of faith. Anyone who simply accepts as 'super-criterion' either the 'Church's present sense of faith' or the ecclesiastical 'magisterium' in one way or the other becomes an apologist for the ecclesiastical system: he is overlooking the fact that, even according to Vatican II, the magisterium is under the word of God and consequently is open to criticism in the light of the normative criterion of Scripture. On the other hand, anyone who neglects the Church's sense of faith and simply makes the gospel the ultimate criterion is in danger of lapsing into an emotional subjectivism: with the air of the historical-critical method he makes light of the ultimate authority of faith. It seems as if a hermeneutical circle cannot be avoided in practice. Unlike the historian of religion, the theologian works within the limits of the Church's faith and presupposes it, but at the same time is expected to study it in a critically scientific spirit. In this respect he or she resembles up to a point the political theorist who is loyal to his state and the constitution and yet has to study it in a critically scientific spirit. This is difficult, but not impossible.

A critically scientific theology is therefore required and not a theology which is part of the 'system', justifying the Church's dogmatic system in every case. The theologian who works in this way from within the system starts out from the 'Church's present sense of faith' or, more precisely, from the 'infallible' official ecclesiastical dogmatic definitions and continually returns to these definitions. Since it is claimed that the latter can never have been false and therefore may not be corrected under any circumstances, only two possibilities remain: either simply to repeat them and support them with any quotations from Scripture and Tradition that can be found (this is how positive neoscholastic theology works), or to 'interpret' them speculatively and try to make it possible for them to be assimilated by the modern mind (this is how speculative neoscholastic theology works). Since such an 'interpretation' lacks any sort of criterion, no limits are set in practice to subjective whim in this 'interpretation' or 'reinterpretation' of dogmas. Thus the axiom 'Outside the Church no salvation' is still used today when it is admitted by Vatican II that vast numbers of people in no way attached to the visible Church can be saved, so that it means in effect:

'Outside the Church there is certainly salvation.' Interpretation is turned into contradiction.

On the other hand, the critically scientific theologian takes account quite concretely of the Church's sense of faith – and not only the present but also the former sense of faith (catholicity in space and time), which, as shown in the question of papal and conciliar infallibility, often includes a critique of the actual sense of faith. This present-day sense of faith must on no account be justified at the expense of truth. It must be measured against the original, authoritative New Testament testimony of faith and, under certain conditions, be very substantially corrected.

Hence various theological *loci* or sources of theology must certainly be considered, but they are not to be artificially harmonized, assimilated and equalized, as if they were all of equal value! No, all ecclesiastical decisions, even the most solemn conciliar ones, on their own admission never possess more than a derived, secondary *standardized authority* by comparison with the original, primary *standardizing authority* of the gospel and Jesus Christ himself who is attested there. It is then only with reference to the gospel of Jesus Christ – to which they always seek to appeal – that councils and other ecclesiastical authorites can demand an unconditional assent. This is also true if it is assumed that councils cannot err, but it becomes even more important if the possibility of error is admitted.

IN WHAT DOES THE CHRISTIAN BELIEVE

What does the Christian actually believe in? Not in propositions certainly, nor precisely in truths (in the plural). It is true that professions of faith, which summarize certain truths or events, can be helpful; but the Christian does not believe 'in' professions. Definitions of faith, which mark off certain points of the Christian message from what is unchristian, are perhaps unavoidable in extreme situations; but Christians do not believe 'in' definitions. Strictly speaking, they do not believe 'in' the Bible or 'in' tradition or 'in' the Church. But the specific danger of Protestant belief in particular is biblicism, the danger of Eastern Orthodox belief is traditionalism, and the danger of Roman Catholic belief is authoritarianism. All these are defective modes of belief. On the other hand, it must be clearly stated:

- The Christian (even the Protestant) believes, not in the Bible, but in him whom it attests.
- The Christian (even the Orthodox) believes, not in tradition, but in him whom it conveys.
- The Christian (even the Roman Catholic) believes, not in the Church, but in him whom it proclaims.

The absolutely reliable reality, to which man can cling for time and eternity, is not the biblical text, nor the work of the Church Fathers, neither is it an ecclesiastical magisterium, but it is *God himself as he has spoken and acted for believers through Jesus Christ*. The texts of the Bible, the statements of the Fathers and of ecclesiastical authorities – in varying importance – are meant to be no more and no less than an expression of this faith.

Consequently, I do not simply believe various facts, truths, theories or dogmas: I do not believe this or that. Neither do I believe merely in the trustworthiness of a person: I do not believe simply in this person or that. What I do is to venture to commit myself quite personally to a message, a truth, a way, a hope, ultimately to someone: I believe in God and in him whom God has sent.

All of this should have brought out the ultimate reason why individual articles of faith are important but not in the last resort decisive. Certainty, dependability and assurance are conveyed – through all the propositions – by the ground of faith: God himself and his Christ, who is proclaimed in propositions, in true propositions, but who is able also to rouse attention by ambiguous and occasionally even false propositions.

Faith is like *love*. If I love someone but have to explain suddenly why I love that person, I may stutter, make mistakes, exaggerate one thing and understate another, say something distorted or even false, stress what is unimportant and even forget what is important. But this is not necessarily detrimental to my love. Love is dependent on statements if it is to find expression. But love is not completely expressed in statements. True love persists even through untrue statements.

It is the same when I have to say why *I believe* in God, in Jesus. I formulate my reasons perhaps obscurely, imprecisely, even falsely. I overlook one thing and overvalue another. In my statement I may miss what is absolutely essential and have to correct myself afterwards. But this need not be detrimental to my belief in God and Jesus. Belief is dependent on propositions if it has to be professed, expressed, proclaimed, taught. But faith is not completely expressed in propositions. True faith is maintained even through untrue propositions. Christian faith is not a closed, quasi-mathematical system of propositions, as a theology infected with rationalism tried to make it, so that it ceases to be true as soon as one of the propositions is found to be incorrect (hence up to a point the anxiety to make sure that all propositions are correct). Christian faith, like love, can be wholly real, even if one of its propositions is not correct.

Is this not a consoling answer? Very much more consoling than the promise at some point of a number of guaranteed, infallible propositions, which still could not save us. If, following Augustine, we say, 'Love, and do what you will', we could perhaps analogously say, 'Believe, and say what you can.' This second brief statement is at least as misleading as the first: the importance of good and true formulations of belief should not be played down. But the essential point should be made clear, that to those who love God (and men) all things – even distorted and false formulations of faith – eventually work for good.

The Opportunities of a Fallible 'Magisterium'

IS THE 'MAGISTERIUM' INCAPABLE OF FUNCTIONING?

The task of the Church, of each individual, and especially of the leaders, is to bear witness to this faith of theirs and give an account of it, to hand on the good news in word and deed, to make clear the grandeur of the cause of Jesus Christ and so too the grandeur of the cause of God and of man, to explain and interpret the meaning of all this quite concretely for modern man and modern society. In this sense there is really no objection to a (pastoral) 'magisterium', even though the term introduced at a late stage and not clear in its connotation, is better avoided, since it suggests an anonymous bureaucracy (particularly if we speak of a 'Teaching Office' as a kind of parallel to a 'Home Office' or a 'Foreign Office') and implies an unbiblical distinction between the Church teaching and the Church taught.

It would be better to speak concretely of leaders and heads of churches and congregations, of parochial clergy (in the widest sense, as including parish priests, curates, and chaplains) and bishops (including the Pope). These leaders and heads of the local, regional, and universal Church have as their great, primary task to see to the proclamation of the gospel publicly before the Church and the world. At the same time the greatest importance is to be attached to the daily, and in particular Sunday, proclamation event, compared to which any kind of solemn, extraordinary acts (a single 'infallible' definition, for instance, in a hundred years) are much less significant. These church leaders should undertake their function of leadership mainly through the daily proclamation of the gospel in a variety of shapes and forms, assisting, encouraging, exhorting and consoling: they should lead their congregations, large or small, in the spirit of Jesus Christ, they should work on individual believers and groups, integrating, coordinating, stimulating, inspiring, and eventually also representing the community internally and externally. In this sense we can speak of a *ministry of leadership and proclamation on the part of priests and bishops* (as also of the Pope).

Here, however, the question repeatedly arises as to whether the magisterium is rendered *incapable of functioning* (incapable of action, checkmated) if it cannot produce any infallible decisions. How are the Pope, the episcopate, the council to undertake their task if in a case of doubt they cannot define infallibly who is right? How, that is, can they function without infallibility? In the first place, of course, we can answer that Pope and bishops are continually exercising their function, even though they produce 'infallible' decisions only in the rarest cases (parish priests, incidentally, produce none at all). There can be no question therefore of paralysing their magisterium if they are denied the power of making infallible decisions. Instead, such a denial implies a positive invitation to them to take even more seriously their fundamental, normal, daily task of proclamation. Nevertheless, we must go briefly into the question of how episcopate (in council) and Pope can function if, like the ordinary priest, they cannot make infallible decisions.

In this connection one thing must be mentioned first. Oddly enough, as the discussion on infallibility has shown, people today scarcely seem to have any difficulties with the fallibility of the *Bible* like those which they have with the fallibility of the Pope or of a council. The Bible anyway functions quite well even without infallible propositions. After all the difficulties with modernism, eventually even with Rome's consent, the historical-critical method came to prevail in Catholic exegesis much earlier than in Catholic dogmatics, where that which has long been taken for granted in the exegesis of the Bible is only now being realized in the history of dogma: truly historical thinking. In historical-critical exegesis it has been shown that the truth of Scripture is not only not destroyed but even emerges with fresh clarity and luminosity when at last we cease to defend every statement of Scripture as infallibly true because 'inspired'. A wholly fresh light was thrown on the great truth of a good God and his good world in the creation account when the attempt was abandoned to establish for apologetic reasons a concordism, with every statement regarded as true in the scientific or historical sense. Even without infallible statements, the Bible was thus able to assert its unsurpassable authority, to make effective its absolute claim to truth, to offer continually a new invitation to faith and radical commitment.

HOW THE COUNCIL MIGHT FUNCTION

If the Bible can manage without infallible propositions, the question naturally arises of whether councils likewise might function without them. How is the infallibility of councils to be substantiated by Scripture if the latter itself shows no signs of possessing such infallibility?

If we want to see concretely how councils can function without infallible propositions, it is best to take a look at the first ecumenical council, that of Nicaea in 325, which managed without making any claim to infallibility. Recent historical investigation has brought out how Athanasius, the leading person at this council, together with the Greek Fathers and also Augustine, established the true, although by no means infallible, authority of a council. A council tells the truth not because its convocation is legally unimpeachable, not because the majority of the bishops of the world are gathered there, not because it is confirmed by any human authority, not because it has the extraordinary assistance of the Holy Spirit, and not because it cannot then be a priori deceived. No, despite the new words, a council does not tell new truths; but it tells the truth because it conveys the old tradition in a new language, because it attests the original message and breathes Scripture, *because it has the gospel behind it.* Why could not a council function in this way even today?

Oddly enough, the first and what is currently the last ecumenical council of the Catholic Church coincide in this respect, that neither wanted to produce definitions which would be a priori infallibly true. The infallible definitions at first envisaged by the curial preparatory theological commission of Vatican II would have been about as much or as little use as Pius IX's long list of condemned errors a hundred years earlier. John XXIII, less as a theologian than as an evangelically minded pastor and man of common sense, had seen that infallible decisions would be of no advantage to the council, that the council would function only if it was *pastorally oriented, giving new currency to the truth of the gospel*, without any claim to infallibility, in the language of people today. As he said in the opening speech to the council, 'The salient point of this Council is not a discussion of one article or another of the fundamental doctrine of the Church which has repeatedly been taught by the Fathers and by ancient and modern theologians, and which is presumed to be well known and familiar to all. For this a Council was not necessary.' What the Pope expected was an up-to-date proclamation: 'a step forward toward a doctrinal penetration and a formation of consciousness in faithful and perfect conformity to the authentic doctrine, which, however, should be studied and expounded through the methods of research and through the literary forms of modern thought'. To those who fear modernism in any reorganization and renewal of doctrine the Pope points out, 'The *substance* of the ancient doctrine of the deposit of faith is one thing, and *the way in which it is presented* is another. And it is the latter that must be taken into great consideration with patience if necessary, everything being measured in the forms and proportions of a magisterium which is predominantly pastoral in character.'

A council then can be of service to Christian proclamation, albeit only to a limited extent (without professional theology) and at best when concentrated on certain important points. It will normally be able to undertake this *theoretical task* credibly only if it works at the same time for the *practical renewal* of the Church in the Christian spirit. The Council of Nicaea itself (this fact is often overlooked) was occupied also with questions of church discipline. And in the tradition of the high mediaeval reform councils, both at Trent and at Vatican I and II 'reform', together with 'teaching', became the second pole of the conciliar efforts. Quite frequently the success or failure, the functioning or non-functioning of a council has been measured more by its results by way of reform than by the effects of its teaching.

All this does not exclude the possibility that a council may produce unambiguous demarcations, not indeed in any questions of theological detail but wherever essential Christian values are at stake, in extreme cases. But even then (the history of the 'reception' or 'acceptance' of councils by the ecclesial community proves this) the council will prevail, not by claiming ecumenicity or infallibility (many councils have tried to do this in vain) but only because and in so far as it has the truth of the gospel credibly behind it. A council then can speak only in a way that relates to the particular situation and not by any means infallibly, but nevertheless *with binding force* and in decisive questions with ultimate binding force. This ultimate binding force can come only from the truth behind which is God himself: from the Christian message which, in a particular situation, does not permit long discussion and careful differentiation, but can demand a completely sincere and absolute assent (on certain occasions as a matter of life or death).

When a child has fallen in the river, we do not discuss the different methods of saving life. If it is really a question of the existence or non-existence of the Church or if the fate of innumerable human beings is directly involved, theological distinctions are out of place and a clear profession of faith must be attempted, even though this might be dangerous. It is of course understood that eventual condemnations must arise out of a real emergency and at some cost to the ecclesiastical representatives; they should not be facile interventions of ecclesiastical bureaucracies in times of peace, seeking to stifle instead of accepting justified criticism. As protection against accidents does not constitute the sum total of children's education, neither does proclamation in the Church consist merely in the condemnation of errors. The *opportunity* of a council today, as Vatican II showed very clearly, lies in making a constructive contribution, without any claim to infallibility and in full awareness of the limited possibilities, to the solution of the great problems of the Church, of Christendom, of society, and of humanity today.

HOW THE POPE COULD FUNCTION

How could the Pope function without infallible dogmatic definitions? In our own time we have seen something of both possibilities. First there was Pope Pius XII, who decided a century after Vatican I to claim the authority ascribed to the Pope by the council but not claimed in the meantime, in order to proclaim *urbi et orbi* an infallible dogmatic definition, a new Marian dogma. And yet none of his dogmatic statements were so disputed in Christendom and even in the Catholic Church as this 'infallible' definition. The pastoral effects on the devotion of the Catholic people and the conversion of the world, expected at the time, are seen in a more sober light at a distance of thirty years. Vatican II dissociated itself from extreme Marian ideas and in practice brought these to an end, making even more obvious the dubiousness of that definition.

The other example is of the next Pope, John XXIII, who from the very beginning had no intention of pronouncing an infallible definition. On the contrary, he repeatedly insisted in one form or another on his own human weakness, limitation, and even from time to time on his fallibility. He lacked the aura of infallibility. And yet none of the Popes of this century exercised a greater influence on the course of the history of the Catholic Church and indeed of Christendom as a whole than did this Pope who attached no importance to infallibility. With him and Vatican II a new epoch of church history was inaugurated. Without any infallible propositions he succeeded in gaining a hearing once more in a variety of ways for the gospel of Jesus Christ in the Church. Consequently he possessed an authority inside and outside the Catholic Church which would have been unthinkable in the time of his predecessor. Anyway, with all his weaknesses and faults, more spontaneously than deliberately, more symbolically than programmatically, he let it be seen in outline how the Pope might be really Pope without any claim to infallibility. Such a Pope would not jealously insist on his powers and prerogatives or exercise authority in the spirit of the ancien régime, but would exercise an authority of service in the spirit of the New Testament related to the needs of the present time. He would enter into fraternal partnership, co-operation, dialogue, consultation and collaboration, especially with the bishops and theologians as a whole; he would involve those concerned in the decision-making process and invite them to share responsibility. The Pope then should exercise his function in this way even in questions of proclamation and teaching: *in* the Church, *with* the Church, *for* the Church, but not *above* or *outside* the Church.

Again, there is nothing to prevent a Pope from occasionally reacting *against* something and under certain conditions being bound to react. No infallible decision would have been required, a clear understandable word in terms of the Christian message spoken by Christ's 'Vicar' would have sufficed in the face of the invasion of Poland or the mass murder of the Jews. It is strange, however, that nothing was said 'infallibly' in recent times at the very moment when countless people might have expected it. On the other hand, despite all fallibility, the Pope (together with the rest of the bishops) can serve the ecclesial community and its unity, inspire the Church's missionary work in the world, intensify its efforts for peace and justice, for disarmament, human rights, the social liberation of peoples and races, its involvement on behalf of the underprivileged of all kinds. Without any claim to infallibility, as mediator and inspirer in the Spirit of Christ and as leader in the Christian renewal, he can constantly make the voice of the Good Shepherd heard in his teaching and working in the Christian *oikumene* and far beyond it. Rome would thus become a place of meeting, for discussion and for sincere and friendly collaboration.

Out of all this it follows that the Pope can function even without infallible dogmatic definitions; indeed, under the present conditions of Church and society, he can fulfil his ministry *better* without infallible dogmatic definitions. If anyone therefore questions papal infallibility in regard to propositions, he is not thereby questioning the papacy as such. So much must be said emphatically against constant confusions, distortions and suspicions. There is a good deal about the Petrine ministry that has become questionable, especially the mediaeval and modern absolutist forms which have been maintained up to our own time. A Petrine ministry has a future only if it is understood in the light of the Petrine symbol in the New Testament. The exegetical and historical substantiation of a *historical* succession of the bishops of Rome has become questionable. But a Petrine ministry has retained its objective meaning if, in its *functional and practical* succession, it is a ministry to the Church as a whole: a *primacy of service* in the full biblical sense.

Such a primacy of service, as it became visible at least in outline in the person of John XXIII, offers a real *opportunity* to the Catholic Church and to Christendom as a whole. A primacy of service would be more than a 'primacy of honour': the latter cannot be condoned in a Church of service, nor in its passivity can it be a help to anyone. A primacy of service would also be more than a 'primacy of jurisdiction': the latter is a complete misunderstanding if it is taken to mean sheer power and authority; literally understood, it conceals the very essence of this primacy, the aspect of service. Petrine ministry, understood biblically, can only be a 'pastoral primacy': a pastoral ministry to the Church as a whole. As such and regardless of all unclarified and indeed unclarifiable questions of *historical* succession, it is supported objectively by the New Testament. In this sense it could be of the greatest value today for Christendom as a whole. It would speak for the great concerns not only of Roman Catholic Christianity but of Christendom as a whole.

In Case of Conflict

DIFFERENT FUNCTIONS

It should be clear by now that the ministries of leadership can function as a service of pastoral proclamation without infallibility. We withdraw nothing of what has been said, we do not weaken but in fact strengthen authority, if, again on the lines of Vatican II, we stress the fact that the ministries of leadership must act continually in collegiality, solidarity, and fellowship with all *other ministries* in the Church. No one in the Church has a monopoly of truth; no one may limit, channel or regularize the diverse charisms.

Among these other ministries, from the very beginning, 'prophets' and 'teachers' in the Church have had a special importance which cannot be superseded by the ministries of leadership. Prophets and theologians in particular are at the service of truth in the Church.

The *prophets*, lesser or greater, men or women, aware of their vocation and responsibility, by letting the Spirit speak directly in a particular situation point the way to the present and the future. Their 'one-sided' warnings and 'harsh' demands on the Church and its leaders – like those of the Old Testament prophets in regard to the hierarchs and the people of Jerusalem – are unwelcome at the time, but they also convey courage, clarity and joy for the renewal of the truth by the power of the Spirit.

The *theologians*, for their part, struggle by different methods to find the authentic tradition and the correct interpretation of the original message, in order to bring the latter out of the past and offer it freshly to Church and society today. By critical scrutiny of current teaching and reflection on the gospel itself they can stimulate and inaugurate better proclamation and action.

And what happens when *conflicts* arise over the question of

truth in the Church, conflicts especially between leaders and
teachers in the Church, between bishops (or Pope) and
theologians? Here we can offer only a few brief observations.

ON COPING WITH CONFLICTS

1. Conflicts are *borderline cases*. In determining the authority
of church leaders and theologians and their relations with one
another, we must not think simply in terms of a case of conflict
and in that light try to establish the dominion in principle of one
group over the other. The case of conflict must remain a
borderline case; it must not be allowed to become a basic model.
Here, too, fear is a bad counsellor.

2. Even in the Church conflicts are *unavoidable*. They are
signs of life and in any case are to be preferred to the deathly
silence of totalitarian systems. Conflicts must be endured and a
fruitful settlement attempted. At the same time no group may
simply outmanoeuvre the other. It is no help to the well-being
of the whole or the freedom of the individual if one group comes
to prevail at the expense of the other; instead there must be
intensive and active collaboration in the service of the common
cause.

3. A solution in principle for cases of conflict, which are
always possible, must be based on the clearest possible
differentiation of areas of competence. Obviously even this will not
lead to an idyllic future for the Church, free from conflict. But
by the clear demarcation of responsibilities and with moderation on the part of each group many conflicts could be
avoided from the very beginning. Leaders on the one hand and
theologians on the other have their own specific charism, their
own peculiar vocation, their proper function. Theologians
should not want to be bishops nor should bishops want to be
theologians. Neither a church of professors nor a church of
hierarchs accords with the New Testament. Both the ministry
of leadership of bishops and priests and the ministry of teaching
of theologians have their particular importance and also their
particular assumptions. From the outset they are dependent on
one another's cooperation, since they both have their origin in
the same gospel of Jesus Christ and both exist for the same
people. Both have to serve the proclamation of the gospel in

their own specific fashion, whether by leadership (preeminently by preaching at the congregational act of worship) or by study and teaching.

4. We cannot discuss here in detail how churches are to be governed or the study of theology pursued in a normal situation. What is *essential* for the church leadership and theology is laid down in the *gospel*. More is left to human regulation than is generally assumed. Normally, for instance, councils in the Catholic Church are convoked according to the rules of canon law; from the Middle Ages the task of convocation has been assigned to the Pope. But this is a question of human law. The possibility of convoking a truly universal council of all Christian churches should not be excluded because of questions of law and protocol.

5. While allowance has to be made for the clear demarcation of responsibilities between the functions of church leaders and theologians, in an emergency under certain conditions the one group must undertake in a subsidiary fashion the functions of the other. When church leaders fail, theologians must talk and act; when theologians fail, church leaders must do the talking and acting. Here everyone – obviously also the lay person – has his own responsibility which he cannot pass on to anyone else. Whenever, as a result of the failure of one group or the other, it is a question of the existence or nonexistence of the Church of the gospel, then a *status confessionis* exists, then people cannot be content to be merely spectators. Then some will have to come to the aid of the others, in order resolutely to do what they can to serve the believing community.

6. Genuine emergencies and emergency situations are such that they cannot be foreseen or *settled in advance* in their concrete shape. Who is to extinguish a fire can be planned in advance only up to a point. When the fire actually breaks out, the person who happens to be available will deal with it, even if he does not belong to the fire department. This is not a plea for abolishing or neglecting the fire department. In an emergency, regardless of questions of legal competence, each and everyone must do what is necessary. In church history there are plenty of examples of subsidiary action of one group for the other. Bishops reacted to a disastrous and dangerous confusion on the part of theologians in questions of faith (in the ecumenical

councils of the first millennium). Bishops and theologians acted when the Popes failed to do so (as in the Great Schism of the West and the reform councils). Pastors and lay people rallied round a theologian of the Confessing Church when Catholic and Protestant bishops and the Pope failed to take action (in regard to National Socialism in Germany).

7. Despite the possibility of distinguishing them in principle, the *frontiers* between the different areas of competence are *fluid* in the individual case and cannot always be clearly defined. In particular, in the individual case, it is not easy to discover whether it is a question of the existence or nonexistence of the Church, whether this question or that is merely a question of theology or really of faith. From the very outset theologians will have to guard against subjectivistic enthusiasm and church leaders against doctrinaire authoritarianism and both against obstinacy. It is not a state of emergency when a curate or teacher of religion in a parish does not speak about the resurrection or the divinity of Jesus with that exact orthodoxy which a theologian or bishop or episcopal theologian might expect in the light of his dogmatic theology. A state of emergency exists in a church when *preaching and action are continually and unambiguously contrary to the gospel.* The essential norm for judging the situation is not some viewpoint of ecclesiastical politics, but the gospel itself. The subsidiary intervention of one group for the other is permissible only as a last resource. A state of emergency may not simply be presumed as a reason for intervention either by church leaders or by theologians. In the first place, in a spirit of self-criticism, all other possible ways and means must be used.

In view of all the unforeseeable, incalculable and uncontrollable conflicts in the Church, a trust emerging from belief in the indefectibility of the Church is particularly important and the development and application of imagination is a real Christian virtue if aid is to be provided for every emergency. Creative imagination can consider models, methods and solutions, can make clear how difficult situations may be managed – even without infallible propositions and authorities. In this way do we not need to be less fearful for the future of the Church?

In Conclusion

LOOKING BACK

The indestructibility of the Church of Jesus Christ as the whole community of believers is itself a truth of faith, rooted in Christian origins, based not only on isolated classical texts but on the Christian message as a whole, which as God's final decisive call will continue to awaken belief and to assemble a community of believers. The conviction of believers from the very beginning was that the Church is maintained quite concretely by God in the truth of Jesus Christ wherever his Spirit, the Holy Spirit of God, is alive and continually bringing fresh guidance into the whole truth; wherever, that is, Jesus himself is and remains the way, the truth and the life for the individual or for a community; wherever people commit themselves in discipleship to his way; wherever they follow his guidance on their own way of life. Consequently this persistence in truth is more a matter of orthopraxy than of orthodoxy, more a matter of individuals and individual communities than of institutions. With the ever-possible failure of hierarchy and theology, this persistence in truth continues to be manifested in the living faith of 'little people' and in fact, not only in the great churches, but occasionally outside these. Here it becomes especially clear that the ecclesiastical ministries do not establish truth in the Church, but are there to serve it and men.

The result is that the Church continues to live even in the event of serious error in a matter of faith or morals, indeed that the Church must continually be learning to live with errors. Errors of the ecclesiastical magisterium are a serious matter, but they are not a threat to the existence of the Church. The Church, however, needs a criterion for what is to be considered as true in the Christian Church: this is the Christian message as originally recorded in the New Testament, ultimately Jesus

Christ himself. This Christian message must be read critically against the background of the ecclesial community and tradition. Precisely in this way it becomes clear that the Christian ultimately believes not in propositions or truths, not even in the Bible, in tradition, or in the Church, but in God himself and in him in whom God revealed himself. Such a faith is indeed dependent on propositions if it is to be expressed, but it need not be destroyed by false propositions.

Hence both the everyday and the extraordinary proclamation can be sustained despite individual errors. In particular it can be made clear that episcopate, council, and Pope can function and undertake their task even though in a case of conflict they cannot define infallibly who is right. In this way it is even easier to cope with cases of conflict, which are always possible in the Church.

LOOKING FORWARD

A fallible magisterium would then have to be seen as an opportunity. Could not the *Church of the future* cope with its errors more easily in this way? That is, it could learn by its mistakes, using the method of trial and error advocated by Karl Popper. Would this not be a way of regaining the old freedom to secure a hearing for the truth of the gospel again and again throughout all the errors? If sin could become a 'happy fault' (*felix culpa*), might not error also (in itself much less serious) become a 'happy error' (*felix error*), since the truth of the gospel shines out all the more brightly through the Church's errors? Could not church history be considered more realistically in this way and yet at the same time belief in the persistence of the Church in truth become more convincing?

A consensus in the direction outlined is possible and seems to be emerging in various publications. It would be an *ecumenical consensus*, for in this way other Christians too could believe in the indestructibility, the indefectibility, of the Church of Jesus Christ in truth. The most serious impediment between the Christian churches would thus be removed. But more importantly, the Christian message, this Jesus himself and the God for whom he stands, would have become more credible again. And for that alone the pursuit of theology is worthwhile in the troubles of the present time.

Does not what has been expounded here deserve to be freshly considered? Following the French theologian *Yves Congar*, one of the great precursors of the Second Vatican Council, in this matter so serious for the Catholic Church and Christendom and also for himself, the theologian may be permitted to put forward a plea:

Let the question of infallibility be freshly investigated – now, under a new Pope – in objective relevance, scientific honesty, fairness, and justice.

Let an ecumenical commission – on the lines of the commission on birth control in the 1960s – composed of internationally recognized experts from the various disciplines (exegesis, history of dogma, systematic theology, practical theology, and the non-theological studies also involved), be appointed to look into this question.

Let there be less importance attached to the negative-critical approach than to the positive-constructive one, and then let the question be asked whether the *persistence of the Church in truth, despite all errors,* is not better substantiated in the Christian message and the great Catholic tradition and whether it would be better to live with this even in the Church today.

After the rejection of any kind of contraception by Pope Paul VI – justified, in the Roman view, by the authority, continuity, traditionality, universality, and consequently in practice by the infallibility and irreformability of the traditional teaching – it might be hoped that a solution of the question of infallibility would carry with it also a solution of the question of contraception. What for countless people in our developed countries with their declining birth rate represents a serious burden of conscience means for the people in many underdeveloped countries, and especially in Latin America, incalculable harm, for which the Church must share responsibility: poverty, illiteracy, unemployment, under-nourishment, and sickness are related to high birth rates as effect to cause. During the past two decades the growth rates of food production (by no means slight) were largely outpaced by the higher birth rates.

Pope John Paul II returned from Latin America with new experiences. There he had spoken out against poverty, under-development, and child misery. In view of all this and in light of the fact that he wants to work for ecumenical understanding, is it too much to expect from him a decisive step toward an honest clarification of the pressing question of infallibility – in an atmosphere of mutual trust, free research, and fair discussion?

Postscript

This theological meditation is not intended to provoke *a new controversy on infallibility*. The most recent debate, which can now be seen at a certain historical distance, has brought out a number of things:

1. No one – neither a theologian nor an ecclesiastical authority – has been able to produce a proof of guaranteed infallible propositions, and the blind alleys to which infallible propositions lead are today more evident than ever (see *Fehlbar? Eine Bilanz*, edited by Hans Küng [Zurich: Benziger 1973]).

2. The ecclesiastical authorities have taken scarcely any notice of the negative result of the debate; they repeated with slight modifications only the magisterial utterances which had been called in question (see the various declarations of the Roman Congregation for the Doctrine of the Faith and of the German Bishops Conference in 1973 and 1974).

3. A constructive Catholic theology, which does not start out from within the system, from certain defined propositions, only to return to them, but which can make the original message of God and his Christ freshly effective for us today, is possible (see the author's *On Being a Christian* [New York: Doubleday 1976; London: Collins 1977, SCM Press 1991] and *Does God Exist?* [New York: Doubleday 1980; London: Collins 1980 and SCM Press 1991]).

4. The questioning of the traditional teaching on infallibility continues even within the Catholic Church and in Catholic theology (see the recent book by August E. Hasler, *Wie der Papst unfehlbar wurde: Macht und Ohnmacht eines Dogmas* [Munich/Zurich: Piper, 1979]).

But the debate about infallible propositions and authorities is not to be continued here (I made some observations on the subject in a preface to Hasler's book). What ought to be done is to process the positive conclusions of the infallibility debate (which have been too little considered) and then, without polemics, to explain how today a persistence of the Church in truth can be believed and understood (see the last chapter of *Fehlbar? Eine Bilanz*). The majority of thinking people today are not concerned whether error can be a priori excluded as a result of the assistance of the Holy Spirit (infallibility of individual propositions or authorities) in certain cases (in practice, extremely rare today). But in view of the new problems assailing the Church in the first, second and third worlds, in view of the numerous ideologies of the left and right, a much more fundamental question arises: whether a persistence in truth can be ascribed to the Church at all or whether this Church and its truth are not coming to an end. The question then is no longer the infallibility of certain ecclesiastical statements of faith and authorities on faith, but the indefectibility of the Church itself.

The French theologian Yves Congar has called for a *re-reception of the papal dogmas of Vatican I*. Congar, who contributed more than anyone to the theological preparation of the new understanding of the Church presented by Vatican II, thinks that the historical relativity of Vatican I has been brought home most effectively by a number of historical studies (Aubert, Torrell, Schatz), by works on the history of theology (Thils, Dejaifve, Pottmeyer) and those that raise radical questions (Küng), also by the fact of Vatican II and the revival of local and partial churches, and finally by the new understanding of the principles of Eastern ecclesiology. He has called – 'in our Catholic loyalty' – for a 're-reception' of the Vatican dogmas and especially the dogma of papal infallibility. According to Congar, keeping in mind a genuine understanding of the magisterium, the best exegetical, historical and theological studies of recent decades, the ecumenical dialogue inaugurated under new conditions, the theology and reality of the local Church, there should be a fresh reflection together with the other Christian churches and a new formulation of what was defined at Vatican I in 1870 and was then accepted by the totality of Catholics in the relativity of that period. According to Hasler, such a re-reception in practice would lead to a *revision* of the decisions of Vatican I, which would provide the Catholic Church and Catholic theology and Christendom as a whole with a new way out of a situation that has become untenable into a new future. But, once again, we have no desire here to provoke a new controversy on infallibility; what ought to be done is to liquidate the old controversy as soon as possible. Hence our suggestion of the appointment of an ecumenical commission.

Tübingen, February 1979

POSTSCRIPT (1989)

The Roman answer to the two 1979 publications included in this documentation was to remove my licence to teach on 18 December 1979. The texts from this period are documented in N. Greinacher and H. Haag (eds.), *Der Fall Küng. Eine Dokumentation*, Munich 1980.

INSTEAD OF AN EPILOGUE

'. . . so that we may enter together upon the path of charity, and advance towards him of whom it is said "Seek his face ever more". And I would make this pious and safe agreement, in the presence of our Lord God, with all who read my writings . . .

'If, then, any reader shall say, This is not well said, because I do not understand it; such a one finds fault with my language, not with my faith: and it might perhaps in very truth have been put more clearly; yet no man ever so spoke as to be understood in all things by all men. Let him, therefore, who finds this fault with my discourse, see whether he can understand other men who have handled similar subjects and questions, when he does not understand me: and if he can, let him put down my book, or even, if he pleases, throw it away; and let him spend labour and time rather on those whom he understands. Yet let him not think on that account that I ought to have been silent, because I have not been able to express myself so smoothly and clearly to him as those do whom he understands. For neither do all things, which all men have written, come into the hands of all. And possibly some, who are capable of understanding even these our writings, may not find those more lucid works, and may meet with ours only. And therefore it is useful that many persons should write many books, differing in style but not in faith, concerning even the same questions, that the matter itself may reach the greatest number – some in one way, some in another. But if he who complains that he has not understood these things never has been able to comprehend any careful and exact reasonings at all upon such subjects, let him in that case deal with himself by resolution and study, that he may know better; not with me by quarrellings and wranglings, that I may hold my peace.

'Let him, again, who says, when he reads my book, Certainly I understand what is said, but it is not true, assert, if he pleases, his own opinion, and refute mine if he is able. And if he do this with charity and truth, and take the pains to make it known to me (if I am still alive), I shall then receive the most abundant fruit of this my labour. And if he cannot inform myself, most willing and glad should I be that he should inform those whom he can. Yet, for my part, "I meditate in the law of the Lord," if not "day and night" at least such short times as I can; and I commit my meditations to writing, lest they should escape me through forgetfulness; hoping by the mercy of God that he will make me hold steadfastly all truths of which I feel certain; "but if in anything I be otherwise minded, that he will himself reveal even this to me," whether through secret inspiration and admonition, or through his own plain utterances, or through the reasonings of my brethren. This I pray for, and this my trust and desire I commit to him, who is sufficiently able to keep those things which he has given to me, and to render those which he has promised.'

ST AUGUSTINE, *De Trinitate*, 1,5.

NOTES

FOREWORD

1. 'Konzil – Ende oder Anfang?', *Frankfurter Allgemeine Zeitung*, 18.11.1964; *Tübinger Forschungen*, No. 19, 1964; *Civitas*, No. 4, 1965, pp. 188–99; *KNA-Sonderdienst zum Zweiten Vatikanischen Konzil*, 8.9.1965; 'The Council – End or Beginning?', *The Commonweal*, No. 81, 1965, pp. 631–7; 'Het Concilie: Einde of Begin?', *Elseviers Weekblad*, 6.2.1965; 'Poczatek czy koniec Soboru', *Życie i Myśl*, Warsaw, No. 1, 1965, pp. 104–13.
2. Cf. 'Was hat das Konzil erreicht?', *Vaterland*, 17.–18.12.1965; *Tübinger Forschungen*, No. 27, 1966; *Universitas*, No. 21, 1966, pp. 171–86; *Deutsche Tagespost*, 8.–9.4.1966; 'The Reform of the Roman Church', *Sunday Times*, 12.12.1965; 'What has the Council done?', *The Commonweal*, No. 83, 1966, pp. 461–8; 'Sobór Jest Poczatkiem', *Tygodnik Powszechny*, Cracow, 13.2.1966; 'Co Sabor osiagnal?', *Kultura*, Paris, 1966, pp. 69–82; a different version, 'Die 16 neuen Pfeiler von St Peter', *Epoca*, 1966, pp. 12–19; *Neue Bildpost*, Nos. 3–8, 1966; also printed separately as *Konzilsergebnis, Dokumente der Erneuerung*, Kevelaer, 1966.
3. Cf. H. Küng, *Truthfulness: The Future of the Church*, London and Sydney, 1968.
4. Cf. the author's 'Aufforderung zur Selbsthilfe', *Frankfurter Allgemeine Zeitung*, 9.5.1970; 'Mischehenfrage: was tun?', *Neue Zürcher Nachrichten*, 16.5.1970; 'Mixed Marriages: What is to be done?', *The National Catholic Reporter*, 30.5.1970; 'Que faire à propos des mariages mixtes?', *Le Monde*, 7.–8.6.1970. Cf. the position taken by the German Bishops' Conference and my reply, *Publik*, 5.6.1970.
5. Cf. J. Neumann, 'Zur Problematik lehramtlicher Beanstandungsverfahren', *Tübinger Theologische Quartalschrift*, No. 149, 1969, pp. 259–81.
6. Full text in *Herderkorrespondenz*, No. 24, 1970, pp. 230–4.

CHAPTER ONE

1. Karl Rahner, 'Zur Enzyklika "Humanae Vitae"', *Stimmen der Zeit*, No. 93, 1968, p. 204. Summarized in *The Tablet*, London, 14.9.1968.

2. J. Neumann, in a radio interview published in *Die Enzyklika in der Diskussion. Eine orientierende Dokumentation zu 'Humanae Vitae'*, ed. F. Böckle and C. Holenstein, Zürich-Einsiedeln-Cologne, 1968, p. 47. This volume will henceforward be referred to as *Dokumentation*.

3. Ibid., pp. 46 f.

4. W. Schaab, *Die Zeit*, No. 32, 1968 (*Dokumentation*, pp. 44 f.).

5. *Osservatore Romano*, 24.6.1964.

6. *Osservatore Romano*, 30.10.1968.

7. 8.9.1968, *Dokumentation*, p. 38.

8. Cf. also Charles Davis, *A Question of Conscience*, London, 1967, pp. 93 f.

9. *Osservatore Romano*, 1.8.1968.

10. *Corriere della Sera*, 3.10.1965.

11. J.-M. Paupert, *Le Monde*, 11.–12.8.1968.

12. A. Müller, *Neue Zürcher Nachrichten*, 10.8.1968 (*Dokumentation*, p. 79).

13. H. Helbling, *Neue Zürcher Zeitung*, 30.7.1968 (*Dokumentation*, p. 81).

14. On what follows cf. H. Küng, *Structures of the Church*, London, 1965, p. 34.

15. *Corpus Iuris Canonici*, ed. A. Friedberg, Leipzig, 1881, Vol. II, p. 287; cf. Vol. II, p. 908.

16. S. Merkle, 'Der Streit um Savonarola', *Hochland*, No. 25, 1928, pp. 472 f.; cf. St Thomas Aquinas, IV Sent. dist. 38, expos. textus in fine.

17. R. Bellarmine, *De summo pontifice*, Ingolstadt, 1586–93, Paris, 1870, Book II, Ch. 29, I, 607.

18. General audience of 31.7.1968; *Osservatore Romano*, 1.8.1968 (*Dokumentation*, p. 33).

19. Ibid., pp. 33 f.

20. Ibid., pp. 45 f.

21. Ibid., pp. 28 f.

22. *Humanae Vitae*, No. 6.

23. *The Tablet*, 6 May 1967, p. 511.

24. *Herderkorrespondenz*, No. 21, 1967, p. 438.

25. Ibid., p. 436.

26. Ibid., p. 432.

27. This information is taken from a well-informed unsigned article in *Herderkorrespondenz*, No. 22, 1968, pp. 525–36, on 'The Post-Conciliar Background of an Encyclical' (quotations from pp. 532 ff).

28. Ibid., p. 530.

29. L. Kaufmann, 'Der Vorhang hebt sich. Zur Vorgeschichte von "Humanae vitae" ', *Publik*, 29.11.1968.
30. *Humanae Vitae*, No. 18.
31. Ibid., No. 28.
32. Ibid., No. 29.
33. Ibid., No. 31.
34. Cardinal Charles Journet, *Osservatore Romano*, 3.10.1968.
35. Cardinal Pericle Felici, 'L' "Humanae Vitae", la coscienza ed il Concilio', *Osservatore Romano*, 19.10.1968. Cf. the same author's 'Continuità, coerenza, fermezza di una dottrina. Dalla Costituzione pastorale "Gaudium et Spes" alla Enciclica paolina "Humanae Vitae" ', *Osservatore Romano*, 10.10.1968.

CHAPTER TWO

1. On the manipulation of the proposition 'Outside the Church no salvation', cf. H. Küng, *Truthfulness*, New York, London and Sydney, 1968.
2. L. Ott, *Fundamentals of Catholic Dogma*, 1960, p. 299. On what follows cf. among recent Latin textbooks, J. Salaverri, *Sacrae Theologiae Summa*, Vol. I, Madrid, 1955, pp. 552–747; T. Zapelena, *De Ecclesia Christi*, Vol. II, Rome, 1954, pp. 7–260 (esp. pp. 171–91).
3. L. Ott, op. cit., p. 300.
4. Ibid.
5. Daniel Callahan, ed., *The Catholic Case for Contraception*, London, 1969, pp. 179–80.
6. Cf. L. Ott, op. cit., pp. 297–9.
7. Ibid., p. 298.
8. Ibid.
9. On the history of the whole Constitution on the Church and the various drafts, cf., in addition to the Council documents used here, the article by G. Philips, second secretary of the Theological Commission, in H. Vorgrimler, ed., *Commentary on the Documents of Vatican II*, Vol. I, London, 1967, pp. 105–37.
10. On the interpretation of Articles XVIII–XXVII, cf. the informative commentary by Karl Rahner, ibid., pp. 186–218.
11. K. Rahner, loc. cit., p. 210.
12. *Schema Constitutionis Dogmaticae de Ecclesia* of 10.11.1962, p. 49.
13. K. Rahner, loc. cit., p. 212.
14. Ibid.
15. Ibid., p. 214.

16. Quoted at length in the revised version of the Constitution on the Church of 1963, p. 41.

17. On the exegetical-historical verification of the not very clear Article XIX of the Constitution on the Church about the calling of the twelve, or the apostles, cf. *The Church*, D IV, 1.

18. On the apostolic succession of the Church as a whole, cf. *The Church*, D IV, 2; the Constitution on the Church in Article X passes directly from the mission of the apostles to the offices of the hierarchy.

19. On the historical development of the episcopal office, cf. *The Church*, E II, 2a–b; this should be compared with the statements on the universal priesthood, which becomes effective in baptism, the celebration of the Eucharist and forgiveness of sin (D I, 2 and E II, 2).

20. On this astonishing backward development of dogma see the notes of the Commission on Faith to the Schema of the Constitution on the Church, Rome, 1964, pp. 87 and 99; also *The Church*, E II, 2c and f.

21. On the question of teachers in the Church, cf. *The Church*, E II, 2a and g.

22. *Schema Constitutionis de Ecclesia*, Rome, 1964, p. 101.

23. Cf. H. Küng, *The Living Church*, London, 1963, Part 4, Chapter 3: 'What is and what is not the theological task of this Council?'

24. Cf. *The Church*, E II, 2e–i.

25. Apart from the earlier tendentious works both of J. Friedrich, *Geschichte des Vatikanischen Konzils*, Vols. 1–3, Bonn, 1867–87, written from the Old Catholic viewpoint, and T. Granderath, *Geschichte des Vatikanischen Konzils*, Vols. 1–3 (ed. K. Kirch), Freiburg, 1903–6, written from the Curial angle, cf. especially C. Butler, *The Vatican Council 1869–1870*, London, 1962, which gives a lively impression of the dramatic course of the Council debates and of individual contributions to it; also the latest critical history of the Council, R. Aubert, *Vatican I*, Paris, 1964, which we follow here particularly for the description of the situation on the eve of the Council. Cf. also the same author's *Le Pontificat de Pie IX*, Paris, 1952.

26. On the question of infallibility at Vatican I, apart from the older literature, cf. the following, which appeared on the eve of Vatican II: R. Aubert, 'L'ecclésiologie au concile du Vatican', *Le concile et les conciles*, Paris, 1960, pp. 245–84; A. Chavasse, 'L'ecclésiologie au concile du Vatican. L'infaillibilité de l'Église', *L'ecclésiologie au XIXᵉ siècle*, Paris, 1960, pp. 233–45; W. Caudron, '*Magistère ordinaire et infaillibilité pontificale d'après la constitution*

"*Dei Filius*" ', *Ephemerides Theologicae Lovanienses*, No. 36, 1960, pp. 393–431; O. Karrer, 'Das ökumenische Konzil in der römisch-katholischen Kirche der Gegenwart', *Die ökumenischen Konzile der Christenheit*, ed. H. J. Margull, Stuttgart, 1961, pp. 237–84, esp. pp. 241–64; G. Dejaifve, *Pape et évêques au premier concile du Vatican*, Paris, 1961, pp. 93–137; K. Rahner, *The Episcopate and the Primacy*, London, 1962, pp. 92–101; G. Thils, 'Parlera-t-on des évêques au concile?', *Nouvelle Revue Théologique*, No. 93, 1961, pp. 785–804; J. P. Torrel, 'L' infaillibilité pontificale est-elle un privilège "personnel"?', *Revue des sciences philosophiques et théologiques*, No. 45, 1961, pp. 229–45; W. Kasper, 'Primat und Episkopat nach dem Vatikanum I', *Tübinger Theologische Quartalschrift*, No. 142, 1962, pp. 68–77.

On the question of infallibility in general, cf. the important symposium, *L'Infaillibilité de l'Eglise, Journées oecuméniques de Chevetogne 25–29 Septembre 1961*, Chevetogne, 1963, with valuable contributions by J.-J. von Allmen ('Über den Geist, der in alle Wahrheit einführt'), B. Reyners ('Irenaeus'), B.-D. Dupuy ('Das Lehramt als Dienst am Wort'), P. de Vooght ('Das Wort "Infallibilität" in der Scholastik'), G. Thils ('Infallibilität auf dem Vatikanum I'), N. Afanasieff (on the Orthodox viewpoint), H. Balmforth (the Anglican attitude), J. Bosc (the Reformed attitude), J. de Satgé (conference report). Latest literature referred to in next chapter.

27. Cf. the Council's own documents in *Structures of the Church*, VII, 2.

28. Cf. the still topical comments on the by no means rare instances of conflict between Pope and Church, on the dubious proposition *Prima Sedes a nemine iudicatur*, on the deposition of popes in the Middle Ages, on the modern canon law answer on the loss of office by the Pope, and finally on the ecclesiological importance of the Council of Constance, which deposed three rival popes and represented an opposite pole to Vatican I, in *Structures of the Church*, VII, 3–5.

29. Cf. 'The Sifting of the Certain from the Uncertain', *The Church*, EII, 3b.

30. Cf. the numerous theoretical and practical implications and consequences of such a transition from a primacy of power to a primacy of service in *The Church*, E II, 3c.

31. C. Butler, *The Vatican Council 1869–1870*, p. 57.

32. Ibid., pp. 59–60.

33. Ibid., p. 61.

34. Reprinted in R. Aubert, *Vatican I*, pp. 261–9.

35. Ibid., p. 33.

36. Latin text in R. Aubert, 'L'ecclésiologie au concile du Vatican', *Le concile et les conciles*, p. 280.
37. Mansi, Vol. 52, pp. 1204–30; Part I, Relatio generalis: (a) Arguments from Scripture and tradition (pp. 1204–12), (b) Explanations of the definition itself (pp. 1212–18); Part 2, Emendationes Nos. 1–79 (pp. 1218–30).
38. Mansi, Vol. 52, p. 1261.
39. Mansi, Vol. 52, p. 1214.
40. Ibid.
41. Mansi, Vol. 52, p. 1213.
42. Ibid.
43. Mansi, Vol. 52, p. 1214.
44. As above, we closely follow Bishop Gasser's and the commission's authentic commentary.
45. Mansi, Vol. 52, p. 1213.
46. Mansi, Vol. 52, p. 1214.
47. Mansi, Vol. 52, p. 1213.
48. Ibid.
49. Mansi, Vol. 52, p. 1215.
50. Mansi, Vol. 52, p. 1214.
51. F. Suarez, *De Charitate. Disputatio XII de schismate*, sectio I, Opera Omnia, Paris, 1958, Vol. 12, pp. 733 f. Our argument here is not based on belated post-conciliar hindsight. It may be pointed out that our analysis of the Vatican's problem of primacy and infallibility and of the possible eventuality of a conflict between Pope and Church was published before Vatican II in *Structures of the Church* (original German edition, 1962) and resulted in inquisitional proceedings being taken against us in Rome. The majority of the Council did not, however, venture to bring out into the open and properly discuss questions so painful to the Curia.
52. Cf. Ch. II, 5.
53. According to a public opinion survey carried out in Germany in 1967, 55 per cent of all Catholics questioned took the view that 'the Pope cannot be infallible, as he is a human being'. It is significant that this view was taken by 44 per cent of practising Catholics. Cf. W. Harenberg (ed.), *Was glauben die Deutschen. Die Emnid-Umfrage. Ergebnisse, Kommentare*, Munich, 1968, p. 42.
54. J. Schmid, *Das Evangelium nach Lukas*, Regensburg, 1960, p. 332.
55. Y. Congar, *L'Ecclésiologie du Haut Moyen Age. De Saint Grégoire le Grand à la désunion entre Byzance et Rome*, Paris, 1968, pp. 159–60.
56. J. Langen, *Das Vatikanische Dogma von dem Universal-Episcopat und der Unfehlbarkeit des Papstes in seinem Verhältnis zum Neuen Testament und der exegetischen Überlieferung*, 4 vols., Bonn, 1871–76, Vol. II, pp. 123 f.

57. Cf. *Structures of the Church*, VII, 6; Y. Congar, op. cit., pp. 226–32. Cf. H. Fuhrmann, 'Päpstlicher Primat und Pseudoisidorische Dekretalen', *Quellen und Forschungen aus italienischen Archiven und Bibliotheken*, Vol. 49 (1969), pp. 313–39.

58. Y. Congar, ibid., p. 230.

59. St Thomas Aquinas, *Contra errores Graecorum*, Pars II, cap. 32–5; the forgeries are frankly dealt with in recent Catholic commentaries, e.g., R.A. Verardo's excellent introduction to *Opuscula Theologica* I, ed. Marietti, Turin and Rome, 1954. The basic work on the subject is F. H. Reusch, *Die Fälschungen in dem Tractat des heiligen Thomas von Aquin gegen die Griechen*, Munich, 1889.

60. St Thomas Aquinas, ibid., cap. 36.

61. F. H. Reusch, op. cit., p. 733.

62. St Thomas Aquinas, *Summa Theologiae* II–II, q. 1, a. 10.

63. Cf. *Structures of the Church*, VII, 6.

64. On the question of Honorius, cf. R. Bäumer, article on Honorius I in *Lexicon für Theologie und Kirche*, Vol. V, Freiburg-Basle-Vienna, 1960, pp. 474 f. (bibliography).

65. On the evaluation of this development we may once again refer to *Structures of the Church*, VII, 3–6, and *The Church*, E II, 3.

66. This view is taken by K. Baus, article on 'Konstantinopel' in *Lexicon für Theologie und Kirche*, Vol. VI, pp. 494–7; J. Alberigo (*et al.*), *Conciliorum oecumenicorum decreta*, Freiburg, 1962, pp. 133–5; H. Alevisatos (Orthodox), 'Les conciles oecuméniques Ve, VIe, VIIe et VIIIe', *Le concile et les conciles*, Paris, 1960, pp. 119–23.

67. R. Aubert, *Vatican I*, pp. 110–11.

68. R. Aubert, ibid., pp. 116–17.

CHAPTER THREE

1. V. Conzemius, 'Das Konzil des Papstes. Vor 100 Jahren begann das Erste Vatikanum', *Publik*, 5.12.1969.

2. Ibid.

3. Ibid.

4. H. Jedin, 'Das erste Vatikanische Konzil im Lichte des zweiten', *Vaterland*, 17.1.1970.

5. W. Kasper, 'Die Kirche in der modernen Gesellschaft. Der Weg vom Vatikanum I zum Vatikanum II', *Publik*, 12.12.1969.

6. Ibid.

7. H. Jedin, op. cit.

8. V. Conzemius, op. cit.

9. W. Dirks, 'Das Dogma von den fehlbaren Päpsten. Die Wandlung

der katholischen Kirche seit 1870', *Deutsches Allgemeines Sonntagsblatt*, 11.1.1970.

10. Quoted in *Publik*, 23.1.1970.

11. Text published in *Publik*, 23.1.1970.

12. W. Küppers, 'Sieben Thesen der alt-katholischen Kirche', *Publik*, 23.1.1970.

13. H. Bacht, 'Dialog mit den Alt-Katholiken aufnehmen', *Publik*, 23.1.1970.

14. In particular *The Church*, E II, 3.

15. H. Bacht, op. cit.

16. Ibid.

17. W. Küppers, op. cit.

18. W. Kasper, op. cit.

19. W. Dirks, op. cit.

20. J. Finsterhölzl, 'Belastung oder Verheissung?', *Publik*, 9.1.1970.

21. Ibid.

22. W. Dirks, op. cit.

23. J. Finsterhölzl, op. cit.

24. Ibid.

25. *Structures of the Church*, VIII, 3, pp. 336–7.

26. Mansi, Vol. 52, p. 1219.

27. H. Fries, 'Das Lehramt als Dienst am Glauben', *Catholica*, No. 23, 1969, pp. 154–72 (quotation pp. 165 f.).

28. Cf. Mansi, Vol. 52, pp. 7, 14, 24, etc.; cf. in the Constitution itself 'Ab errore illibata' (D 1836).

29. *Structures of the Church*, VIII 2c, p. 335.

30. Cf. *The Church*, D III 2c.

31. K. G. Steck, 'Die Autorität der Offenbarung. Das Erste Vatikanum im Urteil evangelischer Theologie', *Publik*, 16.1.1970.

32. Ibid.

33. Ibid.

34. Ibid.

35. Ibid.

36. Ibid.

37. Cf. E. Käsemann, 'Liturgische Formeln im NT', RGG II, Tübingen, 1958, pp. 993–6; G. Bornkamm, 'Formen und Gattungen im NT', ibid., pp. 999–1005. On confessions of faith, cf. O. Cullmann, *Die ersten christlichen Glaubensbekenntnisse*, Zollikon-Zürich, 1943, 1949 (English translation, *The Earliest Christian Confessions*, London, 1949); K. H. Schelkle, *Die Passion Jesu in der Verkündigung des Neuen Testaments*, Heidelberg, 1949, pp. 247–75; J. N. D. Kelly, *Early Christian Creeds*, London, 1950.

38. On the whole problem of Church, heresy and excommunication, cf. *The Church*, C III, 4.

39. On the idea of dogma and the difference between dogma and dogmatism, cf. J. Nolte, *Dogma in Geschichte. Versuch einer Kritik des Dogmatismus in der Glaubensdarstellung* (publication in the series *Ökumenische Forschungen* expected in 1971).

40. St Thomas Aquinas, *Summa Theologiae*, II–II, q.1, a.10 ad 1–2; a.9 ad 2; a.10 *in corp*. Cf. also H. Küng, *The Living Church*, Part 4, Ch. 3: 'What is and what is not the theological task of the Council?'

41. Cf. Chapter II, 3.

42. Cf. Chapter II, 7.

43. Cf. Chapter II, 1.

44. V. Conzemius, 'Das Konzil des Papstes', *Publik*, 5.12.1969.

45. Mansi, Vol. 51, pp. 72–7; on what follows cf. C. Butler, *The Vatican Council*, pp. 236–9.

46. Mansi, Vol. 51, pp. 429 f.

CHAPTER FOUR

1. In what follows I have made use of the five points in which my pupil J. Nolte (*Dogma in Geschichte. Versuch einer Kritik des Dogmatismus in der Glaubensdarstellung*, sums up his linguistic philosophical ideas before considering their far wider philosophical and theological implications.

2. R. Descartes, *Principia Philosophiae*, Vol. I, p. 45.

3. Thus Hegel in his *Phenomenology of Mind*. Cf. H. Küng, *Menschwerdung Gottes. Eine Einführung in Hegels theologisches Denken als Prolegomena zu einer künftigen Christologie*, Freiburg-Basle-Vienna, 1970, esp. Ch. V, 1.

4. Cf. *Structures of the Church*, VIII, 3c.

5. Cf. J. Nolte, op. cit.

6. *National Catholic Reporter*, 19.4.1967, quoted in D. Callahan, *The Catholic Case for Contraception*, pp. 210–11.

7. Cf. *The Church*, C I, 2d. On the idea of the people of God in Hebrews, cf. E. Käsemann, *Das wandernde Gottesvolk*, Göttingen, 1961; F. J. Schierse, *Verheissung und Heilsvollendung. Zur theologischen Grundfrage des Hebräerbriefes*, Munich, 1955.

8. Cf. *The Church*, D III, 2c.

9. Y. Congar, *L'Eglise de Saint Augustin à l'époque moderne*, Paris, 1970, pp. 244–8 (quotation, pp. 244–5).

10. Ibid., pp. 245 f.

11. Ibid., p. 248.

12. Ibid., p. 385.

13. Ibid., p. 386.

14. Cf. *The Church*, D III, 2c.
15. M. Luther, quoted from the complete critical edition of his works, Weimar, 1883 ff., henceforward referred to as WA. Reply to Prierias, WA, Vol. 1, p. 656.
16. WA, Vol. 2, p. 303; cf. WA, Vol. 5, p. 451.
17. Cf. J. Kolde, *Luthers Stellung zu Concil und Kirche bis zum Wormser Reichstag, 1521*, Gütersloh, 1876. On Luther's conciliar theology, cf. *Structures of the Church*, VI, 1.
18. WA, Vol. 7, p. 838.
19. Ibid.
20. Cf. especially his *De Potestate Concilii, 1536*, WA, Vol. 39/I, pp. 181–97, and *Von den Konziliis und Kirchen, 1539*, WA, Vol. 50, pp. 509–653.
21. J. Calvin, *Institutio Christianae Religionis, 1559*, esp. Book IV, Chs. 8 and 9, quoted from *Corpus Reformatorum* (henceforward referred to as CR), Vol. 30, pp. 846–67. English translation, *Institutes of the Christian Religion*, Library of the Christian Classics, Vol. 21, London, 1961.
22. Ibid., Book IV, Chs. 9, 11 (translation, p. 1174).
23. B. Gassmann, *Ecclesia Reformata. Die Kirche in den reformierten Bekenntnisschriften*, Freiburg-Basle-Vienna, 1968, p. 355.
24. Article XIX.
25. Article XXI.
26. WA, Vol. 39/I, p. 48.
27. Cf. WA, Vol. 18, pp. 649 f.; Vol. 51, p. 511.
28. P. Althaus, *Die Theologie Martin Luthers*, Gütersloh, 1963, p. 296.
29. Henry Bettenson, *Documents of the Christian Church*, Oxford, 1943, p. 295.
30. *Die Bekenntnisschriften der evangelisch-lutherischen Kirche*, Göttingen, 1959, Vol. IV, pp. 235 f.
31. CR, Vol. 30, p. 855.
32. CR, Vol. 30, p. 866. Calvin developed a detailed doctrine on the council; cf. *Structures of the Church*, VIII, 1; on Calvin's theory of the Church and office in the Church in general, cf. A. Ganoczy *Ecclesia ministrans. Dienende Kirche und Kirchlicher Dienst*, Freiburg-Basle-Vienna, 1968.
33. Article XIX.
34. Article XXI.
35. Cf. the very stimulating recent work by G. Thils, *L'Infaillibilité pontificale. Source-Conditions-Limites*, Gembloux, 1969.
36. Cf. the pioneering contribution by R. Murray, 'Who or what is infallible?', *Infallibility in the Church. An Anglican-Catholic Dialogue*, London, 1968, pp. 24–46. Cf. also the important criticism by A. Farrer, and the contributions by J. C. Dickinson ('Papal

Authority') and C. S. Dessain ('Newman in Manning's Church').
For the earlier Catholic-Anglican dialogue, B. C. Butler, *The Church and Infallibility*, 1954, new edition, London, 1969, is important.

37. F. Simons, *Infallibility and the Evidence*, Springfield, 1968.

38. *Publik*, 12.12.1969. While this book was in the press I received the important volume, edited by Enrico Castelli, *L'Infaillibilité. Son aspect philosophique et théologique*, Paris, 1970, which includes the proceedings of the discussion meeting on the subject held in Rome in January 1970. No doubt a good deal is included that would confirm our analyses. We refer in particular to the following contributions: from the philosophical-theological viewpoint, those of K. Rahner, C. Bruaire, E. Jüngel, J.-L. Leuba, E. Agazzi, R. Marlé, G. Pattaro, E. Grassi, A. de Waelhens, G. Vahanian, R. Panikkar, J. Lotz, G. Girardi, L. Alonso-Schökel; from the historical angle, those of R. Aubert, R. Manselli, P. de Vooght, K. Kerényi, G. C. Anawati; from the ecumenical standpoint, those of R. Bertalot, B. Ulianich, A. Scrima.

39. Timothy Ware, *The Orthodox Church*, London, 1963, p. 255.

40. Ibid.

41. J. N. Kamriris, 'Abriss der dogmatischen Lehre der orthodoxen katholischen Kirche', *Die Orthodoxe Kirche in griechischer Sicht*, ed. P. Bratsiotis, Stuttgart, 1959, Vol. I, pp. 18 f.

42. In this connection, cf. Karmiris's protest, unsupported by any arguments, against the not unfounded assertion of the Reformed Churchman W. Niesel that 'Orthodox Christendom does not know of any infallible teaching office' (ibid., p. 19).

43. T. Ware, op. cit., p. 256.

44. Cf. the documentation in *Structures of the Church*, IV, 2.

45. Cf. P. Johannes Chrysostomus, 'Das ökumenische Konzil und die Orthodoxie', *Una Sancta*, 14, 1959, pp. 177–86; P. Leskovec, 'Il Concilio Ecumenico nel pensiero teologico degli Ortodossi', *La Civiltà Cattolica*, No. 111, 1960, pp. 140–52; B. Schultze, *Die Glaubenswelt der orthodoxen Kirche*, Salzburg, pp. 149–53.

46. H. Jedin, *Kleine Konziliengeschichte*, Freiburg-Basle-Vienna, 1961, p. 10; it was shown in *Structures of the Church* that papal convocation, direction and confirmation of a council is a matter merely of human law.

47. St Augustine, *De baptismo contra Donatistas*, Book III, Ch. 2, quoted from F. Hofman, 'Die Bedeutung der Konzilien für die kirchliche Lehrentwicklung nach dem heiligen Augustinus', *Kirche und Überlieferung* (Festschrift J. R. Geiselmann), Freiburg-Basle-Vienna, 1960, p. 82; for further interpretation, cf. pp. 82–9.

48. M.-J. Le Guillou, *Mission et Unité*; German edition, *Sendung und*

Einheit der Kirche, Mainz, 1964, p. 574. Le Guillou (p. 579) mentions the important names of P. Afanasieff, A. Schmemann and J. Meyendorff, as being 'suspicious of councils'.

49. Ibid., p. 581.

50. J. Meyendorff, 'What is an ecumenical council?', *Vestnik*, No. 1, 1959 (in Russian).

51. Cf. H. Sasse, 'Sacra Scriptura – Bemerkungen zur Inspirationslehre Augustins', *Festschrift Franz Dornsieff*, Leipzig, 1953, pp. 262–73.

52. *Schema Constitutionis dogmaticae de fontibus revelationis*, Rome, 1962, Article XII.

53. Cf. A. Grillmeier's excellent commentary on Chapter 3 of the Constitution on Revelation in *Commentary on the Documents of Vatican II*, London, New York, Vol. III, 1968, pp. 199–246.

54. Ibid., p. 204.

55. Ibid., p. 206.

56. Ibid., p. 210.

57. Ibid., p. 235.

58. Cf. the various views of inspiration in the encyclopedia articles by A. Bea, *Lexikon für Theologie und Kirche*, Freiburg-Basle-Vienna, 1960, Vol. II, pp. 703–11; by G. Lanczkowski, O. Weber, W. Philipp, RGG, Vol. III, Tübingen, 1959, pp. 773–82; likewise in various manuals of dogmatics, on the Catholic side, S. Tromp, M. Nicolau, L. Ott, M. Schmaus; on the Protestant side, K. Barth, E. Brunner, O. Weber, H. Diem, P. Althaus.

59. On the following cf. the documentation in Y. Congar, *L'Eglise de Saint Augustin à l'époque moderne*, pp. 389, 446.

60. Ibid., p. 446.

61. Cf. Chapter II, 3.

62. Cf. *The Church*, E I, 2b.

63. Cf. the discussion on lay preaching in *The Church*, ibid.

64. On the charismatic structure of the Church, cf., besides *The Church*, C II, 3 and E II, 2, the recent comprehensive and penetrating studies: P. V. Dias, *Vielfalt der Kirche in der Vielfalt der Jünger, Zeugen und Diener*, Freiburg-Basle-Vienna, 1968. Hasenhüttl examines in the light of Jesus' message the free authority residing in the charismatic basic structure of the congregation and the reduction of charisms resulting in the development of a congregation without charisms, thus providing material for reflection on the charismatic structure of the congregation at the present day. On the 'charismatic state' (as Hasenhüttl calls it) of apostles, prophets, teachers, evangelists, pastors, cf. also P. V. Dias, B IV–IX, and G. Hasenhüttl, B III.

65. Cf. what we said in Chapter II, 3.
66. G. Hasenhüttl, op. cit., p. 207.
67. *The Church*, E II, 2g.
68. Cf. the acute analysis by M. Seckler, 'Die Theologie als kirchliche Wissenschaft nach Pius XII und Paul VI', *Tübinger Theologische Quartalschrift*, No. 149, 1969, pp. 209–34, the documentation of which will be very revealing to many, particularly the address by Pius XII *Si diligis*, on the occasion of the canonization of Pius X on 31.5.1954.
69. M. Seckler, ibid., p. 233. Cf. in the same issue P. Touilleux, 'Kritische Theologie' (pp. 235–58); J. Neumann, 'Zur Problematik lehramtlicher Beanstandungsverfahren' (pp. 259–81); H. Kümmeringer, 'Es ist Sache der Kirche, "iudicare de vero sensu et interpretatione scripturarum sanctarum" ' (pp. 282–96); all those are important in relation to the whole problem of theology and the 'teaching office'. A. Auer's inaugural lecture at Tübingen, 'Die Erfahrung der Geschichtlichkeit und die Krise der Moral', *Tübinger Theologische Quartalschrift*, No. 149, 1969, pp. 1–22, is of fundamental importance in coping with the crisis of the traditional moral authority supported by the teaching office that was brought out into the open by the publication of the encyclical *Humanae Vitae*.
70. Cf. the discussion on lay theology in *The Church*, E I, 2b.

Books of Related Interest

Hans Küng
GLOBAL RESPONSIBILITY
In Search of a New World Ethic

Hans Küng and Karl-Josef Kuschel
A GLOBAL ETHICS
The Declaration of the World's Parliament of Religion

Hans Küng
GREAT CHRISTIAN THINKERS

Karl-Josef Kuschel
LAUGHTER
A Theological Reflection

Karl-Josef Kuschel and Hermann Häring, Editors
HANS KÜNG
New Horizons for Faith and Thought